DISCARD

THE CHICAGO PUBLIC LIBRARY

SOCIAL SCIENCES AND HISTORY DIVISION

FORM 19

The Great Illusion

AN INFORMAL HISTORY OF PROHIBITION

BY HERBERT ASBURY

GREENWOOD PRESS, PUBLISHERS
WESTPORT, CONNECTICUT

This book was catalogued by the Library of Congress as follows:

Asbury, Herbert, 1891–1963.
    The great illusion: an informal history of prohibition.
New York, Greenwood Press, 1968 [°1950]

    viii, 344 p. 22 cm.

    Includes bibliographical references.

HV
5089
.A74
1968

Cop. 4

    1. Prohibition—U. S.   ɪ. Title.

HV5089.A74 1968   340   68–8051

Library of Congress   [2]

R0 0027 42488

Originally published in 1950 by Doubleday & Company,
Inc., Garden City, New York

Reprinted with the permission of Doubleday & Company, Inc.

Reprinted by Greenwood Press, Inc.
51 Riverside Avenue, Westport, CT. 06880

First Greenwood reprinting 1968
Second Greenwood reprinting 1972
Third Greenwood reprinting 1975
Fourth Greenwood reprinting 1977

Library of Congress catalog card number 68-8051
ISBN 0-8371-0008-9

Printed in the United States of America

TO MY WIFE
EDITH EVANS ASBURY

Contents

Part 1

CHAPTER ONE

"The Good Creature of God"

The most intemperate era in American history began during the last half of the eighteenth century, when rum had become the principal medium of exchange in the slave trade and was nearing the peak of its importance as a factor of the colonial economy; and when whiskey, first distilled in western Pennsylvania, was beginning to be recognized as the easiest and most profitable way in which to market grain. It ended some fifty years after the Revolution, by which time American drinking habits had been somewhat modified by the first waves of European immigration, and the anti-liquor movement had begun to assume the character of a religious crusade, the basis of its strong appeal to the American people.

During this period of some eighty or ninety years, "the good creature of God," as liquor was called in some of the colonial laws, was considered a prime necessity, an indispensable part of clean and healthy living. It was a common article of diet, in many places almost as much so as bread, while even physicians looked upon it as a preventative of all diseases and a specific for many. Everybody drank—both sexes and nearly all ages. The aged and infirm sipped toddies of rum and water—heavy on the rum; babies were quieted by copious doses of a mixture of rum and opium, and so spent their infancy in a happy fog; and able-bodied men, and women, too, for that matter, seldom went more than a few hours without a drink. The occasional abstainer was considered a crackpot and generally shunned. An article in the *Old American Encyclopedia* (1830 edition) thus described drinking customs in colonial times:

> A fashion at the South was to take a glass of whiskey, flavored with mint, soon after waking; and so conducive to health was this nostrum esteemed that no sex, and scarcely any age, were deemed exempt from its application. At eleven o'clock, while mixtures, under various peculiar names—sling, toddy, flip, etc.—solicited the appetite at the bar of the common tippling-shop, the offices of professional men and counting rooms dismissed their occupants for a half hour to regale themselves at a neighbor's or a coffee-house with punch, hot or cold, according to the season; and females or valetudinarians, courted an appetite with medicated rum, disguised under the chaste names of "Hexham's Tinctures" or "Stoughton's Elixir." The dinner hour arrived . . . whiskey and water curiously flavored with apples, or brandy and water, introduced the feast; whiskey or brandy and water helped it through; and whiskey or brandy without water secured its safe digestion, not to be used in any more formal manner than for the relief of occasional thirst or for the entertainment of a friend, until the last appeal should be made to them to secure a sound night's sleep. Rum, seasoned with cherries, protected against the cold; rum, made astringent with peach-nuts, concluded the repast at the confectioner's; rum, made nutritious with milk, prepared for the maternal office. . . . No doubt there were numbers who did not use ardent spirits, but it was not because they were not perpetually in their way. . . . The friend who did not testify his welcome, and the employer who did not provide bountifully of them for his help, was held niggardly, and there was no special meeting, not even of the most formal or sacred kind, where it was considered indecorous, scarcely any place where it was not thought necessary, to produce them. . . .

This sort of drinking was the fashion, not only in the South, but virtually everywhere else in America, even in New England. The

Puritans passed laws forbidding nearly everything that gave the people pleasure, but let liquor alone, except for the usual regulatory statutes and the ordinances against drunkenness. Whatever their other faults, or virtues, may have been, the Puritans were hard drinkers, as well as being the first distillers of rum in this country. As early as 1630 John Winthrop, governor of Massachusetts Bay Colony, who arrived that year with seven hundred Puritan settlers, recorded in his journal that he had "observed it a common fault with our grown people that they gave themselves to drink hot waters immoderately." A hundred and fifty years Boston manufactured and consumed more rum than any other city in America, while in the back country of Massachusetts the thirst for ardent spirits was so great that farmers frequently sold their wheat for rum in the fall and winter, and in the spring and summer traveled forty or fifty miles to get bread. An early colonial versifier wrote of the New Englanders, specifically of the men of Derry, New Hampshire:

> *It was often said, that their only care,*
> *And their only wish, and only prayer,*
> *For the present world, and the world to come,*
> *Was a string of eels and a jug of rum.*

The custom of closing offices and business establishments each morning at eleven o'clock so that everyone could get a drink—known as Leven O'clock Bitters—prevailed throughout the country, and in most of the colonies there was a similar stoppage of work at four in the afternoon. These practices were also observed when the people assembled for such public and communal tasks as haying, reaping, barnraising, woodcutting, and building and repairing highways. On these occasions liquor was free to all, and enormous quantities were consumed. For instance, when a group of citizens of Schenectady, New York, held a woodcutting bee in 1748 to lay in the local minister's winter supply of fuel, the men who did the sawing and chopping drank five gallons of rum and a half gallon of wine.

Workmen commonly received part of their wages in rum or other ardent spirits, and were given stipulated days off for sprees, or, as most work agreements frankly phrased it, "to get drunk." It was well-nigh impossible for a farmer who didn't provide plenty of liquor to get farm hands to work for him; it was generally agreed that no man could do a day's work on a farm without alcoholic stimulation. Slaves were likewise given large and regular rations of liquor. Business conferences began and ended with slugs of rum, while liquor flowed almost continuously at social functions. Grocers and other merchants kept barrels of rum on tap for customers who came in to settle their accounts or to buy large bills of goods; it was good manners to get groggy on these occasions. Meetings of town and village officials, and even court sessions, were frequently held in the taverns, so that the lawmakers and judges could be close to the source of inspiration. An old New Hampshire court bill, dated April 15, 1772, shows that on that day the judge had been supplied with a bowl of punch, two bottles of wine, and a mug of rum flip, at a cost of eight shillings twopence. A jury bill of the same date shows the expenditure of fourteen shillings fourpence for eleven dinners, five mugs of flip, and two mugs of cider. A mug of flip, incidentally, varied in quantity from a pint to a half gallon.

The result of all this, of course, was a great deal of drunkenness. As the *Old American Encyclopedia* put it, "sots were common in both sexes, of various ages, and of every condition." Some of the gentlemen seem to have been rare old topers. The Rev. Mason L. Weems, celebrated inventor of Washington legends, published in 1812 a curious pamphlet called *The Drunkard's Looking-Glass,* in which he reproduced a tavern bill, dated April 1, 1812, for one day's drinking and feasting by Mr. Thomas C——:

3 mint slings before breakfast, 25 cts.	$0.75
1 breakfast	.50
9 tumblers of Grog before dinner, 12½ cts.	1.12½
3 glasses of Wine and Bitters, 12½ cts.	.37½
Dinner and club	1.25
2 ticklers of French Brandy, 25 cts.	.50
Cigars	.25
Supper and Wine	1.25
Total	$6.00

There was never any shortage of hard liquor; almost every tavern, except the backwoods joints, carried sufficient potables to satisfy even such splendid appetites as that of Mr. C., who was by no means unique. Applejack, better known as Jersey Lightning, was plentiful, and so was gin, popularly called Strip and Go Naked, or Blue Ruin, which sold for a few pence a quart. Because of its cheapness and startling impact—it was of a higher proof in those days—gin was the favorite drink of slaves and servants. It was frequently mixed with beer, and sometimes with a raw, cheap rum called kill-devil; or with blackstrap, a mixture of rum and molasses. These concoctions would have appalled even the most hardened veteran of prohibition speak-easies, but they were drunk with relish by those who couldn't afford anything better. They probably offered the quickest way to achieve temporary paralysis ever devised.

By far the most abundant liquor, however, was rum. The prosperity of New England, especially of Rhode Island and Massachusetts, was largely founded upon rum. The first rum used in this country was imported from the West Indies, where it was distilled to absorb surplus molasses production; domestic distillation on a large scale began when a shipload of molasses was brought into Rhode Island late in the seventeenth century. Distilleries were soon in operation throughout New England, and by the early years of the eighteenth century rum was being manufactured in great quantities for the slave trade. At first the dealers on the African slave coast sold a prime Negro for a few gallons of rum, but eventually, as rum became cheaper and more plentiful, the price of slaves rose to two hundred and fifty gallons each, and the business became unprofitable. Meanwhile rum had become an important article of commerce; during the few years preceding the Revolution more than six hundred thousand gallons were shipped abroad annually, while large supplies were sold for domestic consumption. The industry continued to expand, and as late as 1807, although whiskey had become popular in the East, forty rum distilleries were operating in Boston. At one time so much rum was available in the Massachusetts metropolis that it sold at retail for fourpence a quart. West Indies rum, supposed to be better than the New England product, was only twopence more.

2

The taverns and tippling houses, where the middle and lower classes did most of their heavy drinking, and where the rich bought the bulk of their supplies for home consumption, rapidly increased in numbers as liquor became cheaper and more plentiful. Time has cast a patina of glamour over the drinking resorts of early America; many historians appear to be under a compulsion to describe them as places of mellow charm, presided over by a "fat and genial host," serving the choicest of food and drink, and frequented by the most important men of the day, who gathered before the great fireplace each evening to engage in wise and witty talk over bowls of flip and noggins of toddy.

Such a description may have fitted some of the taverns of the seventeenth century, when licenses were granted only to men of good character and reputation, and when the tavern keeper, operating the only place of public resort in the town or village, enjoyed great prestige and high social standing. In most places, in fact, he was ranked above the local clergyman. But the flood of rum changed the picture; when drinking became more profitable, the issuance of a license was determined by political and other considerations. A lower class of men gradually acquired control of the trade, and a new type of resort began to appear—the dramshop and the gin mill, housed in rude shacks and attracting thieves, ruffians, loafers, and other ornaments of a developing underworld.

The character of the tavern likewise declined; there was so much quick money to be made in the sale of liquor that other features of the establishment were neglected. The taverns of the eighteenth century, except for a few first-class houses in the larger towns of the East, were usually dirty and frequently disorderly, while the accommodations were generally unsatisfactory. The food, nearly everywhere, lacked variety, and was poorly prepared and served. Private sleeping quarters were almost unknown; travelers customarily slept two, three, and even four together, removing only their coats and shoes and fighting a losing battle throughout the night with the original inhabitants of the bed, fleas and bedbugs. By the middle of the eighteenth century the places where liquor was sold in this country had already acquired many of the characteristics of their successor, the saloon, and had begun to present a problem which was destined to plague American lawmakers for two hundred years, and for which a solution, in fact, has not yet been found. A description of eighteenth-century drinking resorts which John Adams, second President of the United States, recorded in his diary in 1760, has a curiously modern note:

> But the worst effect of all, and which ought to make every man who has the least sense of his privileges tremble, these houses are become the nurseries of our legislators. An artful man, who has neither sense nor sentiment, may, by gaining a little sway among the rabble of a town, multiply taverns and dramshops and thereby secure the votes of taverner and retailer and all; and the multiplication of taverns will make many, who may be induced to flip and rum, to vote for any man whatever.

In fifty years Adams could see no improvement. He wrote to a friend in 1811 that he was "fired with a zeal amounting to enthusiasm against ardent spirits, the multiplication of taverns, retailers, dramshops and tippling houses, and grieved to the heart to see the number of idlers, thieves, sots, and consumptive patients made for the physician in these infamous seminaries."

3

Throughout the era when rum was so abundant, it was almost the universal beverage, especially of the middle classes. Rum was to be found everywhere. A jug of rum, flanked by a pitcher of water and a box of sugar, occupied the place of honor on every sideboard, and many taverns sold nothing else. The wealthy classes drank it, too, but they varied their liquid diet with imported brandy; arrack, a distillation of rice and molasses which came from the East Indies; and such famous wines as madeira, canary, port, and malaga, which were mixed with milk and sugar to form a summer drink called sillibub. Domestic wines were available in some localities, but were not first-class. Rum was used in a great variety of ways—straight, hot, and cold, buttered, with water and sugar, and as the principal ingredient of flip, sling, punch, and toddy. These were the most popular mixed drinks, although there was also, in the higher classes of society, a fairly large consumption of mead, a fermentation of honey and water; and of metheglin, made of honey and yeast.

The most famous of colonial drinks was rum flip, made by combining rum, beer, and sugar, about two-thirds beer. The mixture was then stirred with an iron poker, called a loggerhead, which had been brought to a cherry-red heat in the fireplace. When it began to boil, it was drinkable. Properly prepared, rum flip had a slightly bitter, burnt taste, and was very potent. An evening over a bowl of rum flip frequently ended in a brawl, and the loggerheads came in handy to settle disputes. From this came the expression "at loggerheads." Rum sling was made of rum and water, about half and half, with a little sugar added. A toddy was basically the same as a sling, except that lemon juice was used if available. Punch was usually concocted of spices, rum, and lime or lemon juice, with sugar or sirup. It was served both hot and cold.

Cider was the second most popular drink, and was almost as plentiful as rum; a cider press was part of the equipment of every farm, and of many town and village households as well. Since the apple is not native to the American continent, cider was unknown in the colonies for a good many years, except for a few barrels imported from England. But extensive orchards were planted, and soon began to yield fruit. By the early 1700s cider sold in the larger towns at from six to eight shillings a barrel, retail. During the pressing season from six to thirty barrels of cider were laid in by each family, according to size and circumstances, for winter consumption. Very little was used sweet, except by the few moderate drinkers and total abstainers; most people considered that cider was scarcely potable until it had got hard; and the harder the better.

The date in which the distillation of whiskey began in this country has not been preserved, but it was probably around 1760, just in time to play a part in the great wave of intemperance. Whiskey first appeared in western Pennsylvania, where it was distilled by the farmers for their own use. Production on a fairly large scale started when the farmers discovered that a horse could carry four bushels of grain to market over the rough trails of the western country, but could carry the whiskey made from twenty-four bushels. At the time of the Whiskey Insurrection in 1794, which occurred when the federal government imposed an excise tax of nine cents a gallon on all distilled spirits, it was said that every family in western Pennsylvania operated its own still. Whiskey began to spread elsewhere in the country during the Revolution, when it was issued as a ration to troops of the Continental Army at times when good rum was unobtainable. Long before whiskey was used to any large extent in the East, it was a popular tipple throughout the West. In some localities prices of goods were quoted in whiskey, and the liquor was used as currency. A keg of whiskey was an important part of the provisions of every flatboat which went down the Ohio and Mississippi rivers. It was placed in the center of the boat, with a tin cup chained to it, and any member of the crew, or any passenger, could help himself whenever he felt the need of stimulation. The flatboatmen, very rugged characters, always drank it straight, although it was as raw as any liquor could well be.

The supply of beer in this country, before the Teutonic immigration began, was very spotty; it was plentiful in some places and scarce in others. This was due partly to recurrent shortages of barley and malt, and partly to a lack of skilled maltsters, although the establishment of malthouses was encouraged by the colonial governments. But Americans of those times were not greatly concerned over this and other shortages; there was a great deal of home-brewing and home-distilling. The people made brandies and cordials out of cherries and other berries, wine from wild grapes, and a variety of liquors from almost everything else that grew in the woods or on the farms. Their ingenuity in these matters was at least equal to that of their descendants of the twentieth century; and their products were probably more palatable than most of the stuff which burned its way down American throats during prohibition. As a contemporary verse put it:

If barley be wanting to make into malt,
We must be content and think it no fault,
For we can make liquor to sweeten our lips,
Of pumpkins, and parsnips, and walnut-tree chips.

When difficulties of transportation and other factors are taken into consideration, the consumption of hard liquors in early America was truly extraordinary, especially during the thirty years or so that followed the turn of the nineteenth century. In 1792, when the population of the United States was a little more than four million, the per capita consumption of ardent spirits was estimated at approximately two and one half gallons, with a grand total, including imports, of 11,008,447 gallons. Of this quantity, about 5,200,000 gallons were produced in this country by 2,579 registered distilleries. By 1810 the number of distilleries had increased to 14,191 and the consumption had tripled, while the population had not quite doubled. In 1814 the Massachusetts Society for the Suppression of Intemperance published a report dealing with the consumption of distilled liquors in 1810, signed by Samuel Dexter, LL.D., president of the society and formerly Secretary of War and Secretary of the Treasury. It said:

The quantity of ardent spirits consumed in the country surpasses belief. By the marshals' return to the Secretary's office in 1810 of domestic manufacturers in the United States, it is ascertained that 25,499,382 gallons of ardent spirits were distilled in that year, of which 133,823 gallons were exported, leaving 25,365,559 gallons to be consumed at home. Considering the caution with which accounts of property are rendered to government through fear of taxation; considering, also, the quantities distilled in private families, of which no account may have been rendered, there is a high probability that millions might be added to the account rendered by the marshals. Let it stand, however, as it is, and add to it 8,000,000 gallons of distilled spirits in the same year imported, and the quantity for home consumption amounts to 33,365,559 gallons.

The report broke down these figures to obtain a per capita consumption for 1810, of four and seven tenths gallons. The population of the United States in that year was 7,239,903. Thirteen years later, in 1823, the Boston *Recorder,* a temperance journal, said that the total annual consumption of the country was seventy-five million "gallons of liquid fire," although no detailed statistics were published. The first annual report of the Executive Committee of the Connecticut State Temperance Society, dated May 19, 1830, said that "in one of the most moral and regular towns of Litchfield County, whose population is 1,586, the amount of distilled liquors retailed during the last ten years has been 36,400 gallons." These liquors were chiefly rum and gin, other kinds not being reckoned. The report also said that licensed retailers in Hartford County, Connecticut, exclusive of the city of Hartford, sold annually 178,000 gallons of hard liquors, or four and one fourth gallons per capita. In 1826 the nineteen hundred inhabitants of Dudley, Massachusetts, drank ten thousand gallons of rum. In 1827 the town of Salisbury, Connecticut, consumed twenty-nine and one half gallons of rum for each of its thirty-four families. Two years later, in 1829, Troy, New York, with a population of ten thousand, consumed 73,959 gallons of rum. Albany, New York, appears to have been the champion. According to a report of the Albany Temperance Society, which made a careful survey of the town, Albany's twenty thousand inhabitants in 1829 consumed two hundred thousand gallons of ardent spirits. This was an average of ten gallons for each man, woman, and child.

4

Nobody drank harder during the great era of intemperance than the clergy. The autobiographies and other writings of ministers who survived the ecclesiastical guzzling to become leaders of the temperance movement are filled with accounts of gigantic drinking bouts in the homes of their parishioners, at ordinations, funerals, and other religious exercises in which they participated, and elsewhere. There were few who didn't drink at every opportunity, and to excess, while many were engaged in the liquor business, owning interests in distilleries and taverns. Eliphalet Nott, president of Union College at Schenectady, New York, for many years, said in a famous series of temperance lectures in the late 1840s that "not a few pioneer ministers were distillers and sold to their neighbors the products of their stills." The Rev. Nathan Strong, pastor of the First Church of Hartford, Connecticut, about 1800, and a noted revivalist who saved many souls by the fervor of his preaching, operated a prosperous distillery within sixty rods of his church. He was thus able to keep an eye on both his businesses at the same time. The authorities of many towns encouraged the establishment of drinking places conveniently near the churches, so that the preachers and their flocks might be able to refresh themselves before and after services.

A temperance historian of the 1880s, the Rev. Daniel Dorchester, D.D., quoted the Rev. Leonard Woods, a noted professor of theology at Andover Seminary, as saying that: "I remember when I could reckon up among my acquaintances forty ministers, who were either drunkards, or so far addicted to drinking, that their reputation and usefulness were greatly impaired, if not utterly ruined." The same historian quotes "another gentleman" who said in a Boston newspaper that "a great many deacons in New England died drunkards"; he had "a list of 123 intemperate deacons in Massachusetts, forty-three of whom became sots."[1] Edward C. Delavan of Albany, New York, who according to the 1891 edition of *The Cyclopedia of Temperance and Prohibition* amassed a fortune as a wine merchant and then became an ardent temperance worker, wrote to the governor of New York in 1857 that an "aged divine, well acquainted with the clergy in Albany," had found that "fifty per cent of the clergy, within a circuit of fifty miles, died drunkards." This was in the 1820s, when only one of Albany's twenty-eight preachers was willing to say a good word for temperance.

Drinking among clergymen was not confined to the towns and cities; it seems to have been even more prevalent in the country districts, and especially in such border states as Kentucky, Ohio, and Tennessee. The Rev. Peter Cartwright, a noted Methodist circuit rider who traveled the western trails around the turn of the nineteenth century, wrote in his autobiography, "it was almost universally the custom for preachers, in common with all others, to take drams. . . . I recollect at an early age," he continued, "at a court time in Springfield, Tennessee, to have seen and heard a very popular Baptist preacher, who was evidently intoxicated, drinking the health of the company in what he called the health the Devil drank to a dead hog. I have often seen it carried and used freely at large baptizings, where the ordinance was administered by immersion." Baptists were probably the most intemperate of the western preachers, but their church authorities do not appear to have been greatly worried about it. In fact, some of the Baptist sects lagged behind other Protestant denominations in espousing the anti-liquor cause; as late as 1854 Primitive Baptist congregations in Kentucky were expelling members who joined temperance societies.

The Methodists, however, had a great deal of trouble with drunken ministers, especially the local preachers who had been authorized to conduct religious services but were not ordained. Despite the exhortations and example of Bishop Francis Asbury, who occasionally tossed off a little ale and light wine "for my health's sake" but refused to drink ardent spirits even when ordered to do so by his physician, the local Methodist preachers continued to distill and to drink liquor in large quantities. Bishop Asbury finally called upon Peter Cartwright, James B. Finley, and other dependable circuit riders to examine the local preachers and dismiss from the connection such as were found guilty of drunkenness. Cartwright thus described the trial of a local preacher in eastern Tennessee:

> I said: "Brother W., do you drink drams?"
> "Yes," said he.
> "What is your particular reason for drinking drams?" I asked him.
> "Because it makes me feel good," he answered.
> "You drink till you feel it, do you?" said I.
> "Certainly," said he.
> "Well, how much do you drink at a time?"
> He replied, gruffly, that he never measured it.

"Brother, how often do you drink in a day?"

"Just when I feel like it, if I can get it."

"Well, brother, there are complaints that you drink too often and too much; and the Saturday before my next appointment here you must meet a committee of local preachers at ten o'clock, to investigate this matter . . ."

I had hard work to get a committee that were not dram-drinkers themselves. The trial came on, the class leader brought evidence that the local preacher had been intoxicated often, and really drunk several times. The committee found him guilty of immoral conduct, and suspended him till the next quarterly meeting; and the quarterly meeting, after hard debate, expelled him. . . . The poor local preacher, I fear, lived and died a drunkard. . . .[2]

Actually, the preacher in colonial times and during the early years of the Republic was in a difficult position; even if he had wanted to do so, he could scarcely have remained temperate and still performed, satisfactorily, the duties of his office. In those days the clergyman was a man of great importance in the community; to offer him a drink was to show respect and esteem. If he refused it, he was looked upon as a hypocrite, and the donor felt insulted, or at least slighted. If he consistently abstained, he was believed to hold unsound views about everything else, and was lucky to retain his pastorate. If he couldn't hold his liquor, he was a weakling and no true man of God. When he stepped into a store or business office, he was called upon to respond to as many toasts as there were men present. When he called upon a member of his flock, the gratified householder met him at the door with a mug of rum or hard cider. Drinks were served almost continuously during his visit, and when he departed he was expected to quaff a good-by cup. If he made twenty calls in one day, he went through, or tried to go through, the same procedure at each place. It is small wonder that many preachers were continually in a more or less pleasant state of befuddlement.

The Rev. I. N. Tarbox, D.D., a noted temperance lecturer of the 1870s, once said that "ordinations were seasons of festivity, in which copious drinking had a large share, and an ordination ball often ended the occasion." He was being somewhat conservative; in reality many ordinations were drunken routs, at which everybody got well plastered. Funerals were likewise occasions of considerable jollity; once the corpse had been disposed of, everybody pitched in to drink up the potables that had been provided. Sometimes they got away with huge quantities of liquor; for instance, when the funeral of a preacher's widow was held in Boston in 1678, the mourners drank fifty-one and one half gallons of malaga wine. In Virginia it took four thousand pounds of tobacco to pay the liquor costs of a single funeral. The bill for liquor consumed at an ordination was usually paid for by the church, while the costs for liquid refreshment at a funeral were footed by the family of the dead person, or by the town or village if the deceased was a pauper. The custom of drinking at funerals began to decline in the early part of the seventeenth century, and by 1750 had virtually ceased.

At ordinations and other religious functions where liquor was on tap, the preacher was expected to lead the assault upon the jugs and bottles. Even the renowned Cotton Mather, an inveterate foe of intemperance, and of almost everything else, imbibed, though moderately, at such gatherings. In describing a meeting, a "private fast," held ten days after his ordination in Boston, Cotton Mather noted in his journal that following two sermons and four prayers, one of which ran for an hour and a half, "some biskets and beer, cider, wine," were distributed. "The Lord," he wrote, "hear in Heaven his dwelling place."

On May 4, 1784, at the ordination of a new pastor of the South Society in Hartford, Connecticut, twenty-four preachers drank "3 bitters, 15 boles punch, 11 bottles wine, 5 mugs flip, 3 boles toddy, 3 boles punch." At the ordination of the Rev. Edwin Jackson at Woburn, Massachusetts, in 1729, the people drank "six and one half barrels of cider, twenty-five gallons of wine, two gallons of brandy, and four gallons of rum." According to the old record, this bill was paid by the town. At an ordination in New England in 1785, in addition to a goodly supply of cherry rum, the celebrants drank "thirty bowles of punch before they went to the meeting, ten bottles of wine before they went to the meeting, forty-four bowles of punch while at dinner, also eighteen bottles of wine and eight bowles of Brandy." The Rev. Lyman Beecher, one of the great figures of the early temperance movement, thus described an ordination at Plymouth, Massachusetts, in 1810, soon after he had become pastor of the Congregational Church at Litchfield, Connecticut:

> . . . the preparation for our creature comforts, besides food, was a broad sideboard covered with decanters and bottles and sugar and pitchers of water. There we found all the various kinds of liquor then in vogue. The drinking was apparently universal. The preparation was made by the society, as a matter of course. When the Consociation arrived, they always took something to drink round, also before public services, and always on their return. As they could not all drink at once, they were obliged to stand and wait as people do when they go to mill. There was a decanter of spirits also on the dinner table to help digestion, and gentlemen partook of it through afternoon and evening as they felt the need, some more and some less; and the sideboard, with its spillings of water and sugar and liquor, looked and smelled like the bar of a very active grog-shop. . . . And, silently, I took an oath before God that I would never attend another ordination of that kind. . . .[3]

The custom of drinking heavily at ordinations declined rapidly during the first quarter of the nineteenth century, partly because church members protested against the cost of such indulgence, and partly because many preachers were becoming interested in the temperance movement. As late as 1825, however, when the Rev. Leonard Bacon was installed as pastor of the Congregational Church at New Haven, Connecticut, the church bought drinks for all comers at the bar of the local hotel.

5

Historians and psychologists who have studied the habits and customs of American pioneers have ascribed their heavy drinking to various causes. Some say it was due to the emotional impact of the Revolution, others that it was the transference of Anglo-Saxon drinking habits to the New World. Still others believe that liquor was consumed in such large quantities because alcohol offered an escape from the harshness and hardships of frontier life, a theory which scarcely stands up when it is recalled that as living conditions improved, drinking increased. There is another explanation, but it is so dreadfully unscientific that no one has ever dared to suggest it for serious consideration. That is, that the colonists drank heavily because they liked liquor.

CHAPTER TWO

Genesis

Many of the statutes with which the colonial authorities sought to regulate the taverns and discourage the excessive use of ardent spirits were very strict. Curfew laws were rigidly enforced in New England, and also in New York, where Peter Stuyvesant complained in 1630 that one fourth of the town of New York (then called New Amsterdam) was "devoted to houses for the sale of brandy, tobacco, and beer." In most localities, particularly the New England colonies, definite limits were imposed upon the length of time a man might sit tippling in a public house, and upon the quantity of liquor which he might buy at one visit. Violators of these laws were fined, whipped, confined in the stocks or pillory, and, in extreme cases, expelled from the colony. In Massachusetts a man who had been convicted several times of drunkenness was compelled to wear, dangling from his neck, a large "D" painted in red upon a white cloth; or a large placard pinned to the back of his coat and emblazoned, "A DRUNK-ARD." Such punishments, however, were not imposed as often as might be supposed, nor were they notably effective; there was a great deal of surreptitious drinking, and even in those early days the authorities found it difficult to destroy a natural appetite by legislation.

Georgia went further than any of the other colonies in the attempt to curb excessive use of hard liquor. Always a star in the dry crown, Georgia experimented with prohibition for some seven years, from 1735 to 1742. A few days after James Oglethorpe arrived in Georgia with his colonists, in February 1733, he spoke to them about their duties and prospects in the New World, and announced that the Trustees of the colony had been pleased to grant to each settler forty-four gallons of beer and sixty-five gallons of molasses, to be used in brewing more beer. It was hoped that this would encourage the establishment of a domestic brewing industry. Oglethorpe also told the colonists that the manufacture and importation of ardent spirits would not be permitted, and urged them to drink beer and be happy, healthy, and prosperous. Since this pronouncement was made on Oglethorpe's own responsibility and had no legal force, it failed to impress the settlers; many of them proceeded to use their molasses for making rum instead of beer. Large quantities of liquor were immediately sent into the colony from South Carolina and other provinces, and rum and brandy were sold openly at the official trading house. When Oglethorpe reported to the Trustees in London the condition of the colony, which was poor, they wrote to him in November 1733:

> As it appears by your letters that the sickness among the people is owing to the excessive drinking of rum punch, the Trustees do absolutely forbid their drinking, or even having any rum, and agree with you so entirely in your sentiments that they order all rum that shall be brought there to be immediately staved.

The following year, 1734, the British Parliament passed an act prohibiting the "importation of rum and brandies" into Georgia, and the law went into effect in April 1735. Immediately there developed in the colony a situation exactly similar, but of course on a smaller scale, to that which confronted the entire United States in the 1920s. Legally deprived of ardent spirits, the settlers neglected the business of building up the colony and devoted themselves to the more agreeable task of getting liquor. Moonshine stills, possibly the first ever operated in America, were set up in the back country, and produced bad rum for local consumption. But the rumrunners, first of a breed that helped to make the enforcement of the Eighteenth Amendment an exciting adventure almost two hundred years later, were the principal source of supply. They ran boats down from South Carolina, and unloaded their cargoes of rum and brandy on the lonely and unguarded coast of Georgia. There they were met by gangs of armed bootleggers, who carried the heavy kegs of liquor, on foot and on horseback, through the wilderness to the towns and villages. Other bootleggers prowled the country districts, posing as peddlers and ordinary travelers, and selling rum by the drink from their packs. There was even an occasional outbreak of hijacking.

Speakeasies sprang up everywhere—in private homes, in the back rooms of stores and offices, and in hurriedly built huts on the outskirts of the settlements. A representative of the Trustees, in a letter to London, described these places as "nurseries of villainy," and estimated that there were as many illegal tippling houses in Georgia as there were gin shops in London. This was clearly an exaggeration, for England was then at the height of the great gin binge which the historian William Lecky, considering its effect upon the English people, described as probably the most momentous fact of the eighteenth century. The passion for gin began to affect the English masses about 1724, and, as Lecky said, "spread with the rapidity and violence of an epidemic." In many sections of crowded London gin was sold in every house. Gin was extraordinarily plentiful, and so cheap that the proprietors of thousands of London gin shops hung out signs guaranteeing to make their customers "drunk for one penny and dead drunk for two pence," and offering free straw to lie upon. Henry Fielding, in a pamphlet published in 1751, said that gin was the principal sustenance of more than one hundred thousand people in the English metropolis. He predicted that "should the drinking of this poison be continued at its present height, during the next twenty years, there will be by that time very few of the common people left to drink it."

The Georgia colonists brought their appetite for ardent spirits with them, but in the New World seem to have preferred rum, perhaps because very little gin was available. And they firmly refused to believe that there was anything criminal in the sale or use of ardent spirits; their sympathies were with the rumrunners and the bootleggers, and the colonial authorities found them decidedly unco-operative. Violators of the law, when caught, invariably demanded trial by jury, the result being that there were almost no convictions. In several cases where judges ordered verdicts of guilty, the jurors refused to obey. The Savannah magistrates made a vigorous effort to enforce the law in 1739, following a serious riot instigated by drunken ruffians, but failed completely, and soon thereafter reported to the Trustees that they were powerless to check the flow of rum. Another report declared that many officials of the colony were making tidy profits in the illegal trade, an accusation which will be familiar to Americans who lived through the gaudy days of a later era. Meanwhile pressure was being brought to bear in London by British merchants, and in 1742 the Trustees abandoned prohibition, permitted the importation of ardent spirits, and instituted a system of licenses for taverns and tippling houses. The rumrunners, bootleggers, and speakeasies soon vanished, and the colony began to prosper under the stimulus of the rum trade. A report to the Trustees a few years later said that drunkenness had greatly decreased.

2

All of the early laws relating to ardent spirits, with the exception of Georgia's prohibition statute, were directed, not against the use of liquor, but against the misuse of "the good creature." The first feeble outcries of laymen and the clergy, which eventually swelled into a mighty roar, were likewise concerned with excessive drinking. Even Increase Mather and his son Cotton, most famous of Puritan clergymen, although they preached almost incessantly against intemperance, admitted that a well-conducted tavern was an important asset to any town or village, and acknowledged the value of ardent spirits when used in moderation. They greatly feared, however, that drunkenness would ruin the Puritans physically and economically. And more important, from their viewpoint, they were convinced that the almost universal use of rum and the reveling and loose conduct in the taverns were hindering the progress of religion. Cotton Mather expressed in his journal the fear that "the flood of excessive drinking" would "drown Christianity"; he held firmly to the opinion that it was the reason people were turning away from the church. Both of the Mathers urged a more rigid enforcement of the laws regulating taverns and tippling houses, a drastic reduction in the number of these places, and the expulsion of habitual drunkards lest their example inflame others with an uncontrollable thirst. As early as 1673 Increase Mather published a pamphlet in which he vigorously demanded that the colonial authorities take these steps.

Throughout the eighteenth century, while the consumption of ardent spirits increased rapidly among all classes of the people, there was also developing an awareness of the evils and dangers of intemperance. More and more clergymen preached temperance sermons, and themselves, as far as they were able, renounced rum and confined their tippling to beer and light wines. More and more laymen of prominence and influence complained that drunkenness was becoming a national vice, and that it was the cause of much misery and poverty; they protested against the indiscriminate granting of licenses. Their attitude was reflected in the report of a Philadelphia grand jury, of which Benjamin Franklin was foreman, in 1744. The jury found that there were more poor people in Philadelphia than ever before, that the use of profane language had become commonplace, even in the streets and public places, and that the people generally were manifesting an increasing distaste for religion. For these evils the grand jury blamed the taverns and tippling houses, comprising "near a tenth part of The City."

Almost all of these sermons and protests were appeals for moderation; there was only an occasional appeal for abstinence from ardent spirits, usually delivered apologetically and modified by the assurance that no one opposed the use of hard liquor as a medicine or on special occasions. The few champions of abstinence were also careful to say a good word for beer and light wines; there was a strong conviction among temperance advocates that if the national appetite could be transferred to malt beverages, drunkenness would disappear. The notion that the manufacture and sale of all liquor containing alcohol should be prohibited was so preposterous that no one seems to have advanced it for more than one hundred and fifty years after the introduction of rum, one of the great landmarks of American drinking. The only suggestion that legal means be used to curtail the production of liquor was contained in a resolution passed by the Continental Congress on February 27, 1777. It was clearly directed against whiskey, which was being made in large quantities in the western country, and most historians believe that its real purpose was to conserve food sorely needed by the Continental Army. At any rate, no attention was paid to it. The resolution said:

> That it be recommended to the several Legislatures of the United States immediately to pass laws the most effectual for putting an immediate stop to the pernicious practice of distilling grain, by which the most extensive evils are likely to be derived if not quickly prevented.

By the middle 1700s some of the dominant religious sects had begun to discipline members for drunkenness, but it was many years before any of them officially promulgated rules relating to abstinence, or to the manufacture and sale of ardent spirits. The first important sect to make even a roundabout approach to this problem was the Methodist. Francis Asbury, himself a strict abstainer from hard liquor, began to preach temperance as soon as he arrived in this country in 1771 as John Wesley's General Assistant, thirteen years before he was ordained Bishop. In 1780, at a General Conference of the Methodist Societies held in Baltimore, Asbury procured the adoption of a minute in which two questions were asked and answered affirmatively: "Do we disapprove of the practice of distilling grain into liquor? Shall we disown our friends who will not renounce the practice?" Three years later the minute was made stronger by an additional question, "Shall our friends be permitted to make spirituous liquors, sell and drink them in drams?" The answer was, "By no means; we think it wrong in its nature and consequences." This minute produced no practical results, but it expressed the attitude of Asbury and other church leaders, and its adoption indicated their power. The members of the church continued to drink, and the local preachers, despite the expulsion of many for drunkenness, continued to distill and sell whiskey.

The problem of the local preacher was not solved until 1816, the year of Asbury's death, when the General Conference adopted a motion which said that "no stationed or local preacher shall retail spirituous or malt liquors without forfeiting his ministerial character among us." Neither Asbury nor other Methodist churchmen of his time ever suggested prohibitory laws; they advocated the teaching of temperance "by precept and example." It is interesting to note that for many years the Methodist Discipline contained this statement: "We recognize that the Church as an ecclesiastical body may not properly go into partisan politics nor assume to control the franchise of the nation." This was finally eliminated by the General Conference of 1924, long after it had become no more than a curiosity.

3

The temperance reformers of the eighteenth century were a small minority of the population, and their sporadic agitation had almost no effect upon the appetite of the people for ardent spirits. There was no apparent decline in the heavy drinking at ordinations and other religious and social functions, while the protests of the laymen failed to reduce the number of taverns and tippling houses. On the contrary, they continued to increase, as did the consumption of ardent spirits. The scattered opponents of hard liquor sorely needed a Moses to lead them out of the wilderness of ineffectuality and set their feet upon the trail to the promised land. He appeared in the person of Dr. Benjamin Rush, Surgeon-General of the Continental Army during the Revolution, a signer of the Declaration of Independence, the most famous medical man of his time, and a widely known patriot of great influence.

In 1785 Dr. Rush published a pamphlet, *An Inquiry into the Effect of Spirituous Liquors on the Human Body and Mind,* which is still recognized as one of the great temperance documents of the age, and as marking the inception of the movement that eventually brought about prohibition. As a temperance historian said in 1891, "Dr. Rush laid out nearly all the fundamental lines of argument along which the present temperance movement is pressed." Dr. Rush's essay, comprising fewer than forty closely printed pages, was the first comprehensive, uncompromising attack upon ardent spirits ever written; a careful, scientific examination of the problems of drinking in which he cited specific causes to prove his points. His conclusions, briefly, were: that ardent spirits had no food value and were therefore useless even as a supplementary diet; that they aggravated all diseases and were the direct cause of many, both mental and physical; that even the moderate use of spirituous liquors led inevitably to drunkenness and destruction; and that they should be taken only on the advice of a physician.

To prevent and cure intemperance, Dr. Rush urged the people to drink wine and beer. For the transition period between drunkenness and temperance, he recommended the use of laudanum or opium mixed with wine. Included in the *Inquiry* was a *Moral and Physical Thermometer of Intemperance,* which portrayed the downward progress of the drunkard from punch to drams of gin, brandy and rum. The man who drank immoderately of punch, a comparatively mild beverage, was very likely, according to the *Thermometer,* to fall a victim to idleness and gaming, to sickness, and to debt. The drinker who guzzled drams of gin, brandy, and rum, especially in the morning, could almost certainly look forward to burglary and murder, to madness and despair, and, finally, to the gallows. In another striking passage, Dr. Rush thus described the effect of ardent spirits upon a confirmed sot:

> In folly it causes him to resemble a calf; in stupidity, an ass; in roaring, a mad bull; in quarrelling and fighting, a dog; in cruelty, a tiger; in fetor, a skunk; in filthiness, a hog; and in obscenity, a he-goat.

During the next twenty years Dr. Rush's essay was published many times, while extracts frequently appeared in important newspapers and in the almanacs, the most popular publications of the time. It made a tremendous impression throughout the country, and its effects were soon apparent. Within two years Dr. Rush was writing jubilantly to friends that in many localities merchants were refusing to sell ardent spirits, and that in Pennsylvania and elsewhere citizens were forming associations pledging themselves to carry on their business affairs and private lives without the aid of spirituous liquors. Dr. Rush's influence was also seen in a memorial which the College of Physicians of Philadelphia sent to Congress in December 1790, when that body was considering new revenue laws, specifically an act imposing a heavy duty upon West Indies rum and other imported spirits. This memorial followed the arguments and conclusions of Dr. Rush's *Inquiry* very closely. It directed the attention of Congress to "the pernicious effect of distilled liquors upon morals and manners," and declared that they produced "a great portion of the most obstinate, painful, and mortal disorders which afflict the human body." Congress was entreated to "impose such heavy duties upon all distilled spirits as shall be effectual to restrain their intemperate use in our country."

Dr. Rush was vastly encouraged by this acceptance of his principles, and by other successes of the budding temperance movement; he expressed the conviction that the use of ardent spirits would eventually cease altogether. He envisioned a healthy American people bursting with beer, light wines, and happiness, and somewhat rashly predicted that by 1915 the use of spirituous liquors would be "as uncommon in families as a drink made of a solution of arsenic or a decoction of hemlock." A more realistic comment upon the human appetite was made by Fisher Ames of Boston, who had defeated Samuel Adams for Congress in 1788. Ames said, "If any man supposes that a mere law can turn the taste of a people from ardent spirits to malt liquors, he has a most romantic notion of legislative power."

The associations which appeared after the publication of Dr. Rush's treatise were not formally organized with constitutions and bylaws, and for that reason none is credited by temperance historians with being the original temperance society. The first of these groups of which any record remains was formed in Litchfield, Connecticut, in 1789. In its issue of July 13 of that year the *Federal Herald,* published at Lansingburg, New York, reported that "upward of two hundred of the most respectable farmers in Litchfield County, Connecticut, have formed an association to encourage the disuse of any kind of distilled spirits in doing their farming work the ensuing season." Actually, the pledge signed by the Litchfield farmers was a little clearer than that; it bound them to "carry on our business without the use of distilled spirits, as an article of refreshment, either for ourselves, or for those whom we employ."

A similar association, formed in Nelson County, Virginia, by Micajah Pendleton in 1800, went further; it prohibited the use of *all* alcoholic drinks, including beer, wine, and cider. This appears to have been the first mention of total abstinence, and it was not heard of again until 1819, when Judge Thomas Hertell of New York advocated it in an essay called *An Exposé of the Causes of Intemperate Drinking.* Both Pendleton and Judge Hertell were considerably ahead of their times; it was not until the middle 1830s that total abstinence became the guiding principle of the temperance movement.

4

The first temperance society in the world to be organized and its meetings conducted according to the rules of parliamentary procedure was conceived by Dr. Billy J. Clark, described by temperance historians as "a young and an intrepid physician." Dr. Clark lived in the town of Moreau, Saratoga County, New York, and practiced medicine both in Moreau and in the neighboring village of Northumberland. He had read Dr. Rush's essay on ardent spirits, and he had been struck by the fact that his own experience had paralleled that of the Philadelphia physician, especially among the hard-drinking lumberjacks who worked near Moreau during the timber-cutting season. On a cold night in March 1808 Dr. Clark sat comfortably before his fireplace, reflecting upon the state of Moreau and the nation. Suddenly it occurred to him that a well-organized society might help stem the tide of intemperance. He was so excited that he immediately jumped on his horse and rode three miles through deep mud to the home of his pastor, the Rev. Lebbeus Armstrong of the First Congregational Church of Moreau. As he entered the clergyman's study, he raised both hands and cried:

"We shall all become a community of drunkards in this town, unless something is done to arrest the progress of intemperance!"

After several hours' talk, Dr. Clark and Armstrong agreed to meet a few days later at the home of another prominent citizen, Peter L. Manney, for further discussion. Preliminary arrangements were made there, and on April 30, 1808, forty-three men, most of them farmers, met at a schoolhouse and organized the Union Temperance Society of Moreau and Northumberland. A constitution and bylaws were adopted and officers elected, the first president being Colonel Sydney Berry, a former judge of the Saratoga County Court. The aims and some of the rules of the society were set forth in Articles IV and XI of the constitution:

> ART. IV. No member shall drink rum, gin, whiskey, wine, or any distilled spirits, or compositions of the same, or any of them, except by advice of a physician, or in case of actual disease; also, excepting wine at public dinners, under a penalty of twenty-five cents; provided that this article shall not infringe on any religious ordinance.
>
> Sec. 2. No member shall be intoxicated, under a penalty of fifty cents.
>
> Sec. 3. No member shall offer any of said liquors to any other member, or urge other persons to drink thereof, under a penalty of twenty-five cents for each offense.
>
> ART. XI. It shall be the duty of each member to accuse any other member of a breach of any regulation contained in Art. IV, and the mode of accusative process and trial shall be regulated by a By-law.

The Union Society, which Lebbeus Armstrong once called "this little feeble band of temperance brethren," withered away after a few years, but not until it had played its destined part. Although it failed to redeem the intemperate lumberjacks of Moreau and Northumberland, it was of great value to the temperance movement because it encouraged reform elements elsewhere to emulation. Within the next decade temperance societies had been formed in Connecticut, Massachusetts, New York, Rhode Island, Vermont, New Hampshire, Maine, and Pennsylvania. Some of these, notably in Connecticut and Massachusetts, were state organizations, with from thirty to forty town and county branches. Reports received in the East from such faraway places as Ohio, South Carolina, and Illinois gave glowing accounts of the upsurge of temperance sentiment in those localities; and for the first time articles on intemperance, most of them dealing with the economic aspects of the evil, began appearing in religious periodicals. The movement seemed to be making great strides everywhere; many reformers were so sanguine as to believe that complete and total victory was at hand. Actually, however, it was on the verge of disintegration.

Some of the societies advocated a sort of modified abstinence from ardent spirits, their pledges permitting the consumption of liquor on special occasions, at public functions, on the advice of a physician, et cetera, but most of them had been organized on the principle of moderation. It was left to each member to decide for himself what constituted temperate drinking. This decision has always been a very difficult one, and the members of many societies apparently experimented for years without reaching a definite conclusion. In some states the reformers, as their descendants were to do a hundred years later, overestimated their strength; they enlarged their activities and began issuing pronouncements about gambling, profanation of the Sabbath, and other vices. Thus they inevitably became involved in local and even state-wide political bickering, and their usefulness as agents of reform was seriously impaired. A temperance historian wrote about Connecticut, "a serious reaction was soon experienced in that state. A political revolution soon followed, and many of the barriers which had been erected were broken down." By the early 1820s conditions were scarcely better than they had been on the night that Dr. Billy J.

Clark made his famous ride through the mud to the home of Lebbeus Armstrong. Said the Boston *Recorder* in 1823:

> We have to report that the efforts for reform are so few and feeble. The laws are poorly executed. Nothing comparatively is yet actually accomplished. Moral societies which sprung into being a few years ago as if by magic, at the alarming prevalence of vice, are merged nearly all into oblivion. Their influence was gone even sooner than their name. Intemperance now walks at large aided rather than opposed by law.

The temperance movement was threatened with a collapse from which it might never have recovered, and which conceivably could have profoundly influenced the course of American history. Such a calamity was averted principally through the efforts of three men— Rev. Justin Edwards of the Park Street Congregationalist Church in Boston; Rev. Calvin Chapin of Rocky Hill, Connecticut; and Rev. Lyman Beecher, father of Harriet Beecher Stowe, pastor of the Presbyterian Church at Litchfield, Connecticut, and one of the greatest of early American reformers. Beecher had been instrumental in organizing the Connecticut Society for the Reformation of Morals in 1813, and had labored with some success, particularly within his own denomination, to reduce the consumption of spirituous liquors at ordinations and other ecclesiastical gatherings. In the autumn of 1825 he preached a series of six sermons, in which he vividly portrayed the evils of intemperance, urged abstinence from distilled liquors, and called for "the banishment of ardent spirits from the list of lawful articles of commerce, by a correct and efficient public sentiment." He modestly recorded in his autobiography that these discourses "became the most interesting thing ever heard of . . . a wonder of weekly conversation and interest, and, when I got through, of eulogy."

Beecher's sermons were published in pamphlet form early in 1826, about the time that the Connecticut *Observer* was printing a series of thirty-three articles by Calvin Chapin, based on sermons delivered at Rocky Hall and Wethersfield, Connecticut. Chapin's articles developed the theme that "entire abstinence from ardent spirits is the only certain preventive of intemperance." They were widely circulated, and attracted much attention. Beecher's sermons, however, were superior in every respect; they formed the basis of innumerable sermons and lectures during the next twenty years, and were republished in many editions, both here and abroad. Their influence was comparable to that of Dr. Benjamin Rush's essay, published forty years earlier.

Of even greater importance, however, was the work of Justin Edwards, who has been called by a temperance historian "the ablest organizer and promoter of the original temperance movement in America" and "the pivot on which all moved." For some time Edwards had been considering the formation of a national organization which might serve as a clearinghouse and focusing point for temperance ideas and activities. The great interest shown in Beecher's sermons and in Chapin's articles encouraged him to call a state convention of temperance reformers, which was answered by sixteen men, all prominent citizens of Boston and including seven clergymen. On February 13, 1826, they organized the American Society for the Promotion of Temperance, which soon became known as the American Temperance Society. Marcus Morton, an associate justice of the Massachusetts Supreme Court, was elected president, and the sixteen signed the constitution as members. A month later eighty-four additional members were elected from various eastern states. On March 4, 1826, the first temperance paper, a weekly called the *National Philanthropist,* began publication in Boston under the editorship of the Rev. William Collier and with the blessing and support of the society. A score of other journals appeared within the next year or two, but most of them failed to prosper. By 1836 there were eleven, well established, while most of the religious periodicals regularly published temperance articles and announcements. Extracts from all of these papers were printed and circulated by the American Tract Society.

The seven clergymen dominated the meeting at which the American Temperance Society was organized, but only two were elected to office. Justin Edwards and Rev. Leonard Woods, of Andover Seminary, became members of the executive committee, and Edwards was also appointed secretary. The records of the society say that the grand principle of the organization was "abstinence from strong drink; and its object, by light and love, to change the habits of the nation with regard to the use of intoxicating liquors." Actually, the society adopted no pledge, and the early organizers soft-pedaled the matter of abstinence. "Considerations of prudence," wrote the Rev. Daniel Dorchester, "held them back from pledging the people." It was several years before abstinence even from ardent spirits was required.

Edwards agreed to devote his whole time to the business of the society, and did so in fact until 1836, when he retired to become president of Andover Seminary. In the fall of 1826 Edwards raised seventy-five hundred dollars for the support of an agent, or assistant, and Rev. Nathaniel Hewitt of Fairfield, Connecticut, was appointed to the post. Additional agents were employed during the next few years, some of whom worked in the field as organizers and lecturers, while others handled publicity and propaganda under Edwards's direction. Once the money was in hand, early in 1827, Edwards and Hewitt started on a tour of the New England and middle Atlantic states, reviving old societies and organizing new ones, and, in particular, spreading the gospel of temperance among the Protestant churches.

When Edwards returned after several months, he reported that six state and 216 local temperance societies had become auxiliaries of the national organization. At the end of 1829 more than one thousand societies were reported, with a total membership of some one hundred thousand. Eleven were state societies. "More than fifty distilleries had been stopped," said the society's annual report, "more than 400 merchants had renounced the traffic, and more than 1,200 drunkards had ceased to use the drunkard's drink." In less than two years, on May 1, 1831, the society estimated that the number of societies had tripled; there were at least three thousand, with three hundred thousand members. Of the thirteen societies reported from Michigan Territory, one was at Laingsburg, a village in Shiawassee County between the modern cities of Flint and Lansing. The original pledge of this society called for moderate drinking, but in 1826 a new pledge was instituted for those who advocated total abstinence from ardent spirits. The members were listed on the rolls as "O.P.—Old Pledge" and "T—Total." The latter were soon known as "teetotalers," and in time the term came to be applied to those who abstained from all beverages containing alcohol.

These spectacular advances continued during the first half of the 1830s, which was a period of great progress and expansion. By 1836, when the American Temperance Society was succeeded by the American Temperance Union and Justin Edwards retired, some eight thousand societies, with approximately 1,500,000 members, were more or less affiliated with the national organization. Early in the decade Edwards and Rev. John Marsh, an agent of the American Temperance Society who became secretary of the new Union, made a series of fruitful visits to Washington, on the first of which Edwards addressed the members of Congress and organized local societies with more than one thousand members. For several years the temperance reformers had been striving to dry up the United States Army, but had been unable to convince the War Department that liquor was to blame for the frequent desertions, and for the many other troubles in which soldiers became involved. In 1831 Lewis Cass, a statesman of great influence and an ardent temperance advocate, was appointed Secretary of War by President Andrew Jackson, and Edwards returned to the attack. Little persuasion was required to induce Cass to sign an order, dated November 2, 1832, abolishing the liquor ration in the Army and prohibiting the sale or use of ardent spirits at "any fort, camp, or garrison of the United States."

In February 1833 Edwards was again in Washington, and on the twenty-sixth of that month a large group of enthusiastic senators and representatives met in the Senate chamber and organized the American Congressional Temperance Society, with Lewis Cass as president. The prestige which the temperance movement acquired by thus bringing into the fold some of America's most prominent politicians was enormous. Similar societies were organized almost immediately in state legislatures throughout the country, Massachusetts leading the way within a month. On a somewhat lower social level Edwards also met with great success, upsetting a custom which had been prevalent for almost two hundred years. By 1837 hundreds of employers, besides joining their local temperance societies, had agreed not to furnish liquor to their workmen, and to discourage its use, while workingmen's temperance societies were flourishing in New York, Philadelphia, Baltimore, and Boston. One, in Philadelphia, had more than three hundred members, all of whom had signed a pledge to abstain from ardent spirits.

To climax his prodigious labors, Edwards played a prominent part in the organization of the American Temperance Union. He dictated the appointment of John Marsh as secretary, and with Lyman Beecher led the so-called radicals in a fight to compel a complete restatement of the movement's fundamental principles. They were victorious, despite much opposition, and after 1836 the temperance reformers openly advocated total abstinence from all intoxicating liquors, including beer, cider, and wine.

CHAPTER THREE

"Interpose Thine Arm"

The impressive victories won by the American Temperance Society during the regime of Justin Edwards were due almost entirely to his genius for promotion and organization. However, he made a far more important contribution to the phenomenal recovery of the temperance movement than merely forming societies. More than any other one man, he was responsible for the dogma that drinking is a mortal sin, and for the transformation of the movement into a religious crusade. Francis Asbury, the first Methodist bishop ordained in the United States, wrote in his journal a few years after his arrival in this country in 1771 that intemperance was "the prime curse of the United States, and will be, I fear much, the ruin of all that is excellent in morals and government among them." Thereafter he frequently noted that he had implored the Lord to "Interpose Thine Arm." But until Justin Edwards entered the fight against liquor there had been few indications that the Almighty intended to answer the prayer.

In the beginning the anti-liquor agitation was a layman's movement; laymen started it, and laymen organized and supported most of the early societies. In many places the local preacher was little more than a respected adviser. An occasional clergyman advanced the novel proposition that the drunkard could scarcely hope to behold the glories of Heaven, and many temperance advocates shared Cotton Mather's fear that Christianity would be submerged by a deluge of liquor. But the main emphasis was upon the terrible effects of ardent spirits upon the human body, and upon the social dislocations and economic misery which followed excessive drinking.

Edwards disagreed with this approach. He was convinced that man's immortal soul was at stake, and that real progress could be made only if organized religion absorbed the temperance movement and imbued the reformers with a furious fanaticism which would carry them to victory. As a clergyman of wide experience, he knew that men do not, or at least did not in those times, become fanatical over questions of physical welfare, or even over problems of economic security. The sort of frenzied zeal which Edwards felt was required stems from the essential instability of the religious temperament; holy men have always been able to whip it up by promising the most ineluctable of rewards and threatening the most dreadful of punishments. Edwards's viewpoint found wide support among the clergy, and was endorsed by a surprisingly large number of prominent laymen. They were not slow to point out that even the optimistic Dr. Benjamin Rush, though devoted to reason and the scientific method, had written to a friend in 1789, "I am disposed to believe that the business must be affected finally by religion alone."

As agents of the American Temperance Society, Edwards and his organizers traveled throughout the country for almost ten years, forming new societies and bringing the people into the fold. They delivered their message in the churches, crying over and over again that they were engaged upon a divine mission and acting under the awful authority of God, an assertion which was accepted everywhere as inspired truth. Under their prodding, temperance meetings were turned into religious revivals. Reformed drunkards were produced to give testimony to the accompaniment of a mighty chorus of prayers and praise, while clergymen and members of the congregation alike wept and wailed in holy ecstasy. Intemperance was attacked in the sonorous language of the pulpit, and those who signed the pledge or membership rolls were hailed as converts; renunciation of liquor and acceptance of Jesus became almost one and the same thing.

Edwards alarmed the ecclesiastical authorities by pointing out, and proving with carefully prepared statistics, that backsliding and conduct which necessitated disciplinary action against church members were nearly always caused by the excessive use of liquor. He portrayed a dismal and ungodly future in which the church lay trampled in the dust while the rum demon reigned triumphant. These were unbeatable arguments, and by the early 1830s Edwards had succeeded; all of the Protestant churches had endorsed the work of the American Temperance Society, although a few small and unimportant sects such as the Primitive Baptists remained unconvinced for some years that the task was truly of God. Thereafter the temperance reform was under the guidance of the evangelical churches, and anti-liquor agitation became as much a religious activity as Sunday school and prayer meeting.

With organized religion in control, the whole direction of the movement was changed. The human body and impending economic disaster were not ignored, but emphasis was transferred to the soul; drunkenness was identified with damnation and abstinence with salvation. From this developed the propaganda which in time led millions of Americans to the conviction that all evil came from alcohol, and that the downfall of the liquor traffic would usher in the prophesied age of peace, happiness, and universal prosperity. "Who that looks at the progress and present state of the temperance cause," cried the editor of the *Temperance Recorder* in 1832, "at the increasing strength and majesty with which it moves forward . . . without being full in the conviction that this very cause is the harbinger of the millennium . . . ?" Reuben Walworth, Chancellor of the state of New York and an eminent temperance advocate, foresaw the time when "total abstinence" would be inscribed on the banner of every state and nation of the world. "Then, and not till then," he said, "shall the peaceful reign of the Messiah commence and be extended to the ends of the earth."

Lyman Beecher had preached these dogmas in 1826 when he said that "drunkards no more than murderers shall inherit the kingdom of God," and Justin Edwards had reiterated them in a hundred pulpits. They were now kept constantly before the people in sermons and lectures, in statements by prominent lay workers for the cause, in articles in the temperance papers, and in the reports of the societies. "Ardent spirit destroys the soul," said the annual report of the American Temperance Society for 1832, ". . . to use it is an immorality, a violation of the will of God . . . the use of ardent spirit tends strongly to hinder the moral and spiritual illumination of men; and thus to prevent their salvation, and bring upon them the horrors of the second death . . . Great multitudes die the second death, who, were it not for this, might live forever." The *Temperance Manual for Young Men of the United States,* a compilation of early temperance documents, expressed these ideas in 1836 in even more frightening language:

> The Holy Spirit will not visit, much less will He dwell with him who is under the polluting, debasing effects of intoxicating drink. The state of mind and heart, which this occasions, is to Him loathsome and an utter abomination . . . it counteracts the merciful designs of Jehovah, and all the overflowing kindness of an infinitely compassionate Saviour . . . binds the soul in hopeless bondage to its destroyer, awakens the "worm that dieth not, and the fire which is not quenched," and drives the soul away in despair, weeping and wailing, to be punished with everlasting destruction from the presence of the Lord and the glory of His power.

2

Since the publication of Dr. Benjamin Rush's essay upon the effects of ardent spirits, in 1785, there had been a radical change in the attitude of American physicians toward the use of spirituous liquor in the treatment of disease. Medical societies in New Hampshire, Vermont, Connecticut, Massachusetts, and other states had adopted resolutions urging their members to prescribe distilled liquors only in cases of extreme necessity, lest they aggravate the disease under treatment or cause another. Groups of doctors in New York and elsewhere had published statements declaring that alcohol possessed neither preventive nor curative value, and that its use should be sharply curtailed, if not abandoned. Articles were frequently contributed to the temperance and medical journals by famous physicians and professors of medicine, among them Dr. Reuben D. Mussey of Dartmouth College, Dr. Edward Hitchcock of Amherst College, Dr. Francis Wayland of Brown University, and Dr. Thomas Sewell of Columbian College, Washington. All of them went much further than Dr. Rush had gone in describing the horrible and inevitable results of drinking.

Before Dr. Rush produced his treatise, spirituous liquor was hailed everywhere as the great panacea and God's gift to mankind; less than fifty years later it was being condemned as an invention of the devil and the cause of virtually every known disease. Dr. Hitchcock told his students at Amherst that even "a very moderate and prudent use of ardent spirit or wine" would infallibly produce a premature exhaustion which "renders the individual peculiarly liable to attacks of violent and dangerous disorders. He is seized with fever, or dropsy, or apoplexy; but never suspects that his prudent use of ardent spirit or wine is the cause." Dr. Sewell was considerably less restrained and covered much more territory. He wrote:

> ". . . time would fail me, were I to attempt the account of half the pathology of drunkenness. Dyspepsia, jaundice, emaciation, corpulence, rheumatism, gout, palpitation, epilepsy, lethargy, palsy, apoplexy, melancholy, madness, delirium tremens, premature old age, compose but a small part of the endless catalogue of diseases produced by alcohol drinking. Indeed, there is scarcely a morbid affliction to which the human body is liable, that has not, in one way or another, been produced by it . . ."[1]

Dr. Sewell achieved great renown among the reformers because of the violence of his attacks upon spirituous liquors, and his statements and opinions were widely quoted. His most notable effort in behalf of temperance, however, was made in 1842, when he published a series of six drawings of the interior of the human stomach in various conditions, labeled *"healthful, moderate drinking, drunkards, ulcerous, after a long debauch,* and *death by delirium tremens."* Of the last, Dr. Sewell said, "the fearful effects of the alcoholic poison are indescribable in words. In some places the coats of the stomach seem even to be in incipient state of mortification." Thousands of colored reproductions of the Sewell drawings were made, some of great size, and for more than fifty years they were used by temperance lecturers throughout the country. As a temperance historian said, "they formed the basis of a considerable lecture system on the hygienic questions connected with the temperance reform." Almost any American who can remember as far back as the turn of the twentieth century will recall the edifying spectacle, with the lecturer pointing dramatically at the drawings and then at the local drunkard who had been pressed into service as a horrible example, while frightened children screamed and nervous members of the audience shivered in terror.

One of the remarkable results of the changed viewpoint of American medical authorities was the wide acceptance, by eminent physicians as well as by clergymen and laymen, of the curious theory that one of the horrors to which the intemperate person was constantly exposed was death by internal fires, which might be lighted by spontaneous combustion or by breathing near a burning lamp, candle, or other open flame. Accounts of these holocausts appeared in British and French medical journals before 1800, but they seem to have attracted little attention in this country until 1827, when Jonathan Kittredge, a reformed drunkard, referred to them in an address in New Hampshire. Discussing the various ways in which death might come to the heavy drinker, Kittredge said that "some are actually burnt up. I read of an intemperate man a few years since," he continued, "whose breath caught fire by coming in contact with a lighted candle, and he was consumed. At the time I disbelieved the story, but my reading has since furnished me with well-authenticated cases of combustion of the human body from the use of ardent spirits."

Ten or more instances cited by a noted English physician, Dr. Thomas Trotter, were mentioned in considerable detail by Kittredge, who declared that they were "attested by living witnesses, examined by learned men, and . . . attended with all the proof we require to believe any event." Kittredge's address was published by the American Temperance Society, and the reformers suddenly discovered that similar conflagrations were occurring with distressing frequency in both the United States and Canada. During the next three or four years many cases were reported by physicians and others. Some of the unfortunate drunkards exploded like kegs of gunpowder. Others, the alcoholic fumes having seeped through the skin, burned like a torch. In some the blood caught fire, and could be seen bubbling and boiling in the veins; it was presumed to be doing likewise in the arteries. Others simmered quietly, while smoke poured from the apertures of the body. One Canadian case, reported by a doctor, was of a man whose internal organs burst into flames through spontaneous combustion. Since nothing could be done for him, he was thoroughly cooked.

Vivid accounts of the terrible sufferings of the drunkards whose insides had been transformed into roaring furnaces were published in most of the leading temperance papers, and reprinted in pamphlet form for wider distribution. They aroused enormous interest, as might be supposed; and temperance lecturers were quick to point out that such an unusual experience was but a mild foretaste of what awaited the drunkard in hell. The cases soon became so numerous, and apparently so well authenticated, that the theory was endorsed by many famous physicians, among them Dr. Thomas Sewell and Dr. Reuben D. Mussey, who issued solemn warnings that in such emergencies medical science was powerless. Eminent clergymen and educators likewise saw no reason to disbelieve that a drunkard might suddenly catch fire; the former especially readily accepted the phenomena as another of the Almighty's mysterious moves. The learned Dr. Eliphalet Nott, president of Union College at Schenectady, New York, made a comprehensive survey of the theory, citing many cases, in one of a famous series of temperance lectures which he delivered to his students in 1838. He thus expressed his considered opinion:

. . . these cases of the death of drunkards by internal fires, kindled often spontaneously in the fumes of alcohol, that escape through the pores of the skin—have become so numerous and so incontrovertible, that I presume no person of information will now be found to call the reality of their existence in question.

The theory was abandoned within a decade or so, at least as far as the medical profession and the more intelligent of the reformers were concerned, but a belief in the inflammability of the drunkard persisted in many parts of the country for years. In Rev. W. H. Daniels's *The Temperance Reform and Its Great Reformers,* published in 1879, appears this statement to the author from George McCandlish, secretary of the Reform Club of Jackson, Michigan:

> In the fall of 1867, during my drinking days, I was going home one night badly set up, and when I came to the High Bridge, between Oil City and West Oil City, I looked down and saw a man lying at the bottom of the ravine apparently dead. I was a good deal frightened, and went and called the chief of police; and along with two policemen and Drs. Seys and Harding, we picked up the man, and found that he had fallen over, in a fit of intoxication, and broken his neck. I was summoned as a witness before the coroner's jury, and saw the *post mortem* examination performed by these two physicians. After removing the top of the skull, for the purpose of examining the condition of the brain, they tested it for alcohol, by holding a lighted match near it; and immediately the brain took fire, and burned with a blue flame, like an alcohol lamp.

That, it may be assumed, was when McCandlish quit drinking.

3

The official publication of the American Temperance Society, the *Journal of Humanity,* said in 1830 that the society, "it seems to us, stands pledged to the public fully, and we trust irrevocably, never to make any appeal to legislators or officers of the law, for the aid of authority in changing the habits of any class of their fellow citizens." This had been one of the fundamental principles of the temperance reform from the beginning, but by the early 1830s some of the most important leaders were convinced that it must be abandoned, that the regeneration of the American people could never be accomplished by moral suasion alone, and that if the will of God was to be carried out other methods must be pursued. Many felt, indeed, that the war against liquor had been a failure, despite the extraordinary growth of the temperance movement and the continued agitation carried on by the churches and the local and state societies. There had been no noticeable decrease in the consumption of liquor, although well over a million people had signed the pledge, while most towns and cities reported an actual increase in the number of disreputable gin mills and tippling houses operated and frequented by the most lawless elements of the population. There was much evidence of laxity in the enforcement of regulatory laws, and of corruption in the administration of the licensing system by which the sale of ardent spirits was supposedly controlled; even in those early days the liquor industry was busily trying to cut its own throat. In most of the states the power to grant licenses was in the hands of such local officials as aldermen, county judges, and selectmen, who seem to have been peculiarly susceptible to influence.

Legal coercion to save the great mass of unregenerated liquor drinkers was suggested as early as 1826, when Lyman Beecher urged his people to send petitions to Congress and the state legislatures, "praying for the legislative interference to protect the health and morals of the nation." Little attention was paid to Beecher's plea for more than half a dozen years, but about the middle 1830s local societies throughout the country began to adopt resolutions, and temperance journals began to print articles, demanding the repeal or drastic revision of the license laws. A wave of revolt against the arrogance of the liquor dealers and the venality of local politicians was rising everywhere. A New York City grand jury in 1832, after an investigation of conditions in the metropolis, said that "the time has now arrived when our public authorities should no longer sanction the evil by granting licenses for the purpose of vending ardent spirits." In 1833 John Cotton Smith, governor of Connecticut, announced that he was "decidedly of the opinion that all laws licensing and regulating the sale of ardent spirits ought to be instantly repealed." That same year the sixth annual report of the American Temperance Society demanded that "all sanctioning by law of this abominable traffic be forever abandoned."

These and similar expressions by prominent temperance leaders and influential journals stimulated the feeling of dissatisfaction with the license system, but the effect was somewhat lessened by the fact that their approach to the problem was negative. They insisted upon doing away with the existing laws, but offered nothing to take their place. General James Appleton of Massachusetts, however, came forward with a suggestion which was not only constructive, but was destined to establish the pattern of temperance activities forever after; he was the first to advocate outright prohibition. In a series of letters published in the Salem *Gazette* in 1832, General Appleton wrote, "a law should be passed prohibiting the sale of ardent spirits." A year later General Appleton removed with his family to Maine, and in 1836 was elected to the Maine Legislature. In 1837 he was appointed chairman of a joint committee to study the state's license systems, and submitted a report which, after a thorough discussion of the evils of intemperance, said that the committee was "not only of the opinion that the law giving the right to sell ardent spirits should be repealed, but that a law should be passed to prohibit the traffic in them." This was the first such recommendation made by a legislative committee in American history. The report was tabled, but it had so impressed the Maine legislators that in 1838 a law forbidding the sale of liquor in less quantity than twenty-eight gallons was defeated by a single vote.

After about 1835 the local and state temperance societies began to take Lyman Beecher's advice and to bombard the state legislatures with petitions "praying for the legislative interference"; they poured into the state capitals in such numbers that 1838 is known in temperance annals as "petition year." Taking the cue from General Appleton, they now demanded not only the repeal of the license laws, but the enactment of statutes forbidding the sale of ardent spirits. And some results were obtained. In 1838 Massachusetts passed a law, which, from the viewpoint of the liquor dealer and drinker, was very onerous; a man who wanted ardent spirits had to buy at least fifteen gallons and carry it away all at one time. A year or so later Mississippi enacted a one-gallon law, and Tennessee repealed all statutes licensing the tippling houses and passed a law prohibiting the sale of less than one quart. An Illinois law required town and county authorities to suppress the liquor traffic if petitioned to do so by a majority of the voters. Connecticut passed a law which provided that a liquor license could be granted only by a majority vote of the people gathered at town meeting. Rhode Island and New Hampshire passed the first local option laws early in 1839, and several towns and counties immediately voted no license.

The Massachusetts law remained on the statute books a little more than two years. It was repealed by the legislature of 1839 at the request of Governor Marcus Morton, who had been the first president of the American Temperance Society. Morton was a staunch temperance advocate, but he was opposed to "the legislative interference," and described the fifteen-gallon law as sumptuary legislation and an unwarranted interference with business and property rights. He signed the repealer on February 9, 1840, and three days later the incensed reformers, at a state convention held in Boston and attended by some fifteen hundred delegates, adopted a resolution which outlined the political strategy that eventually brought about the adoption of the Eighteenth Amendment. The resolution said:

> Resolved, that until the laws of this state, concerning the sale of intoxicating liquors, are fully established upon the basis of prohibition and sustained by a correct general sentiment . . . it is, in our opinion, the duty of the temperance men, to vote only for those men as candidates for legislative and executive offices, who are known and inflexible friends of such a course of legislation.

Many of the other laws passed during the legislative flurry of 1838 and 1839 were repealed or modified within the next few years. None was ever very effective; the penalties provided for violation were slight, and the authorities found them difficult to enforce. Nevertheless, they were a beginning, and the fact of their enactment was enough to silence the conservative reformers who had objected to legislative action. The principal complaint, that the temperance movement might become involved in partisan politics, no longer possessed any validity; the reformers were now up to their ears in politics of every description. There had also been some objection on the ground that prohibitory laws would violate personal liberty; this was easily disposed of with the assurance that in the service of God the end justifies the means. By 1840 the temperance reform was definitely committed to the prohibition, by law, of ardent spirits—it was some years before beer, cider, and wine were included in the ban—and extensive plans were in preparation for strengthening the laws already enacted and compelling the passage of others.

Before the legislative program could get under way, however, the whole temperance movement was thrown into considerable confusion by the nation-wide uproar known as the Washingtonian Revival, which was started by six old topers of Baltimore—David Anderson and George Steers, blacksmiths; W. K. Mitchell, a tailor; J. F. Hoss, a carpenter; James McCurley, a coachmaker; and Archibald Campbell, a silversmith. These men, all hard drinkers and friends of long standing, met almost every evening at Chase's Tavern, and passed several hours drinking, gaming, and talking. One of their customs was to send a committee of one or two men to hear and report on any public speaker who might be in Baltimore. Thus they were able to keep up with the times without leaving the tavern or the rum bottle.

On the night of April 6, 1840, two men went as usual to hear the Rev. Matthew Hale Smith, a noted temperance lecturer from New York. Much to everyone's surprise, and to their own as well, they were greatly impressed by Smith's arguments, and in their report said that total abstinence seemed to be worth trying. The company thereupon embarked upon a long discussion, in which the landlord of the tavern joined with violent abuse of all reformers, past, present, and future. The result of the talk was that the six men decided to organize a total abstinence club, to be called the Washington Temperance Society. W. K. Mitchell was elected president, and rules were adopted fixing the initiation fee at twenty-five cents and the dues at twelve and one half cents a month. Each of the six agreed to bring a friend to the next meeting, and all signed the following pledge:

> We, whose names are annexed, desirous of forming a society for our mutual benefit and to guard against a pernicious practice which is injurious to our health, standing and families, do pledge our-selves, as gentlemen, that we will not drink any spirituous or malt liquors, wine or cider.

Baltimore greeted the new society with great enthusiasm. Within two months it was necessary to rent a large hall for the meetings, and by the end of 1840 almost one thousand men, all of whom were, or professed to be, reformed drinkers, had signed the pledge and enrolled as members. One of these was John H. W. Hawkins, a hatter by trade, who was reformed in June 1840 after having been drunk almost continuously for fifteen years. His regeneration was brought about by his little daughter Hannah, who reached his heart, as he sat at home in sodden misery, with the plea, "Papa, please don't send me for whis-key today!" Rev. John Marsh immortalized Hannah in a booklet called *Hannah Hawkins, or, The Reformed Drunkard's Daughter,* which went through twenty editions and was widely read and quoted for many years. Rev. W. H. Daniels in 1879 described it as "a book over which many tears have been shed and many good resolutions made."

Hawkins wrote in his journal that after he and his daughter had wept together, he went "to the society of reformed drunkards, where I found all my old bottle companions." He put his name to the pledge, and soon became the most important figure in the Washing-tonian movement. He was a natural leader, and an orator of great power; at speaking extemporaneously he was probably unequaled in his time. Hawkins devoted the rest of his life to the cause of temper-ance; he lectured in every state in the Union, in some of them many times, and obtained thousands of signatures to the temperance pledge. His labors were truly herculean; he noted in his journal that for eight months he spoke at least once a day, while in eighteen years as a lecturer he traveled two hundred thousand miles and made more than five thousand speeches.

The only lecturer of the period who approached Hawkins in industry, and in the ability to sway an audience, was John B. Gough, who was not a member of the Washingtonians but was in sympathy with the aims of the movement. Like Hawkins, Gough was a reformed drunkard, but unlike Hawkins, who never drank a drop after signing the pledge, Gough suffered several relapses. The most spectacular occurred in September 1845, when Gough was at the height of his fame. While on a visit to New York, where he had been booked for several lectures, he disappeared. His friends, fearing that he had been done to death by the liquor interests, asked the police to search for him. After a week Gough was found in a house of prostitution in Walker Street; he was very drunk, and obviously had been in that condition for some time. When he recovered, Gough explained that he had entered a drugstore to have a glass of soda water with an acquaintance, whose name he did not recall, and that after drinking, everything went black. He was convinced, he said, that the soda water had been drugged. He remembered nothing further until the police carried him out of the Walker Street dive. The temperance reformers, with a few exceptions, accepted Gough's story as the truth; they regarded the affair as another manifestation of the terrible power of Satan. But those opposed to the anti-liquor agitation, especially the New York *Herald* and other newspapers, ridiculed Gough unmercifully, reviving the story whenever opportunity offered. He never quite lived it down, although he continued to lecture and to draw large crowds.

By the beginning of 1841, accounts of the work in Baltimore had begun to appear in the newspapers and temperance journals, and in March a delegation of five Washingtonians, headed by John Hawkins, accepted an invitation from several temperance organizations to visit New York. They delivered their message in a dozen Protestant churches, and ended their campaign in the metropolis with a great mass meeting in City Hall Park which was attended by more than four thousand people. The five Washingtonians, each posted atop an empty rum keg, described their experiences with liquor one after another, while agents circulated through the crowd recruiting members for a New York branch of the society. By the time Hawkins and his companions returned to Baltimore, some twenty-five hundred had signed the pledge, and the Washington Temperance Society of New York was flourishing.

On April 5, 1841, the first anniversary of the historic meeting in Chase's Tavern was celebrated in Baltimore with the largest and most impressive temperance demonstration the country had ever seen—a great procession in which six thousand persons marched through the city's principal streets. A thousand reformed drunkards who had signed the pledge within the past year lead the way, followed by representatives of every temperance society in Baltimore, all carrying appropriate flags and wearing handsome badges. The ex-inebriates naturally attracted a great deal of attention, but most of the applause went to a detachment of one thousand boys and girls. These children were members of a juvenile temperance society called the Cold Water Army, which had been organized, beginning in 1836, by Rev. Thomas P. Hunt, a Presbyterian clergyman who for several years was employed as traveling agent by various state societies. In this capacity he visited hundreds of Sunday schools, and formed units of his army in most of them. The youngsters wore bright red-and-blue uniforms, carried banners inscribed with temperance slogans, and chanted their official pledge:

> *We do not think we'll ever drink,*
> *Whiskey or gin, brandy or rum,*
> *Or anything that'll make drunk come.*

A week after the Baltimore celebration Hawkins led another delegation to Boston, where they were even more successful than in New York, and in July 1841 the movement received the accolade of the American Temperance Union, bestowed by the national convention at Saratoga Springs, New York. Fired with proselyting zeal, the Baltimore society now sent out missionary teams, each composed of two reformed drunkards, to preach the gospel of Washingtonianism to all the land. During the next three years the movement spread across the United States like a plague; as a temperance historian put it, "the whole country was in a blaze." Everywhere the Baltimoreans went, drunkards rushed to sign the Washingtonian pledge—sixty thousand in Ohio, thirty thousand in Kentucky, twenty-nine thousand in Pennsylvania; eighteen thousand in Columbia County, New York; from one thousand to five thousand in scores of towns and cities. Hundreds of Washingtonian societies were organized and set to work rounding up the local inebriates, while more than a score of papers—Hawkins listed nineteen in his journal—sprang up to support the new movement.

In most communities the missionaries were greeted by public demonstrations. By far the largest was held in Boston on May 30, 1844. All the Boston banks closed for the day, and most of the business houses dismissed their employees at noon, when the parade started. At least twelve thousand persons were in line, marching in twenty-three sections, each headed by a brass band and comprising delegations from almost every temperance organization in eastern Massachusetts. And, of course, the ubiquitous little ones of the Cold Water Army. The members of the ladies' temperance societies were not permitted to march, but they assembled on Boston Common, and as the head of the procession appeared they raised the cry of "The Teetotalers Are Coming!" The celebration ended with a mass meeting on the Common, which was addressed by the governor of Massachusetts, George N. Briggs, and others. The day's bag of drunkards was several thousand, and the grogshop keepers reported a slump in business.

With the Boston demonstration the Washingtonian movement reached its peak; thereafter it declined almost as rapidly as it had risen. The journals which supported it soon expired from lack of money, and while a few of the new societies were absorbed by older temperance organizations, most of them simply disbanded when interest lagged, especially in the smaller places where there was a natural shortage of drunkards, the raw material of reformation. By the late 1840s Washingtonianism was no longer important as a phase of the anti-liquor crusade. The collapse of the movement seems to have been due to a combination of several causes. In the first place, it was never organized on a national basis, with a central body to plan and co-ordinate the work; each local society was a separate entity and made its own rules and went its own way. The only connection between the various organizations was a common zeal for reformation, and the traveling teams of missionaries.

More damaging to the movement than the lack of proper organization, however, was the hostility of the clergy and the established temperance societies which had been fighting the rum demon for more than a generation. At first the old societies greeted the Washingtonians as brothers, and the clergy enthusiastically opened the churches for their meetings. But widespread dissatisfaction soon arose in temperance circles over the manner in which the Washingtonians conducted these sessions, the pattern of which had been set by the original Baltimore society. When the Washingtonians gathered to do battle with intemperance, the speakers simply related their experiences with liquor, and when it was judged that the emotions of the audience had been aroused to the proper pitch, all drinking men were asked to come forward and sign the pledge. At most Washingtonian meetings there were no demands for legislative action and no denunciation of the liquor seller; many societies, indeed, admitted grogshop keepers to membership, the only condition being that they quit drinking.

Worst of all from the viewpoint of the clergy, religion played almost no part in the movement. With occasional exceptions, the Washingtonians opened and closed their meetings without prayer, and never turned them into religious revivals. Their interest was wholly in the reformation of drunkards, and there was much complaint that they refused to acknowledge God's part in the process. Moreover, they chose speakers from their own ranks, and would have little or nothing to do with the old societies, many of which were compelled to dissolve through lack of popular support. "Clergymen and the earlier temperance speakers were excluded," wrote the Rev. Daniel Dorchester, a noted temperance historian, "for no one was desired to speak who could not relate an experience as a reformed man. The old organizers, under the popular demand, employed the Washingtonian speakers; but, almost everywhere, they reported that the reformed men could not be persuaded to join the existing societies; and, therefore, a 'Washingtonian' society must be formed in each town, and officered with reformed men." It is not strange that the Washingtonians were soon charged with being atheists, and that the movement was looked upon by thousands of pious Christians as a subtle operation of the devil. The editors of the established temperance journals moved forward as one man in defense of religion, and there was a great deal of unseemly bickering between them and the editors of the Washingtonian papers, especially after one of the latter declared that if Washingtonianism was triumphant the religious sects would be blown to the moon.

Although the Washingtonian movement was as ephemeral as any reform endorsed by hundreds of thousands of people could well be, some of its results were more or less permanent. According to temperance records, more than six hundred thousand inebriates signed the pledge during the excitement, and while it was estimated that four hundred and fifty thousand returned to the way of sin, there was a clear gain of one hundred and fifty thousand souls. The movement provided themes for several plays and many books, and inspired Timothy Shay Arthur, perhaps the most noted of temperance authors, to write *Six Nights with the Washingtonians,* which was his most popular work until he produced his masterpiece, *Ten Nights in a Barroom,* in the early 1850s.

Washingtonianism was also responsible for the first of the secret and fraternal temperance orders, the Sons of Temperance, which was organized by sixteen Washingtonians at Teetotalers' Hall, 71 Division Street, New York, in September, 1842. A year later a national organization was perfected, and by 1855 the Sons had more than thirty-five hundred branches and approximately one hundred and fifty thousand members. Within the next three or four decades many similar orders were founded; when the temperance movement began its political maneuvering on a nation-wide scale they provided a large and fairly dependable bloc of voters. The Sons of Temperance in particular became, as a temperance historian put it, "a center of operations for the various efforts to procure prohibitory laws." Probably the most influential of the other temperance secret societies were the Templars of Honor and Temperance, the Independent Order of Rechabites, the Friends of Temperance, the Cadets of Temperance, and the Independent Order of Good Templars, which in 1874 reported 617,000 members. In his *Temperance Reform and Its Great Reformers,* Rev. W. H. Daniels noted that the Sons of Temperance had established separate divisions "for people of the African race." The Friends of Temperance also organized "a separate order, called Sons of the Soil, for colored people."

4

With the decline of the Washingtonian excitement, the so-called radical reformers resumed their efforts to destroy the liquor traffic by legislative action, strengthened by the conviction that the notion of moral suasion had at last been proved fallacious. By the middle 1840s temperance lobbies were busily at work in every state legislature and political pressure was being brought to bear on city aldermen and town selectmen. Notable local option victories were reported from Massachusetts, Connecticut, Indiana, Michigan, Georgia, Iowa, and other states. In New York a local option law was passed in 1845, and in 1846, out of a total of 856 towns and cities (the law did not apply to New York City), 728 voted against licensing grogshops. This was a great victory; its very magnitude, as John Marsh wrote in his *Temperance Recollections,* "placed the friends of temperance at their ease and let them feel that their work had been accomplished." Considering that their successes at the polls had solved the problem of intemperance, they made no effort to compel enforcement of the law, and ignored the flourishing speakeasies and the flood of liquor which poured into the dry communities from those which had voted wet. Instead they abandoned themselves to an orgy of celebration; a grand jubilee, attended by twelve thousand members of the Sons of Temperance, was held in New York City, and similar meetings were called in towns and cities throughout the state. While the drys were rejoicing, their opponents were working, and at another election in 1847 the temperance majorities were overturned almost everywhere. That same year the legislature repealed the local option law.

A far more important victory than any of these was won in Washington, where the United States Supreme Court, in March 1847, handed down a decision in the cases of several liquor dealers who had been convicted of selling without licenses in Massachusetts, Rhode Island, and New Hampshire. The defendants were represented by two of America's most famous lawyers, Daniel Webster and Rufus Choate, but the Court held unanimously that the states had full power to regulate or to prohibit the sale of intoxicating liquors. The chief justice, Roger Taney, said in his opinion, "Every state may regulate its own internal traffic, according to its own judgment, and upon its own views of the interest and well-being of its citizens. I am not aware that these principles have ever been questioned. If any state deems the retail and internal traffic in ardent spirits injurious to its citizens, and calculated to produce idleness, vice, or debauchery, I see nothing in the Constitution of the United States to prevent it from regulating and restraining the traffic, or from prohibiting it altogether, if it thinks proper."

This decision gave great impetus to the movement for state-wide prohibition, which had been gathering momentum since the decline of Washingtonianism. The legislature of Oregon passed a law in 1844 forbidding the sale of ardent spirits anywhere in the territory, but Oregon was so far away that almost no one in the East heard of this action for several years. By 1845 strong temperance lobbies were at work in all of the state capitals, and thousands of dry workers were busily gathering signatures to petitions for presentation to the legislatures. Interest, however, centered in Maine, which even in those early days was recognized as the bellwether of American politics. Many dry leaders were convinced that if a strong prohibitory law could be passed in Maine, the other states would fall into line almost as a matter of course.

Fortunately for the temperance cause, a new champion had arisen in Maine, described by an opponent in the heat of legislative debate as "that prince of fanatics," and as "a pretty little dapper man, goes well dressed, wears a nice blue jacket and fancy vest, and his hat cocked on one side of his head." This man with the fancy vest was Neal Dow, a prosperous merchant and timberland speculator of Portland, and one of the most astute politicians and propagandists the temperance movement has ever produced. Dow had become interested in the dry cause in 1929, when he was twenty-five years old, and thereafter was increasingly active. In 1839 he tried to compel the Portland Board of Aldermen to enact an ordinance making traffic in liquor illegal. He failed, but the board finally agreed to submit the issue to the people. In the special election which followed, Dow developed the doorbell technique of electioneering which is still used so effectively today. His workers visited every house in Portland, while the case for no-license was set forth in thousands of leaflets and pamphlets, and proclaimed almost incessantly from every pulpit in the city. The temperance forces lost by the narrow margin of thirty-five votes, but four years later, when another election was held, Dow obtained the support of the leaders of the Washingtonian societies and the drys won by 943 to 498, almost two to one.

Portland thus became the first important city to outlaw liquor by popular vote, but the results were very unsatisfactory. The Board of Aldermen dutifully refused to issue licenses for grogshops, but the liquor dealers continued to sell without licenses, and when violators were convicted, which was seldom, they were released by local judges upon payment of nominal fines. It soon became apparent that little or nothing could be done upon the municipal level, and that the liquor traffic could be abolished only if it was made illegal throughout the state. Accordingly, in the fall of 1843, Dow and his associates began circulating petitions to the legislature, praying "that the traffic in intoxicating drinks be held and adjudged as an infamous crime." In February 1844 Dow appeared before a committee of the House of Representatives at Augusta, the state capital, and at his behest a bill providing for state-wide prohibition was reported. This measure passed the House, but was defeated in the Senate. Late in the same year Dow was again unsuccessful, but the margin of defeat was smaller.

Dow now organized the state and local temperance societies, and the remnants of the Washingtonians, and devised a system of political maneuvering which in later years was copied and carried to near perfection by the Anti-Saloon League. In every district the temperance forces endorsed a candidate for the legislature who promised to support a prohibition law, and urged the people to vote for him regardless of party lines. Meetings were held in every part of the state; Dow himself addressed hundreds, traveling four thousand miles in two months. The temperance candidates were nearly everywhere successful, and when Dow again appeared before a legislative committee, in July 1846, he controlled a majority in both the House and the Senate. His position was further strengthened by petitions bearing the signatures of forty thousand qualified voters. A bill abolishing the license system and forbidding all sales of liquor quickly passed the House by eighty-one to forty-two, and the Senate by twenty-three to five. It was signed by the governor on August 7, 1846.

Essentially, the new law resembled the bill drafted in 1837 by General James Appleton's special legislative committee, but it had been sorely weakened by amendments; Dow's control of the legislature was not as complete as he had thought. As finally enacted, the statute permitted wholesalers and importers of liquor to operate, provided they sold not less than twenty-eight gallons at a time; and it empowered town selectmen to issue licenses to sell at retail for medicinal and mechanical purposes. The law was thus restrictive rather than prohibitory, and, from the viewpoint of Dow and his associates, virtually worthless. A more stringent statute, which provided, among other things, for the appointment of a horde of special agents to "ferret out and suppress the grog-shops," was passed in 1849, but was vetoed by the governor, John W. Dana.

In August 1850 Dow again made a trip to Augusta, and presented the legislature with a bill of his own drafting; it subsequently became famous as the "Maine Law," and served as a model for prohibition statutes all over the country. This measure was passed by the House, but lost in the Senate by a tie vote. "This indication of a coming victory," wrote a Maine historian, "inspired the friends of temperance with a new hope throughout the state, and in the succeeding elections in the fall, many a zealous advocate of the temperance cause was elected for the express purpose of carrying through the new bill."

Dow was elected mayor of Portland in April 1851, and when he appeared before the legislature for the sixth time on the twenty-fifth of the following month, he was armed with the prestige of the second most important office in the state. Also, and more to the point, he controlled both the legislature and the governor, John Hubbard of Hallowell, a doctor who had defeated Dana on the issue of prohibition. When Dow again demanded that the Maine Law be passed, the legislators hastened to do his bidding. Both houses adopted it without alteration, and the governor signed it, within three days. It became law on June 2, 1851.

There was no nonsense about the Maine Law, and it contained no loopholes through which violators might wriggle. It prohibited the sale, the keeping for sale, and the manufacture of all intoxicating liquors. Heavy fines were imposed for the first two violations, and imprisonment for the third. It authorized search and seizure upon complaint of three persons, and provided for the confiscation and destruction of illegal stocks of liquor. Dow notified the grogshop keepers of Portland that he would give them two months in which to dispose of their supplies, and that thereafter he would enforce the law. This he proceeded to do with great vigor, personally leading raids upon tippling places and with his own hands smashing barrels and kegs; on one occasion he poured two thousand dollars' worth of rum and whiskey into the gutters in front of the City Hall.

Portland was bone-dry by the late summer of 1851, and Dow began to prepare frequent reports of the operation of the law, which he had printed at his own expense and circulated throughout the country. The Maine Law soon became the principal topic of discussion in temperance circles, especially after the National Temperance Convention, held at Saratoga Springs, New York, on August 20, 1851, and attended by three hundred delegates, had adopted a resolution urging other states to follow Maine's example. And as the political experts had predicted, many did so; the four years which followed the enactment of the Maine Law was one of the most triumphant periods in the history of the temperance movement. In that time twelve states and one territory, in addition to Maine and Oregon, adopted prohibitory laws—Minnesota, Rhode Island, Massachusetts, and Vermont in 1852; Michigan in 1853; Connecticut in 1854, and Indiana, Delaware, Iowa, Nebraska Territory, Pennsylvania, New York, and New Hampshire in 1855.

In several other states, among them Wisconsin, New Jersey, North Carolina, and Illinois, the drys lost by very narrow margins. In Illinois, for instance, both houses of the legislature passed a law, the first draft of which had been written by Abraham Lincoln, and it was submitted to the people at a special election on June 4, 1855. It was defeated by some fourteen thousand votes after Stephen A. Douglas had spoken violently against it, urging his adherents to "bury Maine Lawism and Abolitionism all in the same grave." Since events in nearly all of these states were clearly following the pattern which had resulted in such a smashing victory in Maine, temperance leaders were confident of eventual success; there was a general feeling that within ten years the United States would be completely dry and their labors ended.

But suddenly, and almost without warning, the onward march of the dry reform came to an abrupt stop. The New Hampshire Legislature passed a stringent version of the Maine Law in August 1855, and that was the last of the string of victories; not for a quarter of a century did another state adopt prohibition. Moreover, for twenty years the temperance movement declined steadily; it lost almost everything that had been won during its brief burst of glory. Every state except Maine repealed or drastically modified its prohibition law, and even Maine backslid to some extent, reverting to the license system from 1856 to 1858 and then enacting a new prohibitory statute.

Temperance historians are still debating the cause of the debacle, but it seems clear that there were a great many causes. In the first place, many of the important dry leaders were also deeply involved in the abolition movement, and after the middle 1850s the latter absorbed most of their time and attention. The northern churches, too, preached more abolition than temperance. And the people generally simply lost interest in the dry reform; with the fate of the nation at stake, the question of whether a man should take a drink seemed to be a piddling matter. There was a great deal of intemperance in the Army; all ranks were notoriously heavy drinkers, and the mass of returning soldiers retained the habits they had acquired in camp. Great damage was done to the temperance cause by an elaborate investigation of the liquor question by a special committee of the Massachusetts Legislature, conducted by John A. Andrew, wartime governor of that state and a man of great influence. The majority report of the committee, which virtually gave alcohol a clean bill of health, thus summarized its conclusions:

1. It is not sinful or hurtful in every case to use every kind of alcoholic liquors as beverages. It is not, therefore, wrong in every case to sell every kind of alcoholic liquors to be used as beverages.

2. It is the right of every citizen to determine for himself what he will eat or drink. A law prohibiting him from drinking every kind of alcoholic liquors, universally used in all countries and ages as a beverage, is an arbitrary and unreasonable interference with his rights, and is not justified by the consideration that some men may abuse their rights, and may, therefore, need the counsel and example of good men to lead them to reform.

Thousands of copies of this report were printed and widely circulated, and articles based on the investigation, and endorsing the committee's viewpoint, appeared in many important magazines and newspapers. Temperance leaders refuted the committee's conclusions with statements by eminent physicians, scientists, clergymen, and jurists, but as is nearly always the case, the refutation never quite caught up with the original assertions. The report plagued the temperance movement for years.

The successive blows delivered by the abolition movement, the war, and the Massachusetts inquiry made the dry reform more than a little groggy. But the knockout punch, in the opinion of most temperance historians, was landed jointly by the first Internal Revenue Act, passed by Congress on July 1, 1862; the United States Brewers' Association, organized at New York on November 12 of that year; and the so-called "beer invasion," meaning the enormous increase in the national thirst for beer. Between the middle 1840s and 1870 hundreds of thousands of immigrants from Germany and other central European countries landed on American shores, bringing with them their old-world drinking habits and in particular their traditional fondness for malt liquors. Beer had never been of great importance in the United States; in 1850 only 36,678,444 gallons were brewed, with a per capita consumption of one and three fifths gallons. But between 1850 and 1870, when immigration was in full swing, the production of beer increased more than fivefold to almost 205,000,000 gallons, and the per capita consumption to five and one third gallons. By the early 1880s thousands of breweries were producing approximately 550,000,000 gallons of beer a year, or a little more than ten gallons for every man, woman, and child in the country.

In the larger cities, where the immigrants tended to congregate and settle down in national colonies, retail establishments selling nothing but beer were opened. Some of these were called beer gardens; as a rule they were large, fairly elaborate, provided music and sometimes entertainment, and catered to family parties. Smaller places, of varying degrees of depravity, were known as beer saloons. The term "saloon" caught the popular fancy, and was soon applied to every resort where liquor was sold, both malt and distilled.

As adopted in 1862, the Internal Revenue Act imposed a fee of twenty dollars a year upon each retail liquor establishment in the country, and levied a manufacturing tax of one dollar a barrel on beer and ale and twenty cents a gallon on distilled spirits. The latter tax was increased to two dollars a gallon in 1864, but was reduced to ninety cents in 1875 and remained at that figure for many years. Intended as a money-raising measure for the duration of the war, the act was passed by Congress only after bitter and extended debate, in which Senator Samuel C. Pomeroy of Kansas denounced it as simply a disguised national licensing law, and demanded a federal statute prohibiting the liquor traffic altogether. As far as the record shows, this was the first suggestion of national prohibition. According to temperance authorities, Abraham Lincoln opposed the law, and signed it with great reluctance, upon the understanding that at the end of the war the provision for licensing grogshops would be repealed.

Temperance leaders have always blamed the internal revenue law for many of their difficulties; almost continuously thereafter they had to counter the argument that prohibition would mean a serious loss of revenue to the government. Dr. D. Leigh Colvin, prominent in dry circles for fifty years and a candidate of the Prohibition party for President in 1936, wrote in his history of the party that the act "made the government financially interested in the perpetuation of the liquor traffic," and described it as "perhaps the most far-reaching and calamitous in its ultimate effect of any action ever taken by Congress. It served," he continued, "to entrench the liquor traffic in politics and government . . . the effect of the act was to give the liquor traffic the sanction of the Federal government. . . . A still worse effect was its searing of the national conscience . . . The nation was in a sense in partnership with the liquor traffic. The government shared in the profits of the traffic even to the extent of depending upon it for over one fourth of the national revenue through a long series of years."[2]

The United States Brewers' Association provided the first organized opposition against the temperance movement that had ever appeared in the field; the distillers had no effective organization until 1879. To the horrified indignation of the reformers, the brewers immediately proceeded to follow the methods which the drys had developed in Maine and elsewhere; that is, they tried to influence elections and to control political machines. But they went a little further; they put forth very powerful efforts in Washington. "It appears especially necessary," said the association's constitution, "for the brewing trade that its interests be vigorously and energetically prosecuted before the legislative and executive departments." From the beginning the brewers displayed an uncanny affinity for politicians, and a remarkable knack of getting things done in the national capital. In less than a year they had persuaded the government to reduce the tax on beer from one dollar a barrel to sixty cents, and had adopted a memorial demanding a further reduction of ten cents.

In 1864 the secretary of the association's Washington Agitation Committee reported that he was in "almost daily correspondence with members of Congress." A year later, at the 1865 meeting of the association, the Commissioner of Internal Revenue addressed the brewers in his official capacity, pledging himself to "bring about a cordial understanding between the government and the trade." At the sixth meeting of the association, in 1866, the secretary jubilantly reported that "no new imposition or increase of tax will be placed on malt liquors by the government without first communicating with this Association and getting their views upon it." And in 1869 the brewers royally entertained the Commissioner of Internal Revenue and publicly eulogized him for his efforts in their behalf.

5

Only three things occurred during the dismal decade of the 1860s from which the dry leaders were able to extract even the slightest grain of comfort or encouragement. One was the organization of the National Temperance Society and Publication House by the Fifth National Temperance Convention held at Saratoga Springs, New York, in 1865. The society succeeded the American Temperance Union, which had been formed in 1836. The Publication House soon became the principal outlet for temperance propaganda; it has been estimated that in the forty years of its existence it circulated almost 1,500,-000,000 pages of dry literature. Another happening of the 1860s from which great things were expected was the organization of the National Prohibition party in 1869. Unfortunately, it failed completely to fulfill its promise; it was never able to exert any appreciable influence upon the American political scene, or to become more than a small minority party.

More important than either of these was the emergence of the Catholics as a factor in the temperance movement. The Catholic Church never took any official part in the dry reformation, and endorsements of prohibition by Catholic dignitaries have always been few and far between. Perhaps the most important statement on the subject of temperance was that made by Pope Leo XIII in 1887, when he praised the work of the Catholic Total Abstinence Union, and urged the pastors of the church to "do their best to drive the plague of intemperance from the fold of Christ by assiduous preaching and exhortation, and to shine before all as models of abstinence . . ."

Many individual priests and Catholic laymen, however, have won more than local renown as lecturers and workers for prohibition, and a considerable number of Catholic temperance societies have, from time to time, been engaged in the work. The first Catholic societies were organized about 1840 in Boston and Philadelphia, and probably a dozen were formed during the next decade. More were organized after Father Theobald Mathew visited this country in 1849. Father Mathew was an Irish priest who, singlehanded, almost dried up Ireland, inducing more than half a million Irishmen to sign a total abstinence pledge within three years. He was in the United States for two years and aroused great enthusiasm everywhere he went; he is said to have obtained several hundred thousand pledge signers, many of whom never returned to the rum pots.

The interest created by Father Mathew soon subsided, and in 1860 not more than ten Catholic societies were in existence, and few of them were flourishing. In that year the Rev. Patrick Byrne, a young priest stationed at Jersey City, New Jersey, having obtained permission from his ecclesiastical superiors, formed the Parochial Total Abstinence Society. The idea spread, and similar societies were organized elsewhere in New Jersey, and in New York and other eastern states. In 1867 the Paulist, Passionist, and Jesuit orders began to found similar local societies, later combining them into diocesan and state-wide unions. In February 1872 the first Catholic national temperance convention was held at Baltimore, and the delegates organized the Catholic Total Abstinence Union of America. By 1880 the union had almost six hundred affiliated societies, with some one hundred and fifty thousand members. There were also about three hundred independent societies, with about fifty thousand members. The efforts of all these organizations were aimed at promoting total abstinence among Catholics; there is no record that any of them ever co-operated very wholeheartedly with the Protestants.

6

From the beginning of the dry crusade its leaders had more or less ignored what was eventually to become their most important asset— the great mass of American women, nearly every one a potential reformer of almost superhuman energy. The farseeing Justin Edwards, when he organized the American Temperance Society in 1826, proposed that wives and mothers be admitted to membership in local societies on an equal footing with men, but he was voted down almost unanimously. The general feeling was that if woman possessed any influence, which was doubtful, it should be exercised in the home, where she belonged.

In later years, however, the men graciously permitted the ladies to form their own little societies, the Sons of Temperance encouraged the women of their families to form an auxiliary order called the Daughters of Temperance, and during the Washingtonian excitement Martha Washington Societies appeared in many cities. Nearly all of these were conducted under the close supervision of the local clergymen, and one of their principal functions seems to have been the passage of resolutions endorsing whatever the men had decided was right and proper. When a woman ventured to step outside her own small circle, or to question the wisdom of an omniscient male, she was sharply reminded that she was an inferior creature and must stay within the sphere for which the Lord had designed her.

Even Susan B. Anthony, one of America's outstanding reformers of either sex, when she tried to speak to a motion at the convention of the New York State Temperance Society at Albany in 1852, was told that she and other ladies had been invited "not to speak but to listen and learn." Of sterner stuff than most, Miss Anthony promptly led the women delegates out of the hall and held a public meeting in a Presbyterian church, while the men, in a great flurry of indignation, changed the name of their organization to the Men's New York State Temperance Society. A few months later Miss Anthony organized the Women's State Temperance Society, with herself as secretary and Mrs. Elizabeth Cady Stanton as president. A year later, despite the protests of Mrs. Stanton and Miss Anthony, men were admitted to membership. They promptly elected themselves to all of the important offices, and within two years the organization was defunct. Not for twenty years was another women's state or national temperance society formed.

7

Throughout the long, depressing period from the middle 1850s to the early 1870s the liquor traffic, particularly the brewing industry, waxed prosperous, powerful, and arrogant—the brewers even demanded that the government remove all restrictions from their operations and no longer require them to keep books. The temperance reformers, on the other hand, floundered helplessly, stripped of virtually everything save the shining armor of righteousness. Every move they attempted was met by the screaming protest, "Don't destroy the liquor traffic now! The government needs the money!" This cry was to be repeated endlessly, with variations, for many weary years.

CHAPTER FOUR

"Whirlwind of the Lord"

In the annals of the temperance movement Dr. Dioclesian Lewis occupies a somewhat peculiar position. There is no doubt that he qualifies as a hero, because he was personally responsible for one of the most devastating and far-reaching blows the liquor business ever received; he inspired the mighty clamor of the early 1870s known as "The Women's Crusade," and set thousands of furious females marching against the saloon with prayers upon their lips and destruction in their hearts. On the other hand, from the viewpoint of the ardent dry, he possesses many of the attributes of a villain. He fought staunchly for total abstinence, but he ridiculed the dogma that liquor was the source of all crime (which was rank heresy) and violently opposed prohibition; in a book called *Prohibition a Failure* he predicted that it could never be enforced because it violated personal liberty, the "great vital, pivotal fact of human life." Temperance historians have scarcely known how to handle Dr. Lewis, but they have managed to tarnish his crown a little by inventing the legend that his father was a drunkard, and by carefully noting that his maternal grandfather, though a deacon in the Baptist Church, was also a distiller. In general they have labeled him with the damning classification, "a good man, but——"

Fortunately, Dr. Lewis had many other achievements to his credit, so his fame is secure. He invented the beanbag, "a small bag of ticking three-fourths filled with beans, for tossing and catching." He devised a system of physical education upon which modern teaching of the subject is largely based. He made the first wooden dumbbell. He coined the slogan, "A clean tooth never decays." He crusaded against the corset and the three to six long, heavy skirts then in vogue, which he declared were responsible for 90 per cent of the "so-called female weaknesses." He advocated one short skirt only; if women must wear heavy garments, he urged them to use suspenders, thus taking the strain off the pelvic regions and saving them for more worthy purposes. He advised young ladies who yearned for an erect carriage to carry something on their heads, but instead of the book used for this purpose by effete moderns, he suggested twenty pounds of sand in a sheepskin bag. He spoke often in favor of equal rights for women. He was a prolific author, and some of his books, notably *Our Girls, Our Digestion,* and *Chastity, or Our Secret Sins,* were classics in their time, endorsed by such eminent educators as Andrew D. White of Cornell University, Mark Hopkins of Williams, and Edward Hitchcock of Amherst. He tried to teach hygiene and physiology to girls, but here he ran afoul of the clergy, most of whom considered it a sin for a woman to know anything about her body. A Presbyterian minister, who ran a girls' school in Maryland, said to Dr. Lewis, "I wish my young females to consider themselves a mass of animated matter of which God will take care if they love and serve Him."

A phrenologist examined and measured the bumps on Dr. Lewis's head in 1847, when the doctor was fifty-one years old, and published his findings in the *Phrenological Journal and Illustrated Life.* "His large, rotund body and well-formed head," wrote the expert, "make him at once a striking and conspicuous figure. He stands nearly six feet high and weighs over 200 pounds. His complexion is fair, eyes blue, hair formerly auburn, now white. His skin is fresh, with a peachy hue. His nature is peculiarly sympathetic. . . . He experiences the most exalted and rapturous emotions. He is overflowing with good feelings, affection, charity, aspiration, and adoration." Dr. Lewis practiced medicine occasionally—he was a homeopath with two years' study at Harvard—edited magazines, and ran schools, publishing houses, and hotels, but with such characteristics it was only natural that his principal business should be lecturing. He was a standard lyceum attraction, and very popular, especially among the women. His regular fee was fifty dollars a day, but it was his custom, when he spoke in a town, to stay over one day and deliver a temperance lecture to which admission was free.

In the winter of 1873, while on a speaking tour of New York and the Middle West, Dr. Lewis began to end his temperance lecture with a stirring plea to the women in his audience to go into the saloons and pray with and for the saloonkeepers and bartenders. He had a notion that the women of America could conquer the liquor traffic by faith and prayer, and the Christian principles of light and love properly applied by "visitation bands." Something of this sort had been done in 1858, when a group of women had prayed the saloons out of business, for a little while, in Dixon, Illinois, and in Battle Creek, Michigan. And in 1865, after a worthy young man had been accidentally shot in front of a saloon in Greenfield, Ohio, a band of the leading ladies of the town, each carrying an ax, a hatchet, or a hammer, marched to the saloon and proceeded to knock in the heads of casks and barrels and demolish bottles and fixtures. They were all arrested, but the grand jury refused to return an indictment.

Unfortunately, the nation was preoccupied with the Civil War, and these exploits attracted little attention. When Dr. Lewis started his lecture tour, however, the time was opportune. Heretofore the dry crusade had been almost exclusively a masculine business, and intelligent women were becoming very critical of the way in which it was being managed. They had seen the temperance reform climb to the heights of victory in the early 1850s, when thirteen states and two territories adopted prohibition; now they watched the bumbling attempts of the man to halt the plunge into defeat, as state after state repealed or modified its prohibitory laws and returned to the license system.

Meanwhile conditions everywhere were growing worse, especially in the smaller towns and cities. Drunkenness was increasing. The saloon-keepers ignored the laws; they kept open on Sundays and sold liquor to whoever wanted it, regardless of age, sex, or condition. The brewers were arrogantly buying up both politicians and choice business locations, opening unneeded saloons and flooding the communities with beer. In many towns whole blocks were given up to rows of disreputable gin mills, many of them operated in connection with low dance halls, gambling joints, and houses of prostitution; the unholy alliance of liquor, politics, and crime was in visible process of formation. The male leaders of the temperance movement had failed dismally to scotch or even control the evil, and women all over the country were restive; there were many demands for some form of direct action. The ladies were primed and ready to shoot. Dr. Lewis pulled the trigger.

2

Dr. Lewis first suggested that prayer and "visitation bands" be employed against the saloons at Fredonia and Jamestown, in the southwestern corner of New York, about the middle of December 1873. Women in both towns dutifully organized into committees, and while they frightened a few saloonkeepers, their interest was never more than lukewarm and they had little or no success. Dr. Lewis tried again in two or three towns in Pennsylvania, but failed to really strike a spark until he reached Ohio; then he hit the jackpot. On the night of December 23, 1873, he delivered his temperance lecture at Hillsboro, the capital of Highland County in southern Ohio, a "quiet, cultured, and refined" town of some five thousand population, with two seminaries for young females. There were also thirteen places where liquor was sold, and the gentlemen of the community, most of whom were of Virginia descent, maintained the Old Dominion tradition of a well-stocked sideboard. Some of the town's professional men, if a temperance historian is to be believed, "were very dissipated."

The response to Dr. Lewis's plea at Hillsboro was immediate and very gratifying. When he asked how many would undertake the war against the saloons, more than sixty women rose, while as many men stood up to signify that they would act as "backers" should the ladies require financial or strong-arm assistance. Mrs. Eliza J. Thompson, daughter of former Governor Allen Trimble and Hillsboro's most prominent woman, was unable to attend the lecture, but the family was represented by her sixteen-year-old son. When the boy came home he was greatly excited; he told his mother that the women wanted her to preside at a prayer meeting next morning in the Presbyterian church and then lead them against the saloons. Mrs. Thompson's husband, who had been asleep on the living-room couch, roused long enough to mutter that it was "a lot of tomfoolery." Mrs. Thompson promptly shushed him; in a letter to a friend a few months later she wrote that she had rather tartly reminded him that "the men had been in the tomfoolery business a long time," and suggested that "it might be God's will that the women should now take their part."

Mrs. Thompson was a gentle, retiring woman of sixty, deeply religious and widely known for her church and charitable work. She had never taken part in a public demonstration, and had a horror of being conspicuous. Nevertheless, she resolved to undertake the task if God willed it. She spent the night reading her Bible and praying for guidance, but when morning came she was still waiting for a sign. Soon after breakfast her young daughter came into her room carrying a Bible. "I opened it at the 146th Psalm, Mother," she said. "It must be for you." Mrs. Thompson read the Psalm, which later became known as the Crusade Psalm and was recited at all crusaders' meetings: ". . . The Lord openeth the eyes of the blind; the Lord raiseth them that are bowed down . . . The Lord preserveth the strangers . . . but the way of the wicked he turneth upside down. . . ." As Mrs. Thompson finished reading, she received the call.

"Yes," she said. "It is for me. I must go."

At the church Mrs. Thompson, who because of her work in the crusade was never thereafter called anything but Mother Thompson, found nearly seventy women waiting for her, shepherded by several clergymen and local temperance leaders. At her request the men retired, and the women organized by electing Mother Thompson president and Mrs. Joseph J. McDowell, wife of a former congressman, vice-president. Then Mother Thompson addressed the crusaders:

"We will sing the good old hymn, 'Give to the Winds Thy Fears,' and as we all join in singing, let us form in line, two by two, the small women in front, leaving the tall ones to bring up the rear, and let us at once proceed to our sacred mission, trusting alone in the God of Jacob."

Some singing, some praying, some weeping, and all visibly in the transports of religious exaltation, "this band of mysterious beings," as Mother Thompson called them, marched out of the church—and the most remarkable, and hysterical, demonstration of feminine power in American history was under way. With half the town following, the crusaders marched up Main Street to Dr. William Smith's Drug Store, where Dr. Smith took one look at the multitude and quickly signed a pledge to sell no more liquor. "After calling at all drugstores," wrote Mother Thompson, "the pledge being signed by all save one, we encountered various saloons and hotels with varied success, until by continuous daily visitations with persuasion, prayer, song, and Scripture-reading, the drinking places of the town were reduced from thirteen to one drugstore, one hotel, and two saloons, and they sold very cautiously."

Largely because most of the Hillsboro saloonkeepers were of the so-called respectable class, even this partial victory required some two months of constant hounding, in addition to special prayer meetings every morning and mass meetings each evening. One man, a druggist, held out for more than a month, when he went bankrupt and had to close his doors. Another, known as "the witty Englishman," withstood daily visits even longer, but one day he suddenly began to weep, flopped to his knees, and prayed loudly for forgiveness and peace. While some of the ladies prayed with him and sang hymns, the others destroyed his stock of liquors. The worst saloon in Hillsboro, the Lava Bed, run by Joseph Lance, was the first to surrender; after a few days Lance locked his doors and went into the fish business. He may have been influenced somewhat by the fact that he was under two indictments for illegal selling. Two other saloonkeepers shipped their liquors to Cincinnati and sold their fixtures at auction. "The ladies attended in force," said the Cincinnati *Gazette* of January 27, 1874, "anxious to secure mementos. It was fun to see our pious sisters stringing home from this sale, lugging bottles, tumblers, beer mugs, and decanters."

Meanwhile Dr. Lewis had gone on to Washington Court House, in the adjoining county of Fayette, a town of about three thousand population which, according to Dr. Lewis's biographer, was "much given to dissipation." It supported eleven saloons, and three drugstores, the principal business of which was selling liquor by the drink and in bulk. Dr. Lewis lectured there on Christmas Day, 1873, and under the leadership of Mrs. George Carpenter the women of Washington Court House attacked the saloons with even greater vigor than Mother Thompson's cohorts in Hillsboro had displayed. At first the saloonkeepers treated the crusade as a great joke; they and their ribald customers watched in amusement as the ladies knelt on the sawdust-covered floors and prayed and sang hymns. But after a day or two they began to lock their doors whenever they saw the crusaders marching down the street, whereupon the women knelt on the sidewalks and carried on as usual.

Saturday, December 27, was the big day of the crusade in Washington Court House. Although a heavy snow had fallen the night before and the weather was bitterly cold, more than a hundred women assembled at the Presbyterian church early in the morning and moved en masse against the bars. They knelt in the snow all day, praying and singing and reading from the Bible, while all the town's clergymen and a large number of other men remained in the church in continuous prayer meeting, the church bell being tolled at the conclusion of each prayer. Within a few days the saloonkeepers began to give up, signing the pledge and turning their stocks over to the women to be destroyed. An official report of the Washington Court House crusade organization said that when the first saloonkeeper surrendered on December 29 "nearly a thousand men, women, and children witnessed the mingling of beer, ale, wine, and whiskey, as they filled the gutters and were drank up by the earth, while bells were ringing, men and boys shouting, and women singing and praying to God who had given the victory." A similar hullabaloo accompanied each surrender thereafter; according to the Fayette County *Herald,* the "following order of exercises was carried out: 1. Prayer by Rev. George Carpenter. 2. Rolling out of barrels. 3. Ax application to barrel heads. 4. Fire application to old bourbon. 5. Cheers by the multitude." After a week of constant visitation by the ladies, the owner of the largest saloon in town, a man named Smith, asked them politely to stay away; they were ruining his business and the crusade was becoming a bit of a bore.

"Oh, but, Mr. Smith!" said Mrs. Carpenter. "We must come here. We have vowed to Heaven that we would not cease until the selling of liquor was stopped in this town."

"Do you mean to come here and pray every day until I stop?" demanded Smith.

"We do," said Mrs. Carpenter.

Smith sighed and surrendered. He told the women that if they would bring his stock of liquor out of the cellar, without aid from any man, they could do as they pleased with it. Whereupon these "delicately nurtured creatures," as a contemporary writer described them, wrestled eighteen barrels of whiskey up two flights of stairs, borrowed an ax from Smith, and skillfully knocked in the heads.

After December 30 several victories were reported each day, and on Friday, January 2, 1874, one week after Dr. Lewis's lecture, it was anounced at the nightly prayer meeting that the last drinking place had surrendered, and that for the first time in its history Washington Court House was without a house where liquor was sold. There were a few days of rejoicing, and then the crusaders divided into smaller committees and went into nearby towns and villages to hold meetings and get the crusade started throughout Fayette County. Most of them hurried back to Washington Court House in a couple of weeks, however, when the distressing news came that a stranger had taken out a license to operate one of the abandoned saloons and that he was backed to the extent of five thousand dollars by a Cincinnati distillery. Several barrels of whiskey were unloaded at the saloon early in the morning of January 14, but they were met by forty women, who crowded into the place and prayed and sang continuously until eleven o'clock at night, being frequently reinforced by other crusaders. The next two days were the coldest of the winter, and the women found that the saloonkeeper had locked them out; they had kept him from opening for business, but they were mighty uncomfortable. So they employed workmen to build a small hut on wheels, which they called a "tabernacle," and equipped it with a small stove. This they set up in the street in front of the saloon, and warmed themselves between periods of kneeling in the street. After one day the newcomer surrendered.

The crusaders now decided to do something about a beer garden just outside the town limits, which was run by Charley Beck, a German immigrant. Beck seemed to be in a good position to withstand a siege, a judge had granted him an injunction restraining the women from entering his premises, and a group of Cincinnati brewers had promised him free beer and two thousand dollars in cash if he would stay open a year. But Beck and the brewers failed to reckon with the ingenuity of the ladies. The land next door to the beer garden was owned by a man who sympathized with the crusade, and he invited the women to make use of it. They moved the tabernacle to this man's property, and on the roof rigged up a locomotive headlight with a strong reflector, so that the light shone directly into Charley Beck's door. For two weeks the crusaders kept vigil in the tabernacle, in four-hour shifts, praying and singing from dawn until the saloon closed at midnight, while two of the women sat at a bench ostentatiously entering in a big ledger the names of Beck's customers. Beck's business finally vanished; there were days on which the ledger contained no entries at all. One morning the saloonkeeper came to his door with both hands raised above his head.

"Oh, vimmins!" he shouted. "Shut up, vimmins! I quits!"

Charley Beck was a tough nut that required considerable cracking, but the crusaders of New Vienna, a small village in Clinton County, encountered an even tougher one when they went after John Calvin Van Pelt, who ran a disreputable resort known as the Dead Fall and called himself "the wickedest man in Ohio." Van Pelt was a great, hulking brute, described by a reporter for the Cincinnati *Commercial* as "a burly man, with a round knobby head and a bulbous nose." His wickedness seems to have consisted in selling and drinking inferior liquor, and having bad manners and a sulphurous vocabulary. When the women first visited his saloon he received them sullenly, but quietly; when they returned he became very abusive and threatened to hang them from the rafters above his bar. Next day the crusaders found the windows of the saloon decorated with jugs and bottles of whiskey and a great blood-smeared ax, while empty bottles dangled above the doorway and a black flag floated over the one-story shack. Thoroughly frightened, nevertheless the women marched into the resort and began to pray, while a crowd of some two hundred men waited outside, expecting violence.

Van Pelt made no move against the women until they loudly asked the Lord to baptize him with the Holy Ghost. Then, with a violent oath, he seized a bucket of dirty water and shouted, "I'll baptize you!" He flung the water against the low ceiling, and it came splashing down upon the kneeling women. He followed that up with a bucket of beer, and continued to splash the crusaders until one of them courteously offered to relieve him. "You must be tired," she said. "We wish to suffer all things for the Lord's sake." Thereupon Van Pelt flung up his hands and fled into the back room and locked the door. Drenched to the skin, and odorous with the heady fumes of beer, the women finished their exercises and hastened home to change clothing. But their enraged husbands had Van Pelt arrested, and he spent a week in jail, unable to furnish bail. When he was released he reopened the Dead Fall, the women resumed their visits, and he continued to scream insults and throw beer and water at them. Finally, three weeks after the crusaders had begun to torment him, he told them one morning that if they would go away and return at two o'clock he would give them his final decision.

The women now felt certain that victory was theirs, and the rumor spread that Van Pelt would surrender. At noon all the church bells began to toll, and boys with hand bells raced through the village crying, "Everybody meet at Van Pelt's saloon at two o'clock and hear his decision." When the hour came the whole town was there. After the crusaders had prayed and sung, Van Pelt, dressed in his best, came to the door of the Dead Fall and announced that he was surrendering, "not to law or force, but to the labors of love of the women." Two clergymen were appointed to roll out the barrels of liquor, and then Van Pelt stepped forward, brandishing an ax which he said was the same he had used to terrify the ladies. "I now use it," he said, "to sacrifice that which I fear has ruined many souls." Thereupon he smashed the barrels, and the beer and whiskey poured into the gutter. That night Van Pelt spoke at a special thanksgiving service in the Christian Church, and impressed his listeners with his humble and contrite manner.

A few days later Van Pelt went on a lecture tour of Ohio with Dr. Lewis, who said that he was "a coarse man, beside whom you would not choose to sit, yet when he speaks of his experience, you cannot restrain your tears." The Cincinnati *Commercial* correspondent said that Van Pelt's grammar was "horrid," though he was improving. For a while the "reformed saloonkeeper," as he was billed, was an object of great curiosity and attracted large crowds, which contributed freely to his support. But as interest lessened, both audiences and collections dwindled; several times Van Pelt didn't get enough to pay his expenses. He also complained that wherever he went the crusaders watched him so closely, for fear of backsliding, that they made him nervous. Finally he disappeared. "He was heard of afterwards in Wilmington," wrote a historian of the crusades, "keeping a low, disreputable place . . . The last I heard of him he was in a Western penitentiary. Alas, the seed had not depth of earth."

3

Within two weeks after the last saloon had closed its doors in Washington Court House, the excitement had spread throughout Ohio; there was scarcely a community that had not either started a crusade or was anxiously awaiting the arrival of Dr. Lewis. A little astonished at the fury he had evoked, Dr. Lewis canceled his lyceum tour, and thereafter gave his entire time to the crusade, speaking in a different town almost every night and performing prodigies of organization. Although the crusade centered in Ohio, before the uproar subsided the cries of the praying women had been heard in twenty-two states, including Indiana, Michigan, Wisconsin, Iowa, Minnesota, Nebraska, Missouri, Kansas, Colorado, Oregon, and California. Very little was accomplished in the East although there were a few mass meetings and threats of action in New York and Brooklyn. Dr. Lewis attempted to invade Massachusetts and other New England states, but he was not permitted to speak in Boston, and met with a cool reception elsewhere. "I do not find the soil of New England adapted to this new method of warfare," he said.

Dr. Lewis advised the women that the crusade could not succeed in the large cities, where the liquor traffic was strongly entrenched both in politics and business, and he urged them to confine their efforts to small towns and villages. However, so much pressure was brought to bear by the eager crusaders that he soon found himself lecturing and organizing praying bands in Columbus, Cleveland, Chicago, Cincinnati, and Pittsburgh, as well as in such smaller cities as Xenia, Madisonville, Mount Vernon, Akron, and Springfield, all in Ohio. The first sizable place attempted was Xenia, which had about ten thousand inhabitants and one hundred and twenty saloons. Nine of these resorts were on Whiteman Street, within a space of a few hundred yards, and five were of such bad repute that they were known as Shades of Death, Mule's Ear, Hell's Half-Acre, Certain Death, and Devil's Den. One of the unusual features of the crusade in Xenia was the work of forty or fifty little girls, pupils in Laura Hicks's private school. Each afternoon Miss Hicks led the children into Whiteman Street, where they gathered in front of the saloons and sang a song which began, "Say, Mr. Barkeeper, has father been here?" The girls were given much credit for the fact that on March 14, about a month after Dr. Lewis started the work, the last saloon in Xenia closed its doors.

Similar victories were won in Mount Vernon and a few other cities approximately the same size as Xenia; it was estimated that from 60 to 80 per cent of the saloons were closed in Akron, Springfield, and other cities of about twenty-five thousand population. But when Dr. Lewis and his crusaders invaded Columbus, Cleveland, Cincinnati, Chicago, and Pittsburgh, they were soundly trounced, although they caused a great deal of disturbance. In Pittsburgh and Cincinnati the ladies were arrested for violating various city ordinances, but were soon released, and in Cleveland, Pittsburgh, and Chicago they were attacked by mobs which kicked and beat some of them very severely. The only concrete results of the work in these cities were seven out of four hundred saloons closed in Columbus, and 2,932 pledge signers in Cincinnati, of whom it was believed fifty had been "soundly converted." However, very little had been expected of Cincinnati, even by the most optimistic crusaders. With three thousand saloons, a large German population, and forty million dollars invested in the manufacture of liquor, Cincinnati was a brewers' and distillers' stronghold.

4

In many towns in Ohio and elsewhere the saloonkeepers and their friends fought back viciously; in some the crusaders were cruelly misused. They were kicked, pummeled, spat upon, deluged with beer and slops, bombarded with eggs, vegetables, and even stones, and threatened with guns, knives, and pistols. They were often arrested, but were quickly released when they began to hold prayer meetings in the jails. In Cincinnati the proprietor of a beer garden mounted an old cannon at the entrance to his place and threatened to blow the ladies to kingdom come. One of the women promptly clambered upon the gun and led the others in prayer. In some towns the saloonkeepers locked their doors and imprisoned the crusaders; at Adrian, Michigan, two prominent women were held in a grogshop from dawn until ten o'clock at night, when their husbands threatened to smash the doors. In other places the liquor sellers rigged up powerful force pumps and sprayed the kneeling women with water; it quickly froze, so that a line of praying crusaders resembled a row of icicles. After such an experience many had to be carried home to thaw out. At Carthage,

Missouri, the saloonkeepers organized gangs to disrupt the prayer meetings by blowing on tin horns allegedly provided by the mayor; when the women prayed in the streets, uncouth men with fiddles and other instruments played and danced obscenely before them.

A serious riot developed in Alameda, California, when the crusaders erected a tent near a polling place, hoping to influence voters who were casting their ballots in an election held under the provisions of the state's local option law. A mob of several hundred men, headed by the band of the United States Fourth Artillery, destroyed the tent and tried to assault Miss Sally Hart, who had led the women during the crusade work in Alameda. Miss Hart outran them and escaped, but was struck by several stones. Later the mob made an effigy of her and buried it in a sandbank. Mrs. Annie Wittenmeyer, first president of the National Women's Christian Temperance Union, who wrote a history of the crusade, said that "the Alameda outrage, which has no parallel in the history of civilized nations, was perpetrated by members of the San Francisco German Saloon-keepers' Society." She quoted a gentleman who saw the rioting as saying, "It was simply hell let loose. It was a constant series of howlings, cursings, and threats . . . The sight of a lady was a signal of an outburst of obscenity and insult . . . The mob were like a pack of hyenas."

On May 5, 1874, the mayor of Bucyrus, Ohio, issued a proclamation forbidding the crusaders to pray in the streets, and to enforce the edict swore in fifty special policemen, described by a temperance historian as "low, drunken ruffians, armed with hickory bludgeons." The women were set upon by the specials as they marched down the main street of the town, and their leader, a woman of seventy, was dragged into a cellarway and her arm severely lacerated by blows from a club. Another, while on her knees praying, was dragged a block before gentlemen of the town came to her rescue. The Bucyrus *Journal* said that the crusaders "experienced every indignity but a square blow; such cowardly blows as could be secretly given, seizures and violent pushes, amounting in effect to blows, were given continuously . . . A more damnable, iniquitous series of infernal outrages were never offered to ladies." The women stood their ground and defied their assailants, and that night several warrants were sworn out charging the specials with assault and battery. Next morning when the crusaders appeared on the street they were not molested. Here, as elsewhere, the women accepted whatever came their way with true Christian fortitude; the more they were reviled and abused the louder they sang and prayed.

The strange goings on in the Middle West aroused tremendous interest throughout the United States, and were thoroughly covered by important newspapers in New York, Boston, Cincinnati, Cleveland, and other large cities, while *Harper's Weekly* and *Frank Leslie's,* the most popular magazines of the period, sent into the field both special writers and staff artists. Most of the correspondents seem to have sympathized with the crusaders, although some were violently opposed. The New York *Herald,* which had been anti-temperance since it was founded by James Gordon Bennett, took a very dim view of the whole business. "Who shall say," demanded the *Herald,* "that the Ohio reformers, in their ardor to suppress the liquor traffic, may not propose to burn the beer-sellers? . . . We have it on good authority that 'of all cookeries most the saints love a roast,' and it is quite possible that Dio Lewis may yet preside at an *auto-da-fé* for the conversion of beer-sellers."

5

Although the winter of 1873–74 was unusually severe everywhere in the Middle West, and especially in Ohio, as far as the records show, none of the crusaders froze to death, died of exposure, or even caught pneumonia. But this was only one of the many wonders of the crusade. Strange things happened during the six or eight months the movement was in progress, and temperance advocates have never questioned their authenticity because they were reported and vouched for by such eminent leaders as Dr. Lewis, Mrs. Annie Wittenmeyer, Mother Thompson; Mrs. E. D. Stewart of Springfield, who had won the nickname of Mother Stewart for her work with the soldiers during the Civil War; and Frances E. Willard, the most renowned of all American women reformers, who in her *Women and Temperance* described the crusade as "this whirlwind of the Lord."

Such minor miracles as sudden changes in the weather for the benefit of the crusaders, and argumentative saloonkeepers being stricken dumb, falling to the floor in a fit, or bursting into tears, were reported scores of times. On many occasions the liquor men loosed vicious dogs against the women; invariably, as soon as the animals caught the holy scent of the crusaders they turned and ran, yelping in distress, or crawled cringing to the feet of the ladies. In Cleveland a saloonkeeper set three fierce dogs upon Mrs. Charles Wheeler as she knelt on the sidewalk. "Without ceasing her prayer," wrote Mrs. Wittenmeyer, "she gently laid her hands upon their heads, and as though taught of a higher power than their master's, they crouched at her feet and were quiet." The fact that Mrs. Wheeler had only two hands seems to suggest that this took a bit of fast work; the further fact that she walked home followed by the dogs dispels any doubt. A similar wonder, except that only one dog was involved, was reported from Shelbyville, Indiana. In that same town a saloonkeeper's wife rushed upon a kneeling crusader, wildly swinging a hatchet. But as she raised the weapon to strike, her face turned white, she trembled, her arm dropped to her side, and the hatchet clattered to the ground. She immediately turned to her husband and ordered him to bring out his liquors to be destroyed. He refused.

In Bellefontaine, Ohio, another liquor dealer's wife stood in the doorway of her husband's saloon and reviled the crusaders with a flood of very intemperate language. Nothing could be heard above her screams, so after a few moments of patient waiting the leader of the praying women raised her hand to heaven and said, "Lord, silence this woman!" Immediately the woman's mouth shut like a steel trap, and she never spoke another word as long as she lived, which was only a couple of years. In another Ohio town a young man walked calmly between the ranks of kneeling women and started into a saloon to get his morning glass of whiskey. He seemed oblivious to what was going on, which was because he was deaf. Suddenly he felt something like a drill passing through his head. At once his ears were opened, and he heard the songs and prayers. He turned and fled, shrieking, and never took another drink.

The most spectacular miracle of the crusade, or at least the one that involved the most people, occurred in Cincinnati, which in the opinion of the crusaders could have stood a hundred more. On Good Friday of 1874 a band of eighty or a hundred women, led by Mrs. M. E. Winslow, visited fourteen saloons and then marched to the Esplanade, now called Fountain Square, where they planned to hold a thirty-minute prayer meeting. As they approached their objective, however, they found the way barred by a mob of some two thousand desperate-looking men, and Mrs. Winslow heard a voice shout:

"Jack, a woman's foot shall not trod the Esplanade today!"

The praying women dropped to their knees, and Mrs. Winslow raised her hands on high.

"Lord!" she implored. "Give us the Esplanade!"

Immediately she felt a great surge of power sweeping through her body, and she rose to her feet. Standing before her, arms folded, glaring viciously, his lips curled in an uncouth sneer, was a "great, brutal-looking fellow, debauched and degraded." She knew at once that this must be Jack. She touched him on the shoulder.

"Jack," she said, "we are a band of brokenhearted mothers and wives, weeping and praying because you are all going to hell as fast as you can go. We want to pray here, right by this fountain, and I want you to make way for us and keep the men still till we get through our service."

A great change came over Jack. For a moment he seemed bewildered and befuddled; it was obvious that he was in the grip of a power greater than any he had ever encountered. Then he smiled and his face was transfigured; he looked almost human. He patted Mrs. Winslow tenderly on the back, and with a fearful oath cried:

"I'll do it! Men, make way for the crusaders! The crusaders are coming through!" He forced his great brawny shoulders through the crowd, shouting:

"God bless the crusaders!" Other men took up the cry, and the mob parted like the waters of the Red Sea.

"Then," wrote Mrs. Winslow, "we knelt around that central fountain which is the glory of Cincinnati, and two thousand men, mostly reeking with the fumes of rum and tobacco, knelt with us, with sobs and tears."

6

No exact records of the results of the crusade were ever compiled, but it has been estimated that between twenty-five thousand and thirty thousand saloons were closed; Dr. Lewis reported in March 1874 that in the first two months of the crusade seventeen thousand drinking places were abandoned in Ohio alone. Statistics of the Internal Revenue Bureau show that between 1873 and 1875 almost seven hundred and fifty breweries went out of business throughout the country, while the production of malt liquors dropped 5,599,406 gallons. The New York *Tribune* said that during the months of January and February 1874 the collection of liquor taxes by the federal government decreased nearly three hundred thousand dollars in two of the largest revenue districts of Indiana and Ohio. Before the crusade had ended, the loss in revenue amounted to more than one million dollars. A correspondent of the New York *Observer,* writing from Tiffin, Ohio, reported that "the assessors and gaugers of the ninth district of Ohio tell us that, as a result of the temperance movement, not one of the eight distilleries in the district is now in operation. The sale of all kinds of liquors, beer, and ale has fallen off more than 60 per cent."

These were all definite gains for the cause, but they were ephemeral; the crusade failed to affect the laws which permitted the saloons to operate, nor did it destroy the alliance of the politicians and the liquor interests. The uproar began to subside in six or eight months, and within a year after Mother Thompson had set out to turn the way of the wicked upside down, every town which had been involved in the crusade, and of which there is any record, had as many saloons as before the movement. Many, including Washington Court House, had more.

Other results of the crusade, however, were more lasting; some proved to be of great importance in the development of the temperance movement. "It has come and it has gone—this whirlwind of the Lord," wrote Frances E. Willard, "but it has set forces in motion which each day become more potent, and will sweep on until the rum power in America is overthrown. There was but one Pentecost; doubtless history will record but one 'temperance crusade.'" Among other things, the excitement aroused nation-wide interest in the liquor question, which had declined noticeably during the decade of the 1860s; emphasized and exposed the iniquities of the rum traffic; and revived the thousands of moribund men's societies, which began a series of campaigns that brought about important victories within the next fifteen years.

The most important offspring of the crusade, described by Miss Willard as its "sober second thought," was the National Women's Christian Temperance Union, which was organized at the Second Presbyterian Church of Cleveland on November 18, 19, and 20, 1874, after preliminary work had been done during the summer at Lake Chautauqua, New York. Delegates from seventeen states, most of them former crusaders, participated in the organizational meeting, and elected, as first president of the union, Mrs. Annie Wittenmeyer of Philadelphia, secretary of the Home Missionary Society of the Methodist Church and publisher of the *Christian Woman* and the *Christian Child*. A vice-president was chosen from each state. The platform adopted at the first meeting emphasized the religious character of the union, and urged the reformation of the drunkard through faith in God. There was little in it to alarm the liquor industry. But at the second annual convention, in 1875, the union served notice that its goal was legal prohibition of all intoxicating drink, adopting a resolution which said that "while we will continue to employ all moral agencies as indispensable, we hold prohibition to be essential to the full triumph of this reform." The W.C.T.U. has never abandoned this purpose.

Frances E. Willard, who at the age of thirty-four had resigned as Dean of Women of Northwestern University to devote her life to the temperance cause, and had participated briefly in the crusade at Pittsburgh, was elected corresponding secretary at the union's first meeting. Five years later, in 1879, she became president, and held that office until her death in 1898. When Miss Willard took office as head of the W.C.T.U. it was organized in twenty-three states. She proceeded immediately to organize the others, and within a decade had established local branches in virtually every city, town, village, and hamlet in the United States. Under her leadership the union was soon the most powerful temperance organization in the world, with a remarkable propaganda mill second in efficiency only to that developed in later years by the Anti-Saloon League. The record of the union's accomplishments is long and impressive; among other things it compelled the legislature of every state in the Union, after a campaign that lasted from 1880 to 1902, to enact so-called scientific instruction laws. These statutes provided for the compulsory teaching of the dangers of drinking in all American public schools.

Because of her great ability as an organizer, and the extraordinary energy which took her into thousands of cities and towns, Frances Willard became one of the best-known personages of her time. Millions of American Protestant women have regarded her as at least semidivine, and since her death have addressed prayers to her as a Catholic pleads for the intercession of a saint. And if the innumerable legends which have clustered about her are to be believed, she has seldom failed them. For instance, once a woman temperance lecturer bogged down in the middle of a speech. She bumbled along for a few moments, then raised her eyes to heaven and cried, "God or Frances E. Willard, help me!" Immediately she regained her self-possession and triumphantly finished her talk.

CHAPTER FIVE

"Born of God"

Recovery of the temperance movement from the doldrums of the 1860s, begun by the Women's Crusade in Ohio and the Middle West, was given a considerable impetus by the Prohibition party, which in 1876 proposed an entirely new means of combating the liquor traffic. In the platform adopted by its national convention that year, the party denounced the importation, exportation, manufacture, and sale of all alcoholic beverages as "high crimes against society," and demanded an amendment to the national constitution which would render prohibitory measures "universal and permanent." At the same time the convention nominated for the presidency General Green Clay Smith of Kentucky, a Baptist preacher who, before he entered the ministry, had been active as a politician in both the Republican and Democratic parties. As a Democrat he had been a member of the Kentucky Legislature, and as a Republican had served two terms in Congress. At the Republican National Convention of 1864 he had come within one vote of being chosen as Lincoln's running mate.

The election of 1876 was the famous contest which Rutherford B. Hayes won by a single vote in the Electoral College, although Samuel J. Tilden, the Democratic nominee, had received a majority of the popular vote. General Smith was endorsed by most of the important temperance organizations and supported by some forty dry papers and magazines. His advocacy of nation-wide prohibition aroused great interest, but the temperance people failed to cast their ballots for him. His share of the total vote was only 9,737. There were several reasons for this poor showing. In the first place, the Prohibition party, having been in existence only since 1869, was organized in fewer than a dozen states, and was unable to collect enough money to conduct a proper campaign. Also, considerable skulduggery seems to have been practiced, especially in some of the larger communities. In New York and Buffalo, for example, the election returns failed to show a single vote for the Prohibition candidate, although several prominent members of the party lived in these cities and there is no reason to doubt that they voted their own ticket.

Both the Democrats and the Republicans made strenuous efforts to get the dry vote. The Democrats could do little more than urge the drys not to throw away their votes on a minor candidate who had no chance of victory. The Republicans, however, could point out that Hayes's temperance sentiments were well known, and that he was being supported by almost all of the religious periodicals. They also made a great deal of the religious and temperance affiliations of Mrs. Hayes, who was the first president of the Women's Home Missionary Society of the Methodist Church, and had been prominent in the W.C.T.U. since its organization. In several states where the anti-liquor element was particularly strong, Republican spellbinders posed as temperance lecturers and made speeches intimating strongly that if Hayes were elected he would do something about the liquor traffic. Some of these speakers described both Hayes and his wife as ardent prohibitionists, and promised that Mrs. Hayes would dry up the White House, which, in fact, she did. In 1877 she announced that so long as she was First Lady no alcoholic liquors would be served, either at social functions or at the President's private table. William M. Evarts, Secretary of State, once remarked that at Hayes's state dinners "water flowed like champagne."

In December 1876 the first prohibition amendment to the national constitution ever to reach the halls of Congress was introduced in the House by Representative Henry W. Blair of New Hampshire. It was a weak measure which prohibited distilled liquors only, and even if adopted and ratified, would not have been effective until 1900. As had been anticipated, it was buried in committee, a fate which also befell a stronger amendment, prohibiting all alcoholic liquors, introduced by Senator Plumb of Kansas in 1880. Blair, who in the meantime had been elected senator, offered a third amendment in 1887, a comprehensive measure which had been carefully prepared by Frances E. Willard, president of the W.C.T.U.; John B. Finch, national chairman of the Prohibition party; and John N. Stearns, secretary of the National Temperance Society. Because of pressure exerted by the temperance forces, this amendment was favorably reported to the Senate, and was voted upon March 2, 1889. It was defeated thirty-three to thirteen. Congress was not asked to consider another anti-liquor amendment until 1914.

Meanwhile a movement for state constitutional prohibition had been gaining headway in the Middle West. Both Michigan and Ohio—the former in 1850 and the latter in 1851—had abolished the license system by constitutional amendment, but neither state had prohibited the manufacture and sale of liquor. In 1861 both houses of the New York Legislature passed a resolution submitting a prohibition amendment to the people, but because of the Civil War no attempt was made to procure its passage by the succeeding legislature, as was required by New York State law. Nothing more was done until the late 1870s, when the plan was revived by temperance workers in Kansas, Iowa, and Wisconsin.

In nearly every respect constitutional prohibition was superior to the statutory laws which the drys had hitherto supported. The procedure for submitting a constitutional amendment to the people varied in different states, but in each it was long and difficult. Once in a state constitution, however, an amendment was apt to remain, for to repeal it was equally difficult. (Prior to the ratification of the Eighteenth Amendment, twenty states had adopted constitutional prohibition, and only two had repealed it—Rhode Island in 1889 and

South Dakota in 1896.) On the other hand, a statutory law was at the mercy of each succeeding legislature, which could amend or repeal it according to the way the political winds were blowing. Massachusetts provided a perfect example of what might happen to statutory prohibition. In 1852 the law was enacted, in 1868 it was repealed, in 1869 it was re-enacted, in 1871 it was amended, in 1872 it was further amended, in 1873 it was re-enacted, and in 1875 it was again repealed. In Pennsylvania, during the middle 1850s, a prohibition law was repealed even before it went into effect.

Kansas was the first state to adopt constitutional prohibition. In his message to the Kansas Legislature in 1879 Governor John P. St. John, who had been elected as a Republican and later became the presidential candidate of the Prohibition party, asked for the submission of an amendment to the state constitution which would prohibit all forms of alcoholic liquors. He also recommended, as an interim measure, a new local option law to replace the existing statute, which was unsatisfactory to the drys. Both were immediately introduced, and the local option bill seemed likely to pass, especially in the Senate. With characteristic lack of perspicacity, the wets proposed a deal, confident that they could control the House and that in any event the people of Kansas would not vote for the destruction of the liquor traffic. They offered to withdraw their opposition to the amendment, as far as the Senate was concerned, if the drys would abandon the local option law. The anti-liquor forces agreed, and the amendment passed the Senate unanimously. Then, to the surprise of the liquor people, it was pushed through the House. It was voted upon at the general election of November 1880, and received a majority of 7,998. It went into effect on May 1, 1881, and was a part of the Kansas constitution for some sixty-seven years.

In June 1882, two years after the victory in Kansas, Iowa gave constitutional prohibition a majority of almost thirty thousand, but the amendment was held invalid by the courts because three words had been omitted from the text as printed in the *Legislative Journal,* official record of the House. Similar omissions in Oregon and Indiana blocked the submission of amendments in those states, coincidences which brought forth caustic comment from temperance leaders. In Iowa the dry forces, though their efforts to pass a constitutional amendment had been defeated, compelled the legislature to pass a statutory prohibition law. Indiana and Oregon, however, remained wet. An amendment received a majority of eighty-two thousand votes in Ohio, but was defeated because this was not a majority of all the votes cast at the general election. Maine voted for constitutional prohibition in 1884, and Rhode Island did the same in 1886. In other states amendments received majorities, but not large enough to satisfy legal requirements. Only in North Carolina was the dry vote in the minority. In nearly every state where amendments were not voted upon by the people, resolutions providing for submission passed one branch of the legislature, and in most of these more stringent local option laws were enacted.

Contemplating these triumphs, leaders of the anti-liquor forces were confident that the United States was on the verge of another great wave of prohibition comparable to that of the 1850s, when fourteen states and two territories went dry. But they failed to consider the fact that although the reformers were united as to fundamental aims, they were divided as to method. The Prohibition party, the W.C.T.U., and the National Temperance Society advocated an amendment to the national constitution; many of the state and local societies favored the plan which had proven successful in Kansas and, failing that, state-wide statutory prohibition; others insisted that local option laws provided the best solution of the liquor problem; and, finally, a large body of temperance workers, including perhaps most of the Protestant clergy, clung to the principle of moral suasion, confident that in His own good time the Lord would redeem man from his erring ways.

The believers in faith and prayer supported the Red Ribbon Reform Clubs and the Blue Ribbon Reform Clubs founded during the middle 1870s by Dr. Henry A. Reynolds and Francis Murphy. Both Dr. Reynolds and Murphy were reformed drunkards, but Murphy possessed two added distinctions which greatly increased his popularity—he had been a saloonkeeper and had served a term in jail. Dr. Reynolds was merely a graduate of Harvard Medical College who had succumbed to the lure of the whiskey bottle. Both reformers emphasized the necessity of saving the drunkard, and preached that only by embracing religion and signing the pledge could man be rescued from the clutches of the rum demon. The Red and Blue Ribboners set New England and the Middle West ablaze with temperance fervor, but the enthusiasm stopped short of the ballot box.

Between 1887 and 1890 prohibition amendments were voted down in twelve states, while repeal movements got under way in others. The recession thus begun continued for some fifteen years, at the end of which time only Maine, Kansas, and North Dakota remained in the dry column, and even in those states enforcement machinery seemed to be on the point of collapse. Speakeasies ran wide open in the towns and cities, and bootleggers swarmed everywhere. This long series of setbacks appears to have been due largely to lack of financial resources, the absence of a strong central organization, and the increasing power and influence of the liquor interests. Moreover, both the Democratic and Republican political machines were openly antagonistic to the dry cause. A good example of the low esteem in which politicians held even the most important of the temperance leaders occurred at the Republican National Convention of 1884, when Frances E. Willard appeared on behalf of the W.C.T.U. to present a memorial urging the inclusion of a prohibition plank in the party platform. After a great deal of wirepulling and acrimonious discussion, the Platform Committee grudgingly allotted her fifteen minutes. What happened then is thus described by Dr. D. Leigh Colvin in *Prohibition in the United States:*

> She was coldly received. The Platform Committee in its report ignored the subject and when the platform was read not a delegate even from the prohibition states uttered a peep against the omission. Later the Memorial which Miss Willard had presented was found amid the litter on the floor of the committee room aslime with tobacco juice. This was subsequently procured and photographed . . . a facsimile was published broadcast as evidence of the Republican party's disrespectful treatment of the Memorial of the Christian women. . . .[1]

The nearest the drys of this era came to obtaining recognition from either of the major parties was a meaningless plank adopted by the Republican National Convention of 1892: "We sympathize with all wise and legitimate efforts to lessen and prevent the evils of intemperance and promote morality." What the anti-liquor forces sorely needed was an organization which could unify the divergent elements of the movement, raise money, and combat the machinations of the liquor interests and the politicians. And once again the prayers of the faithful were heard and the Lord interposed His arm. Out in Ohio were heard the first faint chirpings of the Anti-Saloon League of America, which was destined to take complete charge of the crusade, intensify its religious character, and lead it to final victory.

2

Actually, the Anti-Saloon League was an offspring of the Women's Crusade, although a somewhat different origin was claimed by F. Scott McBride, who was general superintendent of the league in the middle 1920s. "The Anti-Saloon League," he said, "was born of God. It has been led by Him, and will fight on while He leads." The mundane version, however, traces the organization only as far back as the Oberlin Temperance Alliance, which was formed at a mass meeting in Oberlin, Ohio, in March 1874, when the crusade was at its height. The purpose of the alliance was to support the women in their war against the saloon, and "by all lawful measures to suppress the traffic in and the use of intoxicating liquors." For several years the alliance devoted itself, with considerable success, to purely local problems, but in 1888 it promoted a temporary state-wide organization to fight for a township local option law, which was passed by the Ohio Legislature. On September 5, 1893, this organization was made permanent under the name of the Anti-Saloon League of Ohio, with Rev. David O. Mears of Cleveland as president and Rev. Howard H. Russell of Berea as superintendent. This was the first state-wide league, although a local Anti-Saloon League had been formed at Washington several months before, and had immediately launched a campaign to drive the saloons out of the District of Columbia.

The movement for a national Anti-Saloon League is said to have been the outgrowth of a conversation between Archbishop John Ireland of the Catholic Church and Rev. A. J. Kynett, chairman of the Permanent Committee on Prohibition and Temperance of the Methodist Church, who traveled together from Chicago to Philadelphia late in 1894. In the early fall of 1895 the Anti-Saloon League of the District of Columbia, at Kynett's suggestion, issued a call for a national convention of temperance workers, which was held in the Calvary Baptist Church in Washington on December 17–18. A large majority of the delegates were clergymen. This convention formed the Anti-Saloon League of America by merging the District of Columbia and Ohio leagues, and forty-five other national, state, and local organizations. The first president was Hiram Price, who had been a Republican member of Congress and had held several important political jobs. When he died in 1901 Bishop Luther B. Wilson of the Methodist Church assumed the office. One of the vice-presidents was Archbishop Ireland, who, as far as the record shows, was the first Catholic dignitary to co-operate actively with the Protestant reformers. As general superintendent, the real directing head of the league, the convention chose Rev. Howard H. Russell, who resigned in 1903 and was succeeded by Rev. Purley A. Baker of Ohio. Baker was general superintendent during the fight for the Eighteenth Amendment.

Although many of the officers and most of the field agents were paid employees and gave their whole time to the work, it was almost a decade before the Anti-Saloon League was satisfactorily organized on a national basis. By the middle 1900s, however, strong branches had been formed in forty states, and methods of co-operation had been worked out with all other temperance organizations except the Prohibition party. The league dominated the anti-liquor crusade everywhere in the United States and, as Ernest H. Cherrington put it in his *History of the Anti-Saloon League,* "had come to be recognized as the real agency through which the church was directing its fight against the liquor traffic." It had also come to be recognized by the liquor people as a dangerous and unscrupulous enemy; the more intelligent of the wets looked upon it with "apprehension and alarm."

In 1907 *Bonfort's Wine and Spirit Circular* sounded the warning: "The Anti-Saloon League is not a mob of long-haired fanatics, as some of the writers and speakers connected with our business have declared, but it is a strongly centralized organization, officered by men with unusual ability, financiered by capitalists with very long purses, subscribed to by hundreds of thousands of men, women, and children who are solicited by their various churches, advised by well-paid attorneys of great ability, and it is working with definite ideas to guide it in every state, in every county, in every city, in every precinct. . . ."

From the beginning the officials of the Anti-Saloon League displayed a thorough comprehension of the enormous influence of the printed word, and a large proportion of the money raised was devoted to publishing temperance literature of every description. For more than a decade the printing and distribution were farmed out to commercial firms in Columbus and Chicago, but in 1909 the league established its own publishing house, which was incorporated as the American Issue Publishing Company. A new printing plant was built at Westerville, Ohio, near Columbus, where the citizens had donated a tract of land, and the new house began active operations in October 1909. Under the direction of Purley Baker, and Ernest H. Cherrington, who had resigned as superintendent of the Anti-Saloon League of Washington to become general manager and editor-in-chief of the national organization's publishing interests, the American Issue Publishing Company became the most efficient propaganda machine in American history.

By 1912, after less than three years' operation, the plant at Westerville was turning out forty tons of material a month, or approximately 250,000,000 book pages. The quantity increased every year. According to the *Anti-Saloon League Year Book,* the league in 1916 was publishing a national edition and seventeen weekly, biweekly, and monthly editions of the *American Issue,* the organization's official paper; a national edition and six state editions of the *New Republic,* which was edited by William E. Johnson, the renowned "Pussyfoot"; a monthly edition of the *American Patriot;* a daily edition of the *National Daily;* a monthly edition of the *Scientific Temperance*

Journal; seven other minor periodicals, and millions of books, charts, leaflets, tracts, folders, and pamphlets.

This enormous production was actually only a part, perhaps not more than half, of the anti-liquor propaganda with which the United States was flooded during the pre-prohibition years and, to a somewhat smaller extent, while the Eighteenth Amendment was in effect. The Methodist Book Concern and the W.C.T.U. together probably produced as much material as the Anti-Saloon League, while innumerable smaller organizations published leaflets and pamphlets for local distribution. During the Smith-Hoover presidential campaign in 1928 the W.C.T.U., which for many years has operated its own publishing plant at Evanston, Illinois, printed ten million copies of a leaflet listing Alfred E. Smith's voting record as a member of the New York Legislature. Add to all this the speeches written for the twenty thousand to fifty thousand spellbinders whom the league sent into the field during important elections, the sermons prepared for delivery from thousands of Protestant pulpits, and the articles and editorials published by periodicals which were not directly connected with the cause, and any computation would have to be expressed in astronomical terms.

There never seemed to be any lack of funds to pay for the publishing and other activities of the Anti-Saloon League. Money was raised by a system of monthly subscriptions ranging from twenty-five cents to two dollars, in addition to contributions from church organizations and wealthy laymen. Wayne B. Wheeler, general counsel of the Anti-Saloon League and one of the great driving forces of the dry movement for almost twenty years, testified before a Senate investigating committee in 1926 that in thirty years the anti-liquor forces had expended at least thirty-five million dollars. In a series of articles published in the New York *Times* in 1926, Wheeler wrote that in 1914, when a constitutional amendment was defeated in Congress, the expenses of the drys reached a high mark of $2,500,000 a year, 90 per cent of which came from "the little people of the country. In only one case, as I recall it," he continued, "did the national organization receive so much as $25,000 a year from a single source, and only five persons contributed $10,000 a year or more. This money was spent mainly in educational work and in dry literature . . . As I recall it, we spent less than $100,000 directly in electing drys to Congress. . . ."

3

The Anti-Saloon League always called itself "the church in action against the saloon," and claimed to have brought the Protestant denominations into the fight and into politics. In his *History of the Anti-Saloon League,* Ernest H. Cherrington said, "Many years of difficult and patient endeavor were necessary to line up the church on the right side of this new movement." Actually, the church had never wavered in the battle with the rum demon since the time of Justin Edwards, some seventy years before the national league was organized. Throughout that period it had supported, and in most cases organized and directed, every important move of the anti-liquor forces except the Washingtonian excitement in 1840. Moreover, Protestant clergymen had participated in the political fighting since the late years of the seventeenth century, when Increase Mather tried to compel the colonial government of Massachusetts to enact more stringent laws against the taverns. In more modern times the first important instance of ministerial political activity was Lyman Beecher's famous plea, in 1826, for petitions to Congress and the state legislatures praying for "the legislative interference."

As early as 1854 the General Assembly of the Presbyterian Church, the governing body of that denomination, urged all ministers and churches to support legal prohibition, and declared that "such a law should be universally adopted and enforced." A year later the assembly officially thanked God for having engineered prohibitory laws in more than a dozen states and territories. In a declaration published in 1892 the Methodist Church, afterward the principal supporter of the Anti-Saloon League, said under the heading of *Political Action,* "We recommend all members . . . who enjoy the elective franchise to use that solemn trust so as to promote the rescue of our country from the guilt and dishonor which have been brought upon it by a criminal complicity with the liquor traffic . . . we record our deliberate judgment that no political party has a right to expect, nor ought it to receive, the support of Christian men so long as it stands committed to the license policy, or refuses to put itself on record in an attitude of open hostility to the saloon." The Convention of the Southern Baptist Church said in 1890 that "no Christian citizen should ever cast a ballot for any man, measure, or platform that is opposed to the annihilation of the liquor traffic." That same year the Christian Church, or Disciples of Christ, urged "a political party in power committed to the policy of state and national prohibition and to the enforcement of the law." Similar positions were taken by other Protestant churches.

What the league really did was to co-ordinate and centralize the work of the evangelical denominations and their various temperance organizations, and push them deeper into politics than they had ever been before. Some appear to have been a bit slow to espouse the league; it didn't receive wholehearted ecclesiastical support until 1904, when the churches began appointing members of the league's state boards of trustees. This action followed by less than a year the league's successful attempt to satisfy the moral suasion element, still powerful in the churches, by organizing a "total abstinence department" called the Lincoln Legion. The avowed purpose of the legion was to procure signatures to a total abstinence pledge supposedly written and signed by Abraham Lincoln in 1846. When the South failed to display much interest, the league discovered that Robert E. Lee had also been an abstainer and a firm advocate of temperance, so the name was changed to the Lincoln-Lee Legion. By 1916 the legion had obtained some 3,500,000 pledge signers, mostly through the Sunday schools. Once each year, on World's Temperance Sunday, the legion furnished free to all Sunday schools material for a rousing pledge-signing service. According to the league's *Year Book* for 1916, as many as ten thousand schools "have used these supplies in a single year."

During the formative years when it was still wooing the church, high officials of the Anti-Saloon League, including Bishop James Cannon, Jr., of the Methodist Church, chairman of the Legislative Committee, frequently declared that the league was not a political organization. By 1913, however, this pretense had been abandoned. Ernest H. Cherrington, who published his *History of the Anti-Saloon League* in that year, devoted a whole chapter to "The League Becomes a Political Power," in which he said that the organization held "the political balance of power in a large majority of the states and in the Federal Congress." Soon after the passage of the Eighteenth Amendment the league made an official announcement that it was "the strongest political organization in the world."

The facts are that the league was formed as a political organization and was never anything else. But it was not partisan; it never tried to gain the support of any political party, nor would it form even a temporary alliance with any party. It consistently fought against the inclusion of dry planks in both the Republican and Democratic national platforms. In this the league was strongly opposed by William Jennings Bryan, three times Democratic candidate for President and Secretary of State during the administration of Woodrow Wilson. Bryan was anxious to have the dry issue become the exclusive property of his own party, although at that time few Democratic leaders wanted it. The great Commoner is popularly supposed to have played a prominent part in the final fight for prohibition; actually, because of his insistence upon a tie-in with the Democrats, he became something of a bother. His most important contributions to the dry cause were his golden voice, which he exercised for years as a lecturer on the Chautauqua Circuit, and the serving of grape juice at an official function when he was Secretary of State. By the time the Eighteenth Amendment came before Congress he no longer possessed much influence.

Two things were always emphasized by the Anti-Saloon League— its religious character and the omnipartisan nature of its political activities. According to the *Church in Action Against the Saloon,* also known as the *Blue Book,* this meant that the organization had to do "with candidates and the things they stand for instead of parties." One of the questions in the *Anti-Saloon League Catechism* asked: "May the League, at any time, be identified with any one political party for the accomplishment of its purpose?" The answer was: "No.

The League is under solemn promise not to form affiliations with any political party, nor to place in nomination a ticket of its own. Its plan is to make selections of the most available candidates placed in nomination by existing parties, and to invite persons in all the political parties to unite in securing their election." This advocacy of the so-called "good man" theory sometimes led to curious mix-ups, as in Illinois in 1908, when the league vigorously supported thirty-four candidates for the legislature who had also been endorsed by the liquor interests.

The original and basic plan of the Anti-Saloon League was to dry up the United States in steps—first the towns and the villages, then the counties, then the states, and, finally, the nation. The league's adherence to this idea, especially its early concentration upon local option, estranged the Prohibition party, and there was considerable bad feeling between them until 1913, when the league began to work for a national constitutional amendment. Leaders of the party thought that the league should join them in nominating local, state, and national candidates, and campaign on an out-and-out prohibition platform. In practice this would probably have made the league little more than an appendage of the Prohibition party, and the league would have none of it. It was determined to rule the dry roost, and it did.

The political *modus operandi* of the Anti-Saloon League was a development of the plan advanced in 1840 by a convention of dry workers in Boston, that temperance men should vote only for candidates who were "known and inflexible friends" of their cause; and the doorbell-ringing system devised by Neal Dow when he ran for mayor of Portland, Maine, in 1851. It didn't necessarily include the outright purchase of a politician, nor did it preclude such a buy if the situation warranted. In general, however, and briefly, it consisted in swarming into a contested area and bringing every imaginable sort of pressure to bear upon the candidates and officeholders; in saturating the country with speakers and literature; in laying down a barrage of abuse, insinuation, innuendo, half-truths, and plain lies against an opponent; and in maintaining an efficient espionage system which could obtain reliable knowledge of the enemy's plans. Sometimes the required pressure could be applied through a man's business or professional connections; again, something might be accomplished through his family and relatives, in which case the local clergymen and the ladies of the W.C.T.U. were very helpful.

This method was basic in all of the league's political planning, but the astute agents who directed actual operations in the field worked out variations according to local conditions and the needs of the moment. Perhaps the most illustrious of these agents was William E. Johnson, better known as "Pussyfoot." In the course of a long and distinguished career as a prohibitionist, Johnson edited magazines, wrote articles and lectured for the Anti-Saloon League, dried up Indian Territory as a special officer of the federal government, became an important official of the World League Against Alcoholism, and supervised the campaigns for constitutional prohibition in half a dozen states, in charge of what he described as "publicity and underground activities." In an article published in *Cosmopolitan* magazine for May 1926, Johnson boasted that he had lied, bribed, and drank—"gallons of it"—to put over prohibition. "I have told enough lies for 'the cause,' " he wrote, "to make Ananias ashamed of himself. The lies that I have told would fill a big book." Johnson retired soon after the repeal of the Eighteenth Amendment, remarking that "the devil often gets the best of it."

Although Pussyfoot Johnson's political operations failed by a large margin to conform strictly to the Christian principles upon which the league had been founded, neither he nor others who employed similar "variations" were ever punished or even reprimanded. It was generally felt by prohibition leaders that since the league acted as the agent of the churches and was therefore engaged upon the Lord's business, anything was justified which might help gain the ends desired by the Almighty. Of course the league did nothing that wasn't also done by the forces opposed to prohibition, but politically, and for that matter in every other respect, the drys were incomparably more sagacious than the wets. No proof of actual corruption on the part of the Anti-Saloon League was ever produced, but the liquor interests, specifically the brewers, were not so fortunate; their bumbling attempts to buy politicians and newspapers, control elections, and coerce businessmen and industrialists were constantly being exposed, furnishing excellent material for the league's propaganda mill.

Two of the most important of these exposures came in 1918 while ratification of the Eighteenth Amendment was pending in some thirty-four states—a subcommittee of the Senate investigated the German-American Alliance, which had long been the principal clearinghouse for anti-prohibition work among the foreign-born; and a federal grand jury in Pennsylvania returned indictments charging conspiracy against the United States Brewers' Association, the Pennsylvania Brewers' Association, and almost one hundred corporations more or less connected with the brewing industry. Most of the latter, and both of the associations, pleaded guilty and paid fines of approximately one hundred thousand dollars.

After a series of hearings which were fully reported in the newspapers, and of course in the Anti-Saloon League's publications, the Senate committee declared, among other things, that the brewers had contributed enormous sums of money to political campaigns in violation of the federal statutes and the laws of the several states; and that for the purpose of influencing public opinion they had attempted and partly succeeded in subsidizing the public press. Christian Feigenspan, a New Jersey brewer, testified that in 1915 the brewers had advanced one hundred thousand dollars for the purchase of the Montgomery, Alabama, *Advertiser,* and had financed the Newark, New Jersey, *Ledger* to the extent of one hundred and fifty thousand dollars. In 1917, according to Feigenspan, fifteen brewers and the United States Brewers' Association turned over to Arthur Brisbane $375,000 with which to buy the Washington *Times.* Hugh F. Fox, secretary of the Brewers' Association, testified that he had hired several well-known writers of the period, at an average annual salary of about five thousand dollars, to "write up certain subjects" relating to the brewing industry, and that their articles had been placed in national magazines.

The revelations of most value to the Anti-Saloon League were those concerning the German-American Alliance. The Senate committee found that "with a view of using it for their own political purposes they [the brewers] contributed large sums of money to the

German-American Alliance, many of the membership of which were disloyal and unpatriotic." The investigation showed clearly that the German-American Alliance had been a center for the dissemination of anti-American and pro-German propaganda while this country was at war with Germany, and the organization's charter was revoked by unanimous vote of Congress. Eventually several pro-German propagandists were sent to jail. Since the United States had become involved in the war the Anti-Saloon League had made considerable capital out of the Teutonic ancestry and affiliations of most of the brewers, and had insisted that there was a definite connection between the brewing industry and the un-American activities of the German-American Alliance. Officials of the league were much gratified when a government agency upheld their accusations.

CHAPTER SIX

"The Devil's Headquarters on Earth"

During the post-Civil War period, while the temperance forces were galloping wildly in all directions, the liquor interests were centralizing and consolidating. The brewers had been organized since 1862, but the whiskey manufacturers and dealers failed to pool their interests until 1879, when representatives of three hundred distillers, rectifiers, importers, and wholesalers met at Cincinnati and formed a national association. In May 1882 brewers, distillers, and liquor dealers from all parts of the country conferred at Chicago, and after a flattering speech of welcome by Mayor Carter H. Harrison, Sr., proceeded to organize the National Brewers' and Distillers' Association, the name of which was changed several times in later years. The conference adopted a long resolution which denounced the prohibitory laws already in force as sumptuary and tyrannical, and accused the drys of trying to destroy personal liberty and millions of dollars' worth of property. It concluded:

We propose and mutually pledge ourselves to work harmoniously and assiduously at the ballot-box against the election of any and all candidates or the success of any party who favors the prohibition amendment, and in favor of only those men or that party who are known to represent and advocate the principles embodied in these resolutions.

As its political arm the Brewers' and Distillers' Association organized the National Protective Association, which was rechristened the Personal Liberty League of the United States at a meeting at Milwaukee in October 1882. Branches of the league were formed in most of the states, and some of them promptly announced that they would no longer obey the Sunday closing laws and other statutes designed to regulate and control the sale of liquor. Attempts to enforce these laws resulted in serious rioting in several cities. In July 1889 three hundred Cincinnati saloonkeepers pledged themselves in writing to keep open on Sundays, and when the police tried to shut some of the places threatening mobs formed in front of the Bremen Street and Oliver Street police stations. After severe fighting in which several men were injured, the streets were cleared by the use of high-pressure fire hose.

The Personal Liberty League maintained a large corps of lobbyists in Washington, where they agitated industriously for a reduction in the excise taxes on liquor, and against any measure which seemed to be inimical to the interest of the brewers and the distillers. The latter were comparatively moderate in their demands; they only wanted the tax on whiskey reduced from ninety cents to fifty cents a gallon. The brewers, however, went further; they insisted that the government abolish the tax on beer and refund all taxes paid since the passage of the Internal Revenue Act in 1862.

After the middle 1880s the Personal Liberty League, with the co-operation of state and local liquor organizations, took an active part in political campaigns in which prohibition or local option was an issue. The drys attempted to influence politicians by appealing to their better natures and promising future support. The liquor interests were more practical; they lined the pockets of the political leaders with greenbacks, kept the coffers of both Democratic and Republican machines well filled, and delivered the votes of foreign groups and the riffraff of the saloons. The result was that they played a prominent part in determining policies, and in selecting candidates from president to coroner. On every level in both major parties the liquor men were soon firmly entrenched. They were especially powerful in the large cities. For instance, when New York elected twenty-four aldermen in 1890, eleven were saloonkeepers, while liquor dealers filled 681 of the 4,562 places on Tammany Hall's General Committee. At the same time there were nine saloonkeepers on the Board of Aldermen in Detroit, nine in Chicago, and four in Omaha. Neither the Republicans nor the Democrats made any secret of their alliance with the brewers and the distillers. Sometimes, indeed, they seemed to flaunt it, as in 1884, when 633 out of the 1,002 party conventions and primaries were held in saloons.

To finance these political and other activities, the Personal Liberty League and its affiliated organizations raised huge sums of money by levying a tax on every barrel of beer and whiskey, and by assessing brewers, distillers, wholesalers, importers, hotels, and saloonkeepers. Subscriptions were also solicited from barrelmakers, grain dealers, and others who did business with the liquor industry. To defeat the prohibition amendment in Pennsylvania in 1889 (it was rejected by a majority of 188,027), the liquor people are said to have raised one million dollars in that state alone. Large amounts of money were also sent into Pennsylvania from other states, including one hundred thousand dollars contributed by New York brewers. According to temperance historians, the state committee of the anti-liquor forces was able to collect less than five thousand dollars.

In March 1890 Colonel R. S. Cheves called upon Harry P. Crowell, a Philadelphia brewer who had managed the Pennsylvania campaign for the wets. Colonel Cheves was one of the editors of *The Voice,* official organ of the Prohibition party, but represented himself to Crowell as an expert political manipulator who had been employed by liquor interests to fight a prohibitory amendment which the people of Nebraska were to vote upon within a few months. Crowell gladly described, in detail, how the wets had won the Pennsylvania election, and Colonel Cheves published the interview in *The Voice* of April 3, 1890. Crowell told Colonel Cheves, according to *The Voice,* that the

liquor interests had paid thousands of dollars, in cash, for the support
of high-ranking Democrats and Republicans. United States Senator
Matthew Quay, according to Crowell, "bled us for three years." A
local politician, of either party, received two hundred dollars, while the
standard price for a state leader was five hundred dollars, although
some were paid more. Among the latter were the chairman of
the Republican state and Philadelphia city committees. A prominent
Democratic leader was promised twenty thousand dollars, but settled
eventually for five thousand dollars. The men "who worked and
manned the polls on the day of election" were paid five dollars
each. "We paid the County Commissioners of this county," said
Crowell, "to let us have the poll-list exclusively for our own use with
the understanding that we were not to return the list until after
the election." When asked by Colonel Cheves how the newspapers
had been induced to support the wets, Crowell said:

> Why, we bought them by paying down so much cash. I visited the
> editors in person or had some good man to do so, and arranged to
> pay each paper for its support a certain amount of money. Through-
> out the state we paid weekly papers from $50 to $500 to publish
> such matter as we might furnish, either news or editorial, but the
> city daily papers we had to pay from $1,000 to $4,000, which latter
> amount we paid the *Times* of this city. Other papers we could not
> buy straight out, consequently we had to pay from thirty to sixty
> cents per line for all matter published for us. . . . We paid the
> *Ledger* forty cents per line, and the *Record* we paid sixty cents per
> line, although it did some good work for us for nothing.

2

As the Anti-Saloon League became stronger, and the politicians began to realize that the dry movement was no longer a feeble thing
that could be pushed around at will, signs of disorganization and
distrust appeared among the liquor interests. Such organizations as
the Personal Liberty League lapsed into a condition of innocuous
desuetude, and the spirit of co-operation which had impelled the

brewers and the distillers to form joint associations and work together gradually disappeared. They became more and more inclined
to blame each other for everything that happened; instead of combining to formulate workable plans for defense against the onslaughts
of the league, they wasted time and energy in bickering and
squabbling. "Jealousy and disloyalty in the ranks of our enemies
gave us no little advantage," said Wayne B. Wheeler, "and we tried
always to be on the alert to seize the opportunities thus created."
Bishop James Cannon, Jr., said, "The brewers and the distillers are
not having a very happy time together, for the distillers are very suspicious of the brewers and the makers of light wines." Many distillers,
indeed, were convinced that the brewers would cheerfully throw them
to the wolves if they could induce the drys to agree to the passage of
a law prohibiting ardent spirits but permitting traffic in beer and
wines. As was shown later during the maneuvering over wartime prohibition, there was considerable justification for this fear, and it was
shrewdly fostered by the drys. As a result of all this, a surprisingly
large number of hard liquor men agreed with an official of the National
Liquor Dealers' Association who thus paid his respects to the brewers:
"The average brewer in a mad desire for wealth is careless of public
sentiment. He has no respect for law, regulation, or public decency.
His business is to corrupt public officials that he may thrive. The brewers of the United States are a menace to society."

With the resources of three prosperous industries—whiskey, beer,
and wine—to draw upon, the liquor interests probably raised and expended considerably more money than the Anti-Saloon League;
Wayne B. Wheeler estimated their expenditures, "at the height of the
battle," at from thirty million dollars to forty million dollars a year.
The brewers collected a minimum of $750,000 a year from a barrelage
tax imposed upon the nine hundred or so members of the United States
Brewers' Association, while a similar tax levied by the state associations produced more than two hundred thousand dollars a year in
Pennsylvania and comparable amounts in other states. Almost all of
this money was spent foolishly, much of it upon such fantastic proj-
ects as employing experts to investigate and analyze dry strategy,

which was as obvious as the collar on a glass of beer; and attempting to organize a boycott of industrial and mercantile firms because of their supposed opposition to the liquor traffic. For half a dozen years prior to the passage of the Eighteenth Amendment by Congress, the United States Brewers' Association regularly sent to its members black lists containing the names of some of the country's largest corporations. Among them were the Pennsylvania Railroad, the United States Steel Corporation, the Delaware, Lackawanna & Western Railroad, the Western Union Telegraph Company, John Wanamaker's, the Goodyear Rubber Company, the S. S. Kresge Company, the Grasselli Chemical Company, Procter & Gamble, and the H. J. Heinz Company. Most of these companies were on the black lists because they discouraged, or in some cases prohibited, drinking by their employees; but the reasons for including others were as incredible as the lists themselves. The Heinz Company, for instance, was cited as unfair to liquor because H. J. Heinz was president of the Pennsylvania Sunday School Association which had endorsed prohibition. Several hotels in Chicago were on the lists because they had obeyed the city's Sunday closing ordinance. The Grasselli Company was black-listed because some of its officers had supported a revival meeting at which Billy Sunday preached a temperance sermon.

The net result of the boycott was to irritate the corporations and enrage the members of Protestant denominations all over the country. Other ambitious enterprises set in motion by the brewers similarly backfired. They bought politicians who promptly repudiated them and voted dry. They financed dummy organizations with high-sounding names—Civic Liberty League, Manufacturing and Business Association, National Association of Commerce and Labor—the purpose of which was to oppose liquor legislation, to manipulate elections, and to distribute propaganda emphasizing the nobility and patriotism of the brewers and their vast contributions, in taxes, to the public revenues. They were soon exposed and their usefulness, if any, destroyed.

To offset the vast system of propaganda developed by the Anti-Saloon League, the brewers advertised extensively in foreign-language newspapers, at a cost of some seventy thousand dollars a year; operated a news bureau which sent free a weekly newsletter to fifty-three hundred small-town papers, and published a magazine. They also put out large quantities of booklets, folders, pamphlets, and books, probably the best known of which were the *Anti-Prohibition Handbook—A Textbook of True Temperance,* and the *Year Book* of the Brewers' Association. They estimated in 1915 that their annual distribution of wet literature amounted to almost 450,000,000 pieces. A great deal of the wet propaganda dealt with statistics of employment and business, and emphasized that prohibition would destroy an industry with a capital investment, according to the brewers' *Year Book of 1914,* of $1,294,583,426. The United States Census Reports for that year gave the capital invested in the liquor industry as $915,715,000.

In addition, the various trade organs of the brewing, distilling, and wine industries, and of allied businesses, printed many pages of anti-prohibition material, and expressed their hatred of the drys in terms reminiscent of the days when temperance periodicals applied to beer and whiskey manufacturers every epithet a devout Christian editor could imagine. A typical outburst was a description of the Anti-Saloon League by *Barrels and Bottles* in 1913 as "the most arrogant organization of canting hypocrites and jesuitical grafters the world has ever known." In volume the wet propaganda probably equaled that of the drys, but in quality it was inferior. Many of the accusations made by the drys were unanswerable. For example, clergymen and religious papers constantly charged, as they had been doing for a hundred years, that the liquor traffic was destroying men's souls. How could this be disproven? The beleaguered brewers and distillers could only retort indignantly, "We are not, either!"

3

Inept propaganda, political corruption, and abortive attempts to influence public opinion by bribery and coercion all contributed to the eventual downfall of the liquor traffic. The principal trouble of the brewers and the distillers, however, lay in the simple fact that every time they got wound up for a slashing foray against the drys, they stumbled over the saloon. In season and out, the Anti-Saloon League, the W.C.T.U., and thousands of Protestant clergymen all over the country hammered away at this visible evidence of the liquor interests' iniquity. Deets Pickett, research secretary of the Board of Temperance, Prohibition, and Public Morals of the Methodist Church, wrote that the league "created an emotional abhorrence of the saloon and the liquor traffic, and in doing so it had the essential help of the saloon itself, which was under the eye of every citizen. The people soon came to regard that traffic, and rightly," he continued, "as the crime of crimes, the devil's headquarters on earth, a ponderous second edition of hell revised, enlarged, and illuminated."[1] The league also accomplished something else. As one result of its smashing attacks, "saloon" became one of the most horrid words in the English language; it was officially eliminated from the nation's vocabulary by the Eighteenth Amendment and the Volstead Act, and remained under a ban after the amendment had been repealed. Even today it is nowhere permitted to call a retail liquor establishment a saloon.

There were always from three to five times as many saloons in the United States as were necessary to satisfy the legitimate demand for liquor at retail. On some streets in the large cities, during pre-prohibition times, there was a saloon on every corner, and often two or three in the middle of a block. In proportion to population, the small towns harbored as many saloons as did the bigger communities, and they were all operated with the same arrogant disregard of law and public opinion; their evils, in fact, were even more apparent. Americans who lived in the so-called provinces prior to prohibition will recall the sidewalks slippery with slops and stale beer, the unpleasant odors, the drunks lurching through the swinging doors, the loafers sitting on the curb, and the fighting and cursing inside the saloon. They will remember also that respectable women would go blocks out of their way to avoid passing such a place, and that the buildings on either side of a saloon were generally dilapidated and occupied by businesses which catered only to men. In manufacturing towns there was always a cluster of saloons near the gates of a factory, where they could get first crack at the workingman's pay check. According to the Maryland edition of the *American Issue* for June 1908, "of 3,600 checks paid out in wages by one manufacturer in Joliet, Illinois, on a recent pay day, all but one were returned with the endorsement of some saloon. The single one had been endorsed by a man running both a saloon and a grocery store."

Besides the saloons, there were thousands of speakeasies, known also in those days as blind tigers and blind pigs, which operated not only in such prohibition states as Kansas and Maine, but also in states where the sale of liquor was legal. Incidentally, the saloons which Carry Nation smashed in Kansas were all speakeasies. It seems to be popularly believed that the speakeasy, the bootlegger, and the moonshiner were products of prohibition, and that they were unknown in this country before the beginning of the noble experiment. The truth is that they had existed and prospered since early colonial times. Their numbers increased enormously when the first internal revenue law was passed in 1862, and thereafter government agents waged continuous warfare against them. During the thirty years following 1876, according to a Department of Justice monograph published in 1930, the government confiscated or destroyed more than thirty thousand illicit stills, while fifty-four revenuers were killed by moonshiners or bootleggers and ninety-four wounded. In 1890, when a saloon license in Pennsylvania cost five hundred dollars a year, Pittsburgh had ninety-two legal liquor dealers and seven hundred speakeasies, while the number of speakeasies in Philadelphia was estimated at four thousand. In 1914 investigators employed by the Methodist Board of Temperance, Prohibition, and Public Morals, using government statistics, made a comparison of the number of retail liquor dealers holding federal licenses in five states with the number holding state licenses. In Michigan they found an excess of 3,204 federal licenses; in Rhode Island, 2,105; in Ohio, 6,054; in Illinois, 10,046; in New York, 11,150. Since under the state laws these places were operating illegally, they could only be classified as speakeasies.

The American saloon was probably at its worst from the late 1880s to 1917, when the United States Army improved conditions considerably around the troop-training centers. Some curious legends have grown up around the drinking place of pre-prohibition times; it has been rapturously eulogized as the workingman's club, as a refuge of the harassed male, as the scene of wise and witty conversation, and as the home of sound liquor lovingly dispensed by a generous and understanding bartender. All this is mainly nonsense; it could apply only to the comparatively few barrooms, mostly in the large cities, which obeyed the laws and were operated as decently as any other business. Good liquor was both cheap and plentiful, but it could be obtained, as a rule, only in the high-class resorts and in the retail stores. The stuff served in many saloons was frequently as vile as any of the concoctions guzzled by Americans during prohibition; it was common practice to refill with rotgut bottles bearing labels of good brands. A customer might order Old Crow, but as often as not he'd get Old Corrosive, although it would be poured from an Old Crow bottle.

As an institution the saloon was a blight and a public stench. It was dingy and dirty, a place of battered furniture, offensive smells, fly-blown mirrors and glassware, and appalling sanitary facilities. It encouraged drunkenness; few bartenders hesitated to serve children, idiots, and known drunkards. It ignored the law. It corrupted the police, the courts, and the politicians. It was a breeding place of crime and violence, and the hangout of criminals and degenerates of every type. It was the backbone of prostitution; in every red-light district in the country the fixer, the big boss, was a saloonkeeper. Usually he also owned brothels, and his bartenders were pimps and panders. The Chicago Vice Commission, which made an extensive investigation of prostitution in 1910 and 1911, reported that "the most conspicuous element, next to the house of prostitution itself, was the saloon, and the most important financial interest, next to the business of prostitution, was the liquor interest. As a contributory influence to immorality and the business of prostitution there is no interest so dangerous and so powerful in the city of Chicago." In 1914 the Wisconsin State Vice Committee declared that "the chief cause of the downfall of women and girls is the close connection between alcoholic drinks and commercialized vice."

The Chicago commission also found that harlots were encouraged to solicit customers in the back rooms of saloons, that they received commissions on drinks sold through their efforts, and that when they were arrested the saloonkeepers usually paid their fines. During the investigation the commission's agents counted 928 prostitutes in the back rooms of 236 saloons on a single night. Another commission which investigated the liquor problem in Chicago reported that 3,022 of the city's 7,094 saloons had direct connections with hotels, bedrooms, and private rooms in which prostitution was carried on. In 1914 the Chicago Southside Club, after a survey of the saloons on three important streets, concluded that the back rooms of the 445 saloons investigated contributed to the delinquency of fourteen thousands girls every twenty-four hours. And conditions were no worse in Chicago than in other large cities.

Except among the politicians, the saloon had few friends during the last thirty years of its existence; not even the liquor trade papers had a good word for it. On the contrary, several of them, as well as many individual distillers and even a few brewers, attacked the saloon with a violence scarcely equaled by the Anti-Saloon League. The secretary of the Wisconsin Brewers' Association, W. H. Austin, bitterly denounced the retail liquor dealers as "bums and beggars, not fit to associate with yellow dogs." The *Wholesalers' and Retailers' Review* described the saloons, with a few exceptions, as "houses of drunken men, profanity, and obscenity of the vilest possible type." *Bonfort's Wine and Spirit Circular,* most influential of the liquor periodicals, said: "The modern saloon has been getting worse instead of better. It has been dragged into the gutter; it has been made the cat's-paw for other forms of vice; it has succumbed to the viciousness of gambling; and it has allowed itself to become allied with the social evil."

Liquor *per se* was not to blame for the saloon as this country knew it before the ratification of the Eighteenth Amendment. The brewers were mainly responsible. Before prohibition the big money in the liquor business was in beer, and probably no class in America has ever been more greedy for profits than the old-time brewers. Since the beginning of the so-called "beer invasion" in the late 1850s, and the organization of the United States Brewers' Association in 1862, their sole aim had been to saturate the country with beer. To this end they brazenly corrupted politicians, and encouraged and financed the opening of additional saloons wherever possible. And by the time the Eighteenth Amendment was passed by Congress, they were obviously making great progress. During the sixty years from 1850 to 1910, the per capita consumption of beer increased by at least 1,000 per cent. The consumption of wine doubled, but the consumption of distilled spirits, against which the moral-suasion reformers had directed their heaviest attacks, decreased from 2.24 gallons in 1850 to 1.43 gallons in 1910. The total per capita consumption of all liquors that year was 20.53 gallons. Three years later it had increased to 22.80, but by 1917 it had declined somewhat to 19.95 gallons. At least 90 per cent was beer.

When the Eighteenth Amendment was ratified the United States had almost 180,000 licensed saloons and a good many thousand speakeasies, all supplied, for the most part, by 1,217 legal breweries and 507 distilleries. At a conservative estimate, 80 per cent of the saloons had been financed by the brewers under mortgages. Many thousands were owned outright by brewers; the licenses were issued in their names, they held the leases to the premises, and retained title to the fixtures. In Chicago in 1916, according to the Chicago Commission on the Liquor Problem, the breweries owned 3,043 licenses, 2,232 leases, and the fixtures in 4,687 saloons. Dry investigators reported, about 1912, that the breweries owned 65 per cent of the saloons in St. Louis, 70 per cent in Kansas City, 75 per cent in Toledo, and 90 per cent in Indianapolis, St. Paul, and Minneapolis. In effect, the keepers of these places simply acted as agents of the breweries. The comparatively few saloons owned by independents, and the speakeasies also, were controlled by the brewers, and there was nothing to stop them from withholding supplies from any saloonkeeper who displeased them. In that case the retail dealer would have closed his doors, regardless of any action the distillers might take; a saloon without beer could not prosper.

At any time during the thirty or forty years preceding prohibition the brewers could have done whatever they pleased with the saloon; they could have altered its character or abolished it altogether. But instead of reforming the institution which had been the focus of the dry attack for so many years, the brewing industry in general, and most of the distillers as well, took the extraordinary position that there was nothing wrong with the saloon! It was not until 1916 that they began to realize that the retail end of their business was dragging them down to ruin. Then they made a few futile gestures, most of which displayed even less intelligence than the measures which had been used to combat the Anti-Saloon League. The brewers advertised in the newspapers that they were ready to reform the saloon and to "promote temperance," while the National Retail Liquor Dealers' Association solemnly endorsed the Anti-Profanity League of America and urged all saloonkeepers to display the league's cards in their windows and behind their bars.

4

It was while the saloon was at the nadir of respectability, in the late 1890s and early 1900s, that Carry Nation started the "hatchetation," as she called it, which put her, and the saloon, on the front pages of newspapers all over the country. This redoubtable destructive, perhaps the most remarkable of the many extraordinary characters that the temperance movement has produced, was a native of Kentucky, and lived for many years in Missouri, but it was in Kansas that she earned her reputation as liquor's most violent foe. She began her crusade in 1899, a few months before her fifty-third birthday, in the village of Medicine Lodge, in Barber County, Kansas, where she was living with her second husband, David O. Nation. With the aid of members of the Barber County chapter of the W.C.T.U., of which she was president, Carry Nation closed the speakeasies in Medicine Lodge and drove the bootleggers out of town in less than a year by using tactics similar to those which had been so successful during the Women's Crusade in 1874. She smashed her first saloon in the summer of 1900 at Kiowa, a small but wicked town a few miles from Medicine Lodge, where she destroyed bottles, kegs, and fixtures in three speakeasies and aroused great excitement.

From Kiowa, Carry Nation went to Wichita, second largest city in Kansas, which boasted more than fifty speakeasies and half a dozen large wholesale liquor houses, as well as swarms of bootleggers. There she was arrested after smashing the largest and finest speakeasy in town, and was kept in jail until her release was obtained on a writ of habeas corpus. She made another attack upon Wichita on January 21, 1901, when she abandoned the stones and bricks and iron bars which had hitherto comprised her arsenal, and for the first time used the hatchet which became internationally known as the symbol of her crusade. Less than a week after her second appearance in Wichita, she was in Topeka, the state capital, where she smashed several saloons and sorely distressed state and city officials; they arrested her, but dared not treat her too harshly for fear they would have to acknowledge the existence of an illegal liquor traffic in Kansas, which had been under constitutional prohibition since 1880. Thereafter Carry Nation was in and out of Kansas and all over the country. She roared through the land for ten years; her flashing hatchet destroyed scores of Kansas speakeasies, and did considerable damage to a few legal saloons in other cities. She was fined and imprisoned many times for disorderly conduct and destruction of property, but as soon as her fine was paid or she was released from jail she renewed her warfare against the saloons with great vigor. Wherever she went she made news and caused an uproar. The newspapers in general regarded her as a comic figure, and assigned their staff humorists to cover her activities. They devoted a great deal of space to her, and published her spectacular denunciations of the liquor traffic, which were widely quoted and used for propaganda purposes by various branches of the temperance movement. More than any other one person, she called attention to the saloon, already a bit groggy from a hundred years of incessant attack, at a time when that institution could least afford to be in the limelight. She thus made a valuable contribution to the prohibition cause.

The Anti-Saloon League, which was doing the same thing less violently, ignored Carry Nation, but she had the enthusiastic support of the W.C.T.U. and of most of the Protestant clergy, especially in the small towns; these sources usually provided the money to pay her fines. The liquor interests greeted her exploits with their usual arrogance and lack of sagacity. The brewers and the distillers sent her telegrams and letters jocosely thanking her for advertising their products, and offering to finance further smashings; one brewer in Missouri offered her five hundred dollars if she would confine her destruction to kegs containing his beer. Saloonkeepers decorated their bars with hatchets and signs saying, "All Nations Welcome but Carry," while bartenders concocted special Carry Nation cocktails and highballs. Such gestures were considered uproariously funny and were duly reported by the newspapers, but all they really did was to insure more publicity for Carry Nation, and to increase the anger of temperance workers.

Troubles and misfortune beset Carry Nation all her life, and for all of them she blamed liquor. She was a sickly child, subject to mysterious illnesses accompanied by convulsions, and to prolonged lapses of memory. In later years she decided that all this was due to the drunken habits of her ancestors. Her first husband was an alcoholic; he was so drunk on their wedding day that he could scarcely stand at the altar. Her second husband, a preacher and a lawyer, didn't drink, but he was an impractical man who was seldom more than one jump ahead of actual want. She was a religious fanatic—in her autobiography she wrote that she was "often considered crazy on the subject of religion"—and throughout her life, waking and sleeping, she was tormented by visions in which she fought hand-to-hand combats with Satan, and talked on even terms with God, Jesus, the Holy Ghost, and various of the disciples. She was frequently called mad, but no one ever proved that she was insane, although a broad streak of madness ran through her family. Her grandmother, her mother, and several of her uncles, aunts, and cousins were insane, and so was her daughter, who also had "a great craving for stimulants." She died on June 2, 1911, of "nervous trouble," in the Evergreen Hospital at Leavenworth, Kansas, and was buried at Belton, Missouri. Four years after the triumph of the cause for which she had worked so hard, prohibition agents found, on her father's old farm not far from Carry Nation's grave, the largest moonshine still ever discovered in that part of Missouri.

CHAPTER SEVEN

"Burying Congress Like an Avalanche"

One of the most important sources of the Anti-Saloon League's strength was its flexibility; it was prepared to take advantage of every opportunity, and it could change direction at a moment's notice, even when such a change involved the apparent reversal of policies which had long been regarded as fundamental. For a dozen years the league devoted its efforts almost entirely to local option, and discouraged state-wide and national prohibition movements on the ground that the country would not be ready for them until the drying up of the towns and counties, or at least of a sizable majority of them, had been accomplished. During the middle 1900s, however, the dry leaders seemed suddenly to discover that their omnipartisan method of supporting candidates for office had been so successful that they controlled the legislatures of half a dozen southern states. The league promptly subordinated its local option activities, and switched to a vigorous advocacy of state-wide prohibition. In 1907 the Georgia Legislature passed a dry law, and that same year Oklahoma voted for a constitutional amendment by a majority of 18,103. Mississippi and North Carolina adopted statutory prohibition in 1908, Tennessee did the same in 1909, and in 1912 an amendment was added to the constitution of West Virginia by a dry majority of 92,342. Two years later the Virginia Legislature passed an enabling act which imposed prohibition upon the Old Dominion, and Oregon, Washington, Colorado, and Arizona were likewise added to the dry column.

The wave of state-wide prohibition begun by Georgia continued to roll across the South, the West, and the Middle West until the entire country had been won. When ratification of the Eighteenth Amendment was completed, in January of 1919, thirty-three states were already dry, in addition to Alaska, Puerto Rico, and the District of Columbia, and the Anti-Saloon League said officially that if the local option districts in wet states were included, 95 per cent of continental United States, with 70 per cent of the population, was dry. Only thirteen of the thirty-three states, however, could be classed as bone-dry—Arizona, Arkansas, Colorado, Georgia, Idaho, Kansas, Montana, Nebraska, Oklahoma, Oregon, South Dakota, Utah, and Washington. From the fact that twenty of the dry states permitted the manufacture and sale of liquor under various restrictions, the wets argued vehemently that the American people were not ready for prohibition and didn't want it. On the other hand, the drys contended that the presence of thirteen states in the bone-dry column showed conclusively that the people had always wanted more prohibition than their legislatures had been willing to give them. Each side proved its point to its own satisfaction.

The victories in the six states which adopted prohibition between 1907 and 1914 were the first of importance that the drys had ever won in the South. Except in the great days of the rum trade, when New England held the championship, the South had always been the hardest-drinking section of the country. Moreover, the southerners were ardent advocates of personal liberty; they deeply resented any attempt to interfere with their traditional rights and customs, one of which was to drink what and when they wished. The dry movement started in the East, and spread quickly to the West and the Middle West, but except for local successes it made little headway south of the Ohio River until the Anti-Saloon League flooded that part of the country with propaganda and sent expert organizers into the field to form branches of the league and to co-ordinate the work of the churches and the local temperance societies. After Georgia came into the fold, the South became one of the two great strongholds of the dry movement—the other was the rural Middle West—while the principal opposition to prohibition came from the East and North. The wetness of these areas gradually increased as they became more industrialized and the influx of foreign immigration became greater.

In the annals of the Anti-Saloon League most of the credit for leading the six southern states into the dry column is given to Rev. George Young of Kentucky and Bishop James Cannon, Jr., of Virginia, with a deep bow to Pussyfoot Johnson, who directed the important West Virginia campaign in 1912. In 1904, after a splendid career as head of the Kentucky Local Option League, which he finally merged with the Kentucky Anti-Saloon League, Young became assistant superintendent of the national league. Thereafter he had charge of the work of organizing the southern states. Bishop Cannon first came into prominence in 1909, when he was chosen superintendent of the Virginia Anti-Saloon League, and immediately began to teach Virginia's politicians how to play their own game. Soon afterward he was appointed a member of the executive committee of the national league, and for the next few years was very active throughout the South. However, he didn't neglect Virginia; by 1914 he had become the undisputed political boss of the state, and that same year compelled the Virginia Legislature to enact a state-wide prohibition law. Soon after this victory he became chairman of the league's National Legislative Committee, and thereafter exercised his remarkable talents as a lobbyist in Washington, where he soon became known as one of the slickest political strategists who had ever operated in the capital.

2

One of the most important years of the dry movement was 1913. No additional states were added to the prohibition column, but it was the year in which the Anti-Saloon League, for the last time, again elevated its sights; and in which Congress was at last compelled to at least make a gesture toward correcting what the authorities of dry states had long contended was the most frustrating feature of the whole liquor problem—the interstate shipment of liquor under the protection of the federal government. Since 1898, when the Supreme Court held that the Wilson Law of 1890 did not prohibit the shipping of liquor into dry states for personal consumption, a vast mail-order business in bottled beer and hard liquor had sprung up, most of it handled by wholesale houses which had been established in wet areas. Drinkers marooned in prohibition states could thus get all the liquor they wanted, and the shipments also provided a reliable source of supply for bootleggers and speakeasies. Competition was so keen that mail-order liquor houses advertised all sorts of attractive bargains. One such house was very successful with its special combination offer of "a quart of whiskey, a box of cigars, and a revolver."

Beginning in 1902, the drys waged a continuous fight for a law which would prohibit the interstate shipment of liquor when such shipments violated state laws. Bills were introduced in almost every session of Congress, but the few which the drys managed to get out of committee were easily defeated. None of these, however, were Anti-Saloon League measures. The league took charge of the fight late in 1912, following a meeting of league officials with high dignitaries of the Protestant churches, and the results were quite different. In February of 1913 Congress passed the Webb-Kenyon Law, which President William Howard Taft vetoed when his Attorney General, George W. Wickersham, expressed the opinion that it was unconstitutional. Both branches of Congress immediately passed the bill over the President's veto, the Senate on February 28 by a vote of sixty-three to twenty-one, and the House on March 1 by a vote of 244 to ninety-five. Some years later the law was upheld by the Supreme Court.

What the Webb-Kenyon Law did was to take interstate commerce in liquor out of the hands of the federal government, and make it possible for the drys to enforce their own laws dealing with such shipments. In practice, however, it proved disappointing, for it provided no penalties, and for many months Congress neglected to appropriate funds for its enforcement. The drys tried to strengthen it, but with little success until 1917, when they received aid from an unexpected source. Senator James A. Reed of Missouri, one of the most brilliant of the wet leaders, firmly believed that the drys were insincere and didn't want real prohibition. To test his theory he introduced a bill which became known as the Reed-Randall Bone Dry Act; it prohibited entirely all shipment of liquor into dry territory, and provided heavy penalties for violations. The bill was sponsored in the House by Representative Charles H. Randall, the only Prohibition party member, and much to Senator Reed's astonishment, the drys rushed it through both houses of Congress.

Despite the shortcomings of the Webb-Kenyon Law, the leaders of the Anti-Saloon League joyfully hailed it as the first great national victory of the dry movement. They were enormously impressed by the fact that they had possessed sufficient strength to pass the law over the President's veto, so much so, in fact, that when the league's National Board of Trustees met early in 1913 to make arrangements for the forthcoming Twenty-Year Jubilee Convention, Wayne B. Wheeler and Purley A. Baker easily convinced the members of the board that the time had come to strike for national prohibition.

A few weeks later, as a trial balloon, the *American Issue,* official organ of the Anti-Saloon League, published an editorial advocating a prohibition amendment to the federal constitution, and a canvass was made of dry leaders throughout the United States. "The overwhelming urge," wrote Wayne B. Wheeler in the New York *Times* of March 28, 1926, "was for national prohibition. The canvass of public sentiment was astounding in its approval of the idea." On November 13, 1913, former Governor J. Frank Hanly of Indiana concluded his speech before the Jubilee Convention, at Columbus, Ohio, by offering a resolution declaring for a prohibition amendment. "For a moment there was silence, deep and tense," wrote Wheeler. "Then the convention cut loose. With a roar as wild as the raging storm outside it jumped to its feet and yelled approval. The first shot in the battle for the Eighteenth Amendment had been fired." The decision of the Anti-Saloon League to amend the federal constitution was perhaps the most momentous in the history of the temperance movement, but the liquor press in general greeted it with hoots and hollers; their attitude was, "Who do they think they are?" A few trade-paper editors, however, realized what it meant. The *National Liquor Dealers' Journal* made this comment: "To us there is the handwriting on the wall, and its interpretation spells doom."

On December 10, 1913, almost five thousand men and women, summoned to Washington by the Anti-Saloon League and the W.C.T.U., paraded up Pennsylvania Avenue carrying banners inscribed "National Constitutional Prohibition," and wearing white satin badges bearing a similar inscription. As they marched, the ladies of the W.C.T.U. sang their favorite song, "A Saloonless Nation in 1920." The title of this prophetic ditty, the words and music of which were written by Professor J. G. Dailey of Philadelphia, was taken from a slogan adopted by the Christian Endeavor in 1911—"A Saloonless Nation in 1920, the 300th Anniversary of the Landing of the Pilgrims." On the east steps Dr. Purley A. Baker presented to Senator Morris Sheppard of Texas and Representative Richmond P. Hobson of Alabama petitions asking Congress to submit to the people a constitutional amendment prohibiting the traffic in intoxicating liquors for beverage purposes. That same day submission resolutions were introduced in the Senate by Senator Sheppard and in the House by Representative Hobson.

No effort was made by the Anti-Saloon League to get either of these resolutions out of committee for a year. Instead it concentrated its efforts on the congressional elections of 1914, conducting a campaign which was a revelation to capital politicians and which caused lines of anxiety to furrow the brow of many a thoughtful wet. Wayne B. Wheeler described it in the New York *Times* of March 29, 1926:

> Congressional elections were to be held in November, 1914, and the consensus of opinion was that we should concentrate our fire nationally on them and on the preceding primaries at which the candidates were to be nominated. . . . Back of the drive were virtually all the Protestant denominations which compose and control the League, and through the churches of the country the Washington headquarters was in close touch with every section of the

United States. Through the state leagues, which directed the campaign locally, we were at all times intimately in touch with the battle on all fronts.

. . . we started out to let Congress hear from the people back home. Word went out from Washington and state headquarters to the field to send letters, telegrams, and petitions to Congressmen and Senators in Washington. They rolled in by tens of thousands, burying Congress like an avalanche. . . . Until the final vote of submission the country kept up a drumfire upon Washington.

We started off with about 20,000 speakers, mostly volunteers, all over the United States. They spoke at every opportunity, at every sort of gathering. . . . During the final stages of the battle there were approximately 50,000 trained speakers, volunteers and regulars, directing their fire upon the wets in every village, town, city, county, and state. . . . There was literature, too. . . . We already had a big printing establishment at Westerville, Ohio, but soon it became a bigger one . . . for a time the world's largest prohibition establishment ran three shifts a day, every hour of the twenty-four, grinding out dry literature. . . . This literature found its way to every spot in the United States. It was no uncommon thing for carloads of printed material to roll out of Westerville in one day for the front.

We went into every Congressional district where there was a chance to elect a dry and waged as strong a fight as candidates have ever seen. . . . While we were fighting back in the districts, we were also bombarding the House and Senate at Washington. . . . Our Washington headquarters opened correspondence with every possible friend in Congress. We also went to see them personally. . . . The information obtained in our correspondence with members of Congress at Washington was sent back to the states. We kept the field workers advised of the attitude of every individual member of Congress and suggested ways to the local workers of winning converts. . . .

While all this was going on, we kept informed daily as to what the wets were doing. We knew what their arguments would be every time they changed them. . . . We also knew, often in advance, just what their plans were for influencing this, that, or the other member of Congress. Whenever they opened up on a member of Congress we would wire back to that member's state or district and tell the local drys to start a counterattack. They would do the rest. Within twenty-four hours a storm of telegrams would break over that member's head and he would realize that a revolution had broken loose back home. We confirmed it at Washington.

In the 1914 elections the drys, as Wheeler put it, "triumphed even beyond our hopes . . . we gained many seats." But the leaders of the Anti-Saloon League were under no illusion as to their strength in Congress; they didn't control two thirds of the votes in either house, and knew they couldn't hope to do so for at least another two years. Nevertheless, they determined to make a trial run, apparently to observe the reaction of the wets, and to find out how many of their own people they could depend upon when pressure was applied. Accordingly the Hobson resolution was reported to the House of Representatives by the Judiciary Committee, to which it had been referred, in December of 1914, a little more than a month after the elections and before the excitement had subsided. Although the drys had no hope of passing the resolution, they put up a vigorous fight. The House remained in continuous session from 10:30 A.M. to 11 P.M., and 105 speeches were made, the time being equally divided. When the tally was finally taken, constitutional prohibition received a majority of seven; the vote was 197 to 190. However, since it failed to receive the necessary two thirds, it was defeated.

The wets expected the drys to make another attempt in 1915, and again in 1916, and made elaborate plans to give them the works. But in neither of these years did the Anti-Saloon League make any moves in Congress. "Had we pressed in 1915 or 1916 for the submission of the amendment and failed," Wheeler wrote in the New York *Times,* "we might have delayed its passage for several years . . . the strategy of the day dictated holding off, so far as rushing Congress was concerned.

"But back in the field we did get busy again. All the energy we put into the 1914 election campaign boiled and bubbled with hotter fire in the campaign of 1916. We laid down such a barrage as candidates for Congress had never seen before. . . . On election night the lights burned late at our Washington office. . . . We knew late election night that we had won. . . . We knew that the prohibition amendment would be submitted to the states by the Congress just elected. . . ."

3

The Sixty-fourth Congress adjourned on March 4, 1917, and almost at once President Woodrow Wilson called the Sixty-fifth—the one elected in 1916—into special session to declare a state of war with Germany, which was done on April 6, 1917. "Once the war declaration was out of the way," wrote Wayne B. Wheeler, "the dry leaders could have rushed through a resolution submitting the amendment to the states, had it been desirable to do so. Such a course was delayed by the request of President Wilson himself. The country had just declared war, and the White House had a war program for Congress to act upon. That program, the President held, came ahead of dry legislation. The dry leaders agreed to hold off and give the President a chance to get his program through before pressing for the submission of the prohibition amendment."

It was at this point that the issue became somewhat confused by the interjection of wartime prohibition, which was kicked around by Congress for considerably more than a year, and served as the medium of several attempted trades and compromises in which the drys outsmarted the wets at every turn. One of the important measures in President Wilson's war program was a food control bill, which was introduced early in the special session. Without consulting the White House, dry members of the House of Representatives—Wheeler said they were all Democrats—amended the bill to prohibit the use of grain and other foodstuffs in the manufacture of beverage alcohol. In this form the measure passed the House on June 23, 1917. Immediately there was great excitement, and the frightened brewers abandoned the distillers and set out to save themselves. A group of wet senators headed by Boies Penrose of Pennsylvania announced that they would filibuster against the entire bill unless it was modified to permit the manufacture of beer and wines.

Through Senator Thomas S. Martin of Virginia, the Democratic floor leader, President Wilson asked the Anti-Saloon League to yield in the interests of harmony and patriotism. The league suggested that an appeal be made to the patriotism of Senator Penrose and his associates. Senator Martin replied that such an appeal, "when liquor is at stake," would be hopeless. Officials of the league then said that perhaps they would consent to modification of the bill if President Wilson would make a formal request in writing. The President did so in a letter to Bishop James Cannon, Jr., as chairman of the league's National Legislative Committee, and the committee replied that "as patriotic Americans . . . we will not, for our constituency, offer any obstruction to the prompt passage of the Food Control Bill." Without cracking a smile, the committee informed the President that "we cannot presume to indicate to members of Congress what action they should take . . . they will doubtless act in accordance with their convictions of duty." Finally the committee served notice upon both President Wilson and the wets that the last word regarding wartime prohibition had by no means been spoken. "We are glad," said the letter to the President, "that your request applies only to the pending food administration legislation. It will be our purpose to urge the passage of legislation prohibiting the waste of foodstuffs in the manufacture of beer and wines at the earliest possible date, either in the form of a separate bill or in connection with other war legislation."

The food control bill was rewritten in the Senate, and in its final form prohibited the manufacture of distilled liquors but left the question of beer and wine to the discretion of the President. It was passed by both the Senate and the House, with many prominent drys, among them Senator Morris Sheppard of Texas, voting with the wets in accordance with the promise given by the Anti-Saloon League. The law went into effect on September 8, 1917. It was generally understood that the White House, at an opportune moment, would apply the provisions of the law to beer.

In the meantime the letter of the Anti-Saloon League to President

Wilson had been made public, and the wet leaders in both the Senate and the House became extremely jittery over the clear threat to outlaw wine and beer "at the earliest possible date." Even before the passage of the food control bill Senator Penrose had let it be known that the wets were prepared to withdraw their objections to a vote on the resolution submitting the Eighteenth Amendment to the states, which had been introduced by Senator Sheppard soon after the beginning of the special session. The wets knew that they couldn't hope to prevent the passage of the submission resolution; they hoped that the task of getting it through would absorb the attention of the dry leaders and take their minds off wartime prohibition, which was the immediate danger. They reasoned that even after the amendment had passed Congress, ratification would require majorities in both houses of thirty-six state legislatures, while it could be blocked by a majority in either house of only thirteen states. The wets were confident that they could hold thirteen states till doomsday. They seem to have ignored completely the plain fact that the Anti-Saloon League had been manipulating state legislatures for some ten years, and that the drys had brought most of them into the fold before they went after Congress.

While the Senate was preparing to consider the submission resolution, Senator Warren G. Harding suggested to several dry leaders that a time limit be placed on ratification; without such a limitation he feared that several senators who were known to be wobbling between wet and dry might definitely turn wet. The Anti-Saloon League knew all about this scheme; several months before, a lawyer representing prominent liquor interests had discussed it with a leading dry senator, who promptly branded it as a trick and part of the wet plan to distract attention from wartime prohibition. Wayne B. Wheeler, knowing with great exactness the strength of the dry movement in the state legislatures, told Senator Harding that he was in some doubt as to the legality of such a provision, but, anyway, how much time did the senator have in mind? Harding replied that various wet leaders with whom he had discussed the matter thought five years would be about right. After a few days' consideration, officials of the Anti-Saloon League agreed to a six-year limitation, and an amendment was proposed on the floor of the Senate by Harding and adopted by a large majority. Several other amendments designed to weaken the submission resolution were easily voted down, and a final vote was taken in the Senate on August 1, 1917. The Eighteenth Amendment was adopted by a vote of sixty-five to twenty.

On December 17, 1917, the submission resolution came before the House of Representatives, where another compromise was made. The Anti-Saloon League agreed to give the liquor interests a year in which to get out of business and wind up their affairs, in return for another year added to the time limit for ratification. As thus amended, prohibition must be ratified within seven years, and would go into effect one year after ratification had been completed. The House also added a new section to the amendment: "The Congress and the several states shall have concurrent power to enforce this article." In later years this section was to cause endless bickering among those who believed it meant that the states *must* help enforce prohibition and those who thought it meant that they *may*. In its final form, the resolution submitting the Eighteenth Amendment to the states was voted upon in the House on December 18, 1917. It was adopted by 282 to 128.

While the Eighteenth Amendment was pending in the House, Senator Harding met Bishop James Cannon, Jr., in one of the corridors of the Capitol and remarked that the time limitation meant the end of prohibition; it could not be ratified within six years.

"Senator," said Bishop Cannon, "the amendment will be ratified within two years. We know that three-fourths of the states are ready to ratify."[1]

As a matter of fact, the amendment was ratified in twelve months and twenty-nine days. The first state, Mississippi, ratified on January 8, 1918, and the thirty-sixth, Nebraska, on January 14, 1919. On January 16, 1919, the Secretary of State announced that the amendment had been ratified by the required number of states, and would go into effect everywhere in the United States one year from that date. Twelve more states ratified the amendment within the next three years; New Jersey, the forty-sixth, taking the plunge on March 9,

1922. Only two, Rhode Island and Connecticut, refused to ratify.

Once the Eighteenth Amendment had been adopted by Congress and was safely on its way to the states, the Anti-Saloon League repudiated its promise to give the liquor interests a year's grace, and renewed the agitation for wartime prohibition. In an article published in the New York *Times* on March 30, 1926, Wayne B. Wheeler strongly intimated that the reason for this repudiation was that President Wilson had failed to keep faith with the drys. "For nine months," he wrote, "the Legislative Committee of the Anti-Saloon League stood by, in accordance with its promise to the President. During this period the entire nation was called upon to preserve food. It seemed to us an anachronism that the President, after calling on 100,000,000 people to save food, should permit its waste in the manufacture of beverage intoxicants. With growing impatience, therefore, the dry leaders in and out of Congress witnessed the complacence of the White House toward this continuing waste of foodstuffs." Actually, the President had done a great deal toward hampering the operations of the breweries. He had issued a proclamation on December 8, 1917, which prohibited the manufacture of malt liquors containing more than 2.75 per cent of alcohol, and had ordered a 30-per-cent reduction in the quantity of foodstuffs which could be used. On September 16, 1918, another proclamation prohibited, after December 1, 1918, the manufacture of all malt beverages, including near beer, and on October 1, 1918, the Food Administration prohibited the use of grain in the production of beer.

During the nine months in which the drys watched President Wilson "with growing impatience," they had attempted nothing in Congress, but the country had been heavily propagandized. Consequently, when the Anti-Saloon League decided to press the issue, the campaign for wartime prohibition had become more than a drive by the dry forces; it had been endorsed by such prominent men as Theodore Roosevelt and Herbert Hoover, and Congress had been swamped under petitions bearing more than six million signatures. Different versions of a wartime prohibition measure were passed by the House and the Senate in the summer and early fall of 1918, and the differences were reconciled and the law was enacted by both houses on November 21, 1918, ten days after the signing of the Armistice in Europe. The statute prohibited the manufacture of beer and wine after May 1, 1919, and outlawed the sale of all liquors on July 1, 1919. Since for many months no provision was made for enforcement, the country generally paid little attention to wartime prohibition. Consumption of liquor declined, however, because the beer and whiskey interests immediately increased their prices; the reason they gave was that they hoped to conserve large stocks of liquor for sale should constitutional prohibition be miraculously prevented from going into effect.

In May 1919 the National Prohibition Act, better known as the Volstead Act, was introduced into the House by Representative Andrew J. Volstead of Minnesota, chairman of the Judiciary Committee and a member of Congress for some sixteen years. This was the last chance of the wets to modify the Eighteenth Amendment, and the Anti-Saloon League anticipated, and prepared for, a hard fight in both the House and the Senate. But the wets were so dispirited and disorganized that they made little resistance, and the Volstead Act passed the House in October 1919 by a vote of 287 to 100. The Senate inserted a provision giving farmers the right to possess cider which might or might not turn hard, and then passed the bill without a roll call. On October 27 President Wilson unexpectedly vetoed the Volstead Act because it provided for the enforcement of both wartime and constitutional prohibition; he pointed out that the war emergency no longer existed, and urged the repeal of that section of the law. Two hours after Congress received the President's message, the House voted overwhelmingly to override his veto. Similar action was taken next day by the Senate.

Responsibility for the enforcement of the Volstead Act was lodged by Congress in the Bureau of Internal Revenue, a subdivision of the Treasury Department. As the first Prohibition Commissioner, the Secretary of the Treasury appointed John F. Kramer of Mansfield, Ohio, an ardent prohibitionist, and a lawyer who had formerly been a member of the Ohio Legislature. With the advice and assistance of the Anti-Saloon League, which was consulted on all phases of enforcement, Kramer proceeded to form the Prohibition Unit, the name of which was changed in 1927 to Prohibition Bureau. He described his organization in the New York *Times* of January 11, 1920. "The machinery will consist of two branches," he said. "One branch will operate in the states as units, the other in districts of which there will be ten in the United States. . . . In each state there will be a Federal Prohibition Director. Under each director there will be inspectors, the number varying with the problem facing the state. . . . The state organization will have charge of the permissive features of the law. It will issue all permits for the sale and use of beverage alcohol. It will inspect the records of physicians, druggists, sanitariums and the like. . . . The state director will also have charge of all soft drink manufacturers. . . . At the head of each of the ten districts will be a prohibition agent. Under each prohibition agent will be a staff of men . . . All these men will be experienced in police and Secret Service duties. They will have particular charge of the discovery of the illicit sale and illicit manufacture of intoxicating liquors. They will make raids and arrests. . . ."

To pay the expenses of this setup from January 17, 1920, to the end of the fiscal year on June 30, Congress appropriated two million dollars, supplemented later by a deficiency appropriation of two hundred thousand dollars. For 1921, the total allotted to enforcement was $6,350,000, including two deficiency appropriations aggregating $1,600,000. These sums were suggested by the Anti-Saloon League, which declared officially that the Volstead Act would be no more difficult or expensive to enforce than any other law. In a letter read on the floor of the Senate, Wayne B. Wheeler said, "I think five millions a year appropriated to enforce this law would be ample, and if the liquor dealers suddenly become law-abiding it can be reduced when the need disappears." The Prohibition Unit as finally organized comprised 1,520 enforcement agents, or approximately one to every seventy thousand of the population. Nearly all were paid less than two thousand dollars a year, and most received the minimum of $1,680. All authorities agreed that it was impossible for a man with a family to live decently on these salaries in any large city in the country.

4

The wets have long since abandoned the notions that prohibition was the work of a small group of fanatics, and that it was foisted upon the United States without warning. They still insist, however, that the drys were successful only because the people were preoccupied with the first World War, and that the Eighteenth Amendment was slipped over while "our boys" were away fighting for democracy. The wets base these theories upon the unreasonable assumption that in more normal times all of these preoccupied citizens, and all of the men in the armed forces, would have rushed en masse to the support of the liquor traffic, although they had not done so before the war, and argue that in some mysterious fashion "our boys," if they had been at home, would have blocked the ratification of the amendment.

Actually, the fight for national prohibition was won at the elections of 1916, which were held five months before the United States entered the war, six months before the first American registered for the draft, and more than a year before any large number of American troops landed in Europe. In every contest in 1916 prohibition was the principal issue, and "our boys," and the preoccupied as well, had as much chance to vote as anyone else. Since a normal number of votes was cast throughout the country, it must be presumed that they did so. What happened after November 1916 was really a mopping-up operation, the consolidation of a triumph already won. As Wayne B. Wheeler said, there was never any doubt that the Congress elected in 1916 would submit the Eighteenth Amendment to the states. Nor was there ever any doubt that the states would ratify it. The drys had planned it that way.

At most the war may have hastened ratification by a few years; it is extremely doubtful if anything could have stopped it. It seems clear that the American people wanted prohibition and were bound to try it; for more than a hundred years they had been indoctrinated with the idea that the destruction of the liquor traffic was the will of God and would provide the answers to most, if not all, of mankind's problems. It is even clearer that they had no conception of the fearful mess they were getting into, and that their revulsion was thorough once they had seen prohibition in action. They had expected to be greeted, when the great day came, by a covey of angels bearing gifts of peace, happiness, prosperity, and salvation, which they had been assured would be theirs when the rum demon had been scotched. Instead they were met by a horde of bootleggers, moonshiners, rum-runners, hijackers, gangsters, racketeers, trigger men, venal judges, corrupt police, crooked politicians, and speakeasy operators, all bearing the twin symbols of the Eighteenth Amendment—the tommy gun and the poisoned cup.

Part 2

CHAPTER EIGHT

"A New Nation Will Be Born"

At exactly 12:01 A.M. on January 17, 1920, constitutional prohibition went into effect everywhere in the United States, and the American people, 105,000,000 strong, began the joyous march into the never-never land of the Eighteenth Amendment and the Volstead Act. Everything was ready for the great transformation. More than fifteen hundred enforcement agents, badges shined, guns oiled, and fingers trembling upon the triggers, were on their toes, ready to pounce upon the rum demon wherever he showed his ugly mug. The Coast Guard, the Customs Service, and the various agencies of the Bureau of Internal Revenue were standing by. The police of a thousand cities and the sheriffs of a thousand counties were on the alert. Judges were pondering the probability of history-making decisions, and prosecuting attorneys were thumbing their lawbooks and briefing their publicity staffs. Political bosses were happily grabbing jobs for the faithful in the many departments of the new Prohibition Bureau. Statements, predictions, and pronunciamentos were flying thick and fast. And behind this imposing array, their nostrils quivering eagerly to catch the first faint whiffs of illegal hooch, crouched the Allied Citizens of America and the embattled members of the Women's Christian Temperance Union, the latter more dangerous to the politicians than ever, now that Congress had passed the woman-suffrage amendment to the constitution and submitted it to the states for ratification. The Allied Citizens, formed by the Anti-Saloon League to help the government enforce the law, had long since served notice upon prospective evildoers that it was a militant organization that would tolerate no nonsense.

Entranced by the shining vision of an America forever free from the thralldom of the rum pot, the Anti-Saloon League of New York enthusiastically anounced that "a new nation will be born," and wished every man, woman, and child "a Happy Dry Year." William H. Anderson, superintendent of the New York league and an important figure in the councils of the drys, sternly admonished the wets to be good sports and take their medicine. "Shake hands with Uncle Sam," he said, "and board his water wagon." Had Anderson been able to look four years into the future, he would have seen himself taking a little medicine—a prison sentence for forgery. In New York, Colonel Daniel Porter, supervising revenue agent temporarily in charge of enforcement, expressed the opinion that the penalties provided by the Volstead Act were so severe that the people would not attempt to violate the law; no one, he declared, would risk a fine up to one thousand dollars and imprisonment up to six months (for first offenders) for the sake of a few drinks. "There will not be any violations to speak of," he said.

From Washington came the ominous warning that prohibition officials would keep the liquor traffic, or what was left of it, under close scrutiny at all times. The United States Government, through Daniel C. Roper, Commissioner of Internal Revenue, urged every clergyman in the country to observe January 18 as Law and Order Sunday, and "participate in the moral suasion movement for the upholding of law and order with reference to making America dry under the Eighteenth Amendment." John F. Kramer, the new Prohibition Commissioner, said that he had virtually completed the organization of his anti-liquor forces, and was prepared to handle any problem which might arise. He supplemented the prosaic official statements with a ringing personal pronouncement which reached new heights of rhetoric and optimism. "This law," he proclaimed, "will be obeyed in cities, large and small, and where it is not obeyed it will be enforced . . . The law says that liquor to be used as a beverage must not be manufactured. We shall see that it is not manufactured. Nor sold, nor given away, nor hauled in anything on the surface of the earth, or in the air."

The brewers and the distillers, cowering among their barrels and bottles, said nothing, or at least nothing that was recorded for posterity.

2

In thousands of Protestant churches throughout the country, and in every town which had a chapter of the W.C.T.U., the drys greeted the coming of the great day with thanksgiving and watch-night services, at which the Lord was publicly praised for His share in the victory. In Tennessee there were parades and mass meetings as well. In Denver and San Francisco the ceremonies were elaborate and the meetings remained in session for several days; in the latter city a national official of the W.C.T.U. described prohibition as "God's present to the nation," and the head of the California State Anti-Saloon League declared that San Francisco was "complacently joyful that John Barleycorn had been laid to rest." In Chicago the W.C.T.U. announced that, having brought prohibition to America, it would now proceed to dry up the rest of the world. In Washington, D.C., temperance reformers from all parts of the United States, in the capital to attend meetings of the National Temperance Council and the National Legislative Conference, attended a watch-night service and cheered a rousing oration by William Jennings Bryan. The great Commoner spoke from Matthew 2:20: ". . . for they are dead which sought the young child's life." His audience included such notables as Wayne B. Wheeler, Bishop James Cannon, Jr.; Josephus Daniels, Secretary of the Navy; Clarence True Wilson, of the Methodist Board of Temperance, Prohibition, and Public Morals;

Representative Andrew J. Volstead of Minnesota, author of the Volstead Act; and Senator Morris Sheppard of Texas, author of the Eighteenth Amendment. Incidentally, only a few months after the dry era began, a moonshine still was found neatly hidden in a thicket on Senator Sheppard's farm near Austin. It was producing one hundred and thirty gallons of alcohol a day.

There were a few meetings in New York churches, but no extensive ceremonies had been planned, a circumstance which, among other things, impelled one thousand rural clergymen to sign a statement denouncing the metropolis as "the center of nullification and seditious activity designed to prevent the enforcement of the Eighteenth Amendment." The upstate pastors also reminded would-be nullifiers that "the same power that brought about enactment of prohibition is pledged to its enforcement," a bit of information which didn't make the wets any easier in their minds. The statement further implied that the ministers of New York were cringing before the wealthy, guzzling members of their congregations, and shielding them "from realizing and discharging their responsibility as citizens and as Christians."

The governor of New Jersey had rashly promised, when runing for re-election, that he would ignore the Eighteenth Amendment and make the state as wet as the Atlantic Ocean; the drys laughed at him and celebrated with a great victory banquet in Newark and the ringing of church bells in Atlantic City. In Norfolk, Virginia, Billy Sunday, noted evangelist and always a master showman, entertained a congregation of ten thousand with a funeral service for John Barleycorn. From the Norfolk railroad station, where it had arrived "on a special train from Milwaukee" in a casket twenty feet long, the body of old John was hauled in a truck to Sunday's tabernacle, escorted by twenty pallbearers and followed by a man dressed as a devil and simulating extreme sorrow. Sunday conducted the service while the devil and a group of liquor addicts, sottish and bedraggled, gabbled and squirmed on the mourner's bench and bemoaned the untimely death of their old pal. "Good-by, John," said the evangelist. "You were God's worst enemy; you were hell's best friend. I hate you with a perfect hatred. I love to hate you." Sunday then preached a sermon on the glories of prohibition. "The reign of tears is over," he cried. "The slums will soon be only a memory. We will turn our prisons into factories and our jails into storehouses and corncribs. Men will walk upright now, women will smile, and the children will laugh. Hell will be forever for rent."

3

The wets, or at any rate the drinking segment of the population, appeared to have no doubt whatever that prohibition would really prohibit; they envisioned the future, once hoarded stocks of liquor had been consumed, as dry and bleak and well-nigh unbearable. And governmental action on January 15 didn't make them feel any better. Supported by a decision handed down by Judge John C. Knox of the United States District Court in New York, enforcement officials in Washington announced that all privately owned booze in warehouses and safety-deposit vaults would be liable to seizure when prohibition became effective. There was never any way of knowing how much liquor had been squirreled away in anticipation of the great drought, but everybody who could afford it had been buying feverishly since the ratification of the Eighteenth Amendment by the thirty-sixth state in January 1919. For months the hoarding of whiskey and other drinkables had been one of the principal subjects of conversations; a common greeting was, "Got any good stuff put away?" Few admitted possessing more than "a little."

Editions of the newspapers containing the government's ukase and an account of Judge Knox's decision were scarcely off the presses when a great rush began to get the supplies of liquor into their owners' homes, the only sanctuaries. Vehicles of every description were pressed into service; the New York *Tribune* noted an eagerness "to hire trucks or baby carriages or anything else on wheels." The New York *Evening Post* said that "probably never before had so much bottled liquor been in transit in this city." A dispatch from Chicago said that "trucks and automobiles and vans scurried over the city all day transporting liquor." The San Francisco *Chronicle* described the movement of liquor as "gigantic"; the streets were jammed with trucks and wagons, and the sidewalks were crowded with men lugging heavy suitcases and boxes. "Fair ladies sat in limousines behind alluring barricades of cases," said the *Chronicle*. "Business men in runabouts had cases on their knees. . . . On every face was stamped that extraordinary and inexplicable expression of triumph mingled with apprehension which the possession of irreplaceable treasure in a predicament of extraordinary peril is wont to imbue." This passage would seem to mean that in San Francisco, at least, liquor hoarders were proud but scared. In a list of dry law "don'ts" published in the New York *Tribune* of January 16 was the warning that only in the home could intoxicating beverages be given away, and that the recipient of the gift must drink it immediately. This was probably the only provision of the Volstead Act that was universally obeyed.

As the fateful hour approached, many of the activities of the liquor people took on a quality of desperation. A brewery in Providence, Rhode Island, announced that in lieu of a final dividend, two barrels of beer would be shipped to every stockholder. "Many members of the General Assembly," said the New York *Tribune,* "also shared in the distribution, being among the first to be cared for." In New Jersey a brewer threatened to dump his entire stock into the Passaic River, whereupon hundreds of men hurried to the stream with buckets and pans, hoping to salvage at least a little foam. However, the brewer changed his mind and said that instead he would "de-authorize" his beer. In Denver bootleggers said that they "were through with the game forever," and would sell their liquors at reduced prices; they changed their minds also. In California the owner of a vineyard, convinced that prohibition would bankrupt him and every other grape grower in the country, committed suicide; he had failed to foresee the golden years that lay ahead. In New York two prohibition agents were threatened by a crowd when they seized a truck loaded with twenty thousand dollars' worth of whiskey; but it was never clear whether the crowd wanted to manhandle the officers or grab the liquor. Another hopeful crowd gathered on a Hudson

River pier when a big cake of ice sank a barge loaded with whiskey worth one hundred and fifty thousand dollars. The owners of the liquor, the Green River Distilling Company, tried desperately to raise the barge and get it out of the harbor before prohibition became effective. They failed, and the liquor was confiscated by the government.

When the prohibition authorities notified the vintners of western New York State that they could legally sell their stocks of wine, thousands of motorists set out for the wine districts with the enthusiasm of prospectors rushing to a new Klondike. Many headed for the village of Hammondsport, in Steuben County, where seventy thousand cases of champagne had been placed on sale, but found the highways blocked by the heaviest snowfall of the year. Their yelps of despair were heard by the State Highway Department, and crews and emergency equipment were hurriedly sent to clear the roads. In the forlorn hope that something might happen, members of retail liquor dealers' associations in New Jersey decided to keep their saloons open and sell near beer, an insipid but legal beverage containing a maximum of one half of one per cent of alcohol. More general, however, was the feeling expressed by John S. Bennett, counsel for saloonkeepers' organizations in Brooklyn, which before prohibition had supported some two thousand saloons. Bennett declared that at least 75 per cent of the Brooklyn saloonkeepers would close their doors. "As sensible men," he said, "most of our members know that the public will not buy this one half of one per cent stuff. As law-abiding citizens they cannot sell anything else. So there is nothing to do but close up."

Everybody expected that on the night of January 16, 1920, saloons, cafés, cabarets, restaurants, and hotels all over the country would be crowded with liquor slaves having a last fling before prohibition settled "like a blight upon the entire joyous side of human existence," as Senator W. Cabell Bruce of Maryland put it in testifying before a congressional committee in 1926. But the nation-wide binge failed to occur. Newspaper reports described the last fling as "very tame," even in such notoriously wet cities as New York, Chicago, Detroit, Louisville, Baltimore, New Orleans, Philadelphia, and San Francisco. In Boston it was excessively tame; policemen were stationed in all of the well-known drinking places to prevent guzzling after midnight, and to seize all liquor on tables or otherwise in sight after that hour. In Atlantic City, home of the famous boardwalk and as wet a town as could be found anywhere, virtually every place that sold liquor closed at midnight after a quiet evening; some of the resorts gave their customers milk bottles as souvenirs. Things were a little better in San Francisco; the *Chronicle* reported that many "saw it through with glorious festivals wherein corks popped and siphons fizzled and glasses clinked long after the legal hour." Nothing out of the ordinary occurred in New Orleans; that city simply ignored prohibition, both on the night of January 16 and thereafter. In Washington, D.C., the saloons were crowded all day and all evening, especially those of the Wet Mile, a stretch of Pennsylvania Avenue between the Capitol and the White House, which boasted forty-seven barrooms. When midnight struck on January 16, a final toast was drunk, and glasses and partially emptied bottles were given to favorite customers with the compliments of the saloonkeepers. The bars of the Willard, the Raleigh, and other big Washington hotels had closed several days before the Eighteenth Amendment became effective.

A dispatch to the New York *Times* said that in Chicago drinkers "cheered the final moments of a moist United States in a more or less tame celebration in the cafés and restaurants." But a gang of six masked men gave Chicago a foretaste of what was to come within another few years; they invaded a railroad yard, bound and gagged a yardmaster and a watchman, locked six trainmen in a shanty, and stole whiskey valued at one hundred thousand dollars from two boxcars. In a smaller enterprise of the same sort, several men held up a watchman and rolled four barrels of alcohol from a warehouse into a truck. More than a hundred thefts of large quantities of liquor had been reported during the two or three months prior to the advent of constitutional prohibition; the authorities at Washington admitted that they were investigating seventy-five cases in which whiskey worth several hundred thousand dollars had been stolen, or at least removed, from warehouses heavily guarded by watchmen and enforcement agents. In one of these thefts sixty-one barrels of fine bourbon, valued at one hundred and fifty thousand dollars, disappeared from a government warehouse at Bardstown, Kentucky. The news that so much good liquor had fallen into the hands of men who, presumably, would sell it was greeted by drinkers with quiet chuckles of contentment, but screams of anguish came from the distillers who owned the whiskey. Under the bond placing the liquor in the warehouses, they were required to pay a tax of $6.40 a gallon if it was withdrawn for sale. The Prohibition Bureau ruled that thefts would count as withdrawals.

Almost everywhere the drinking on the last night of the old order was dull, dogged, and expensive, and the celebrants, or mourners, seemed tired and discouraged. They had already participated in three farewells to liquor—when wartime prohibition went into effect on July 1, 1919, when the Volstead Act was passed by Congress late in October, and on New Year's Eve, just sixteen days before the Eighteenth Amendment superseded the wartime act. Physically and financially, they were beginning to feel the strain. Moreover, there seems to have been a shortage of booze, which fortunately proved to be only temporary. The operators of cabarets and retaurants in many cities declared that the previous celebrations, particularly that of New Year's Eve, had exhausted their stock of potables, and that they had been unable to obtain fresh supplies, largely because of the frantic private buying that had been going on for several months. At three of New York's best-known hotels—the McAlpin, the Claridge, and the Waldorf-Astoria—a pint of champagne was given free on New Year's Eve to each pair of diners. The managers of these places were quoted in the New York *Tribune* of January 16 as saying that their cellars were empty, and that on prohibition night they would have nothing but soft drinks for sale. Many resort owners were afraid to sell, although the government had let it be known that there would be no raids until after dawn on January 17, and in several large cities the police had refused to assist in the enforcement of the Volstead Act.

No one who wished to observe the passing of the old era away from home could be certain of getting a drink unless he carried his own liquor, and Americans had not yet acquired the habit of lugging bottles and pocket flasks. Nor had they become accustomed to paying dollars for drinks which only a few years before could be had for nickels. When the United States entered the first World War the standard price of a cocktail or a highball at first-class bars was fifteen cents or two for a quarter. On the night of January 16, 1920, an ounce or so of dubious whiskey cost from forty to sixty cents in the cheapest saloons, and from one to three dollars in the swank cabarets and restaurants. The price of a fifth of whiskey ranged from twelve to eighteen dollars in New York, and from ten to fifteen dollars in San Francisco. In some of the southern cities rotgut moonshine, considered very choice stuff within another year, was available at from four to six dollars a bottle.

4

When New York, the nation's night-life and amusement center and by far the wettest city in the country, was preparing to welcome the Eighteenth Amendment, the newspapers and the police predicted that Broadway would usher the rum demon into limbo with the biggest drunk of all time. The police had announced, unofficially, that since New York had no state prohibition law, they would not attempt to enforce the federal statutes. They prepared to handle crowds larger than those which surge through Times Square on election nights and on New Year's Eve. But none of the prophets had considered the weather. At six o'clock on the morning of January 16, 1920, the official Weather Bureau temperature was six degrees above zero. At noon it was fourteen, with a cold, raw wind blowing from the north. By 11 P.M. the mercury had risen to twenty degrees, but the wind was still howling through the streets and a fine, stinging snow was falling. It was not a fit night for man or drunkard.

Partly because of the weather, and partly because of the same shortages and high prices which affected the celebration of liquor's final night in other cities, the performance in the metropolis failed by a large margin to live up to its advance notices. The New York

Tribune spoke next day of "the sad scenes witnessed on Broadway," and the *Evening Post* said that "the big farewell failed to materialize." The *Times* noted that "the spontaneous orgies of drink that were predicted failed in large part to occur on schedule. . . . Instead of passing from us in violent paroxysms, the rum demon lay down to a painless, peaceful, though lamented, by some, death." The *Sun* reporter could find "no pep anywhere. The much talked of grand, final, tenth edition celebration," he wrote, "from which thousands were to go home with aching heads but almost merry hearts never materialized. There was no organized observance of the last hours of booze, and the few parties that were held in the hotels were rather sad affairs. A walk through Broadway at midnight, the hour when all anti-prohibitionists should have been reeling home, revealed an almost empty thoroughfare." Only the *Herald* dissented; its reporter donned his rose-colored glasses and slipped a purple ribbon into his typewriter. "Oh," he cried, "how New York City's Great Glittering Way did feast and drink! Broadway was agleam with the spirit of the last night of the bubbling glass! . . . all evening long, and all night long, they laughed and drank and bade godspeed to old John Barleycorn. They bade farewell in a royal manner, nor thought of the morrow and its black despair."

Whatever lamentations there were occurred in New York's famous restaurants and cabarets, many of which had promised special programs of "great daring, originality, and imagination." At most of the resorts these ceremonies consisted of mock funerals, and skits involving coffins, death, gloom and despair and hopelessness, all of which caused Billy Sunday's admirers to complain indignantly that the booze hounds had stolen the master's ideas. Considerable originality was displayed, however, at a farewell party given in one of the large dining rooms of the Park Avenue Hotel by a Philadelphia publisher. The walls were covered with black cloth, as were the tables and other fixtures, the waiters, musicians, and all the guests wore solid black, the napkins were black, the tableware had black handles, the main dish was black caviar, and the liquor was served in black glasses specially manufactured for the occasion. In the center of the floor was a huge black coffin filled with black bottles. During the evening the orchestra alternated dance tunes and funeral dirges. At midnight the publisher and his guests marched solemnly around the coffin, and after they had resumed their seats the lights were extinguished and the orchestra played a few bars of a dirge. Then a spotlight picked up the final spectacle—two young men and two girls, all clad in black, sitting at a black table and pouring the last drops from four black bottles, while they held their pocket handkerchiefs before their streaming eyes. A newspaperman who wandered into this party for a few minutes reported that it was "the damnedest thing I ever saw."

The only free liquor in New York on prohibition night, as far as the reporters could discover—and it is reasonable to suppose that they would have found it—was available in the Della Robbia Room of the Hotel Vanderbilt. According to the *Herald,* "one hundred cases of the finest champagne ever held in any cellar" were served to the celebrants at midnight, while the orchestra played "Good-by, Forever." This was the only unusual feature offered by the Vanderbilt. At Thomas Healey's Golden Glades Restaurant, famous for its ice-skating entertainment, a coffin was wheeled around as the clock struck twelve, and the customers filled it with broken bottles and glassware. Mock funerals were held at Maxim's and Murray's Roman Gardens, and songs and skits were presented at the Café des Beaux Arts operated by André Bustanoby, a celebrated restaurateur of the period. At the Pré Catelan, run by André Bustanoby's brother, Jacques, the program was climaxed at midnight by a burlesque funeral oration. A similar celebration was staged at the Garden Cabaret. Both the Garden and the "Pré Cat" were notoriously "fast" resorts and favorite rendezvous for college boys and chorus girls; their farewells to booze were noisy and a bit rowdy. Alderman Louis Zeltner acted as master of ceremonies at Little Hungary, a noted wine-house on the lower East Side, and led the mourners in drinking toasts to every notable who had ever entered the place, from Theodore Roosevelt to Alderman Louis Zeltner. At Delmonico's, Sherry's, Churchill's, Jack's, and Luchow's, among the city's finest restaurants, there were no special ceremonies; the diners just sat and ate and drank and sorrowed.

Two of New York's renowned resorts, Reisenweber's and the Café de Paris, formerly Rector's, celebrated the end of liquor on the night of January 15. The latter gave a Cinderella Ball, with a cover charge of ten dollars, and it was a big success. "When dawn came," said the *Tribune,* "there wasn't enough salable alcohol left in the place to jingle a six-year-old child." There was a great deal of spirited argument, however, between two young actresses and their friends as to which should wear the golden slippers. However, the discussion never reached the slugging, biting, hair-pulling stage so common in modern café society. For the record, the slippers left Rector's upon the dainty feet of Miss Violet McMillan.

Reisenweber's function was a "John Barleycorn Funeral Ball," and the cover charge was a modest five dollars. Invitations to the affair were engraved on elegant stationery, bordered in black, and announced the "last rites and ceremonies attending the departure of our spirited friend." One of the invitations was sent to William H. Anderson, who replied, "I am heartily in favor of the funeral, but am not so sure about the ball." However, he didn't appear, although the Reisenweber management announced that one hundred other guests named Anderson would be on hand to make him feel at home. The usual coffin was the center of Reisenweber's entertainment; it was carried into the main dining room by six waiters acting as pallbearers, and followed by two hundred others marching to the strains of Chopin's Funeral March. Dan Healey, a popular entertainer of the times, impersonated a "prohibitionist," with a bottle protruding from his hip pocket. Favors for the lady mourners at Reisenweber's were vanity cases in the shape of coffins, and each customer received a small flask containing cold tea. Most of them took a hearty swig before they realized it wasn't whiskey. It was probably the last pure liquid that many poured from a bottle in fourteen years.

CHAPTER NINE

"An Era of Clear Thinking and Clean Living"

The invitation to a non-denomination service in the Presbyterian Church at Hempstead, Long Island, on the night before the Eighteenth Amendment went into effect, said, "Let the church bells ring and let there be great rejoicing, for an enemy has been overthrown and victory crowns the forces of righteousness." As well as anything else that was said at the time, this expresses the attitude of the drys, and the state of bedazzlement into which the magnitude of their victory had thrown them. To a man the forces of righteousness were profoundly convinced that "they which sought the young child's life" were truly dead, and that Satan would never be powerful enough to resurrect them. They believed that the Volstead Act, and all other dry laws, could easily be enforced, and that the anti-prohibitionists and the liquor interests would live up to the highest traditions of American sportsmanship and gracefully accept the inevitable. There had been a liquor problem in America for more than two hundred years, but the voice of the people had at last spoken loudly in favor of prohibition; therefore the liquor problem no longer existed. Henceforth whiskey and rum and brandy and gin and beer and wine would be as if they had never been. "Now for an era of clear thinking and clean living!" jubilantly cried the Anti-Saloon League of New York. None of the dry leaders, and for that matter very few of the wets, had any idea that the questions raised by the Eighteenth Amendment would keep the United States in an uproar for fourteen years, and beget a welter of crime and corruption such as the country had never seen. Of all the prominent men and women who participated in the fight, only William Howard Taft appeared to understand clearly what was coming. While the Eighteenth Amendment was pending before Congress, the former President, who supported prohibition once it had been adopted, made this prophetic statement:

> A national prohibition amendment to the Federal Constitution will be adopted against the views and practices of a majority of the people in many of the large cities and in one-fourth or less of the states. The business of manufacturing alcohol, liquor, and beer will go out of the hands of the law-abiding members of the community, and will be transferred to the quasi-criminal class . . . In the communities where the majority will not sympathize with a federal law's restrictions, large numbers of federal officers will be needed for its enforcement. . . . The reaching out of the great central power to brush the doorsteps of local communities, far removed geographically and politically from Washington, will be irritating in such states and communities and will be a strain upon the bond of the national union. It will produce variations in the enforcement of the law. There will be loose administration in spots all over the United States, and the politically inclined national administration will be strongly tempted to acquiesce in such a condition. Elections will continuously turn on the rigid or languid execution of the liquor law, as they do now in the prohibition states.[1]

The afternoon newspapers of January 17, 1920, and the morning journals of the next day, reported that prohibition agents had seized trucks loaded with liquor in New York City and Peoria, Illinois, raided stills in Detroit and Hammond, Indiana, and issued twelve warrants for the arrest of liquor-law violators in New York. These were the first infractions of the Volstead Act, or at least the first to be detected by enforcement officers, and all had occurred within a few hours after the dry era began. Such news soon became commonplace. Until the repeal of the Eighteenth Amendment in 1933, there was never a moment when the law was not being flouted and openly violated, and when the federal government was not frantically trying new schemes to control the flood of illegal liquor with which the country was inundated. In considerably less than a year the whole pattern of prohibition had been established, and all of the problems with which the authorities were to wrestle for fourteen years, and which were to leave a blighting scar upon every phase of American life, had made their appearance.

2

Before prohibition nearly all of the heavy drinking in the United States was done in the saloons, the cafés, the cabarets, and the restaurants; in a vast majority of American homes liquor presented no problem. The rich and the well-to-do drank cocktails, had wine with their meals, and served champagne and hard liquors at their parties. The families of the so-called laboring classes used little spirituous liquor at home, but were fond of beer and light wines, and usually kept supplies on hand. Those of recent foreign origin often made their own wine, and brewed a little beer, but not enough to alarm the Internal Revenue Bureau. In the homes of the middle and upper lower classes, especially in the small towns, liquor of any description was seldom found, except a half pint or so of whiskey or brandy, which was tucked away in the medicine chest and used only in emergencies. At their social functions, lemonade was the great stand-by. But as soon as the saloon was outlawed, and liquor became illegal and comparatively difficult to get, almost everybody was bound to have it.

Those who couldn't afford to buy it, or didn't trust the bootleg stuff, tried to make it. If they were vague as to procedures, they could learn everything they needed to know at any good library; there were thousands of books and magazine articles which described methods of distilling alcohol in such ordinary household utensils as coffee percolators and wash boilers. Or they could find out from the government itself. The Department of Agriculture published several pamphlets containing information about manufacturing liquor from almost every sort of produce, including the "pumpkins and parsnips and walnut-tree chips" of colonial times. One told in detail how to make alcohol by cooking a quart of corn meal in a teakettle, catching the steam in a bath towel, and then wringing out the towel. The stuff thus produced smelled terrible and tasted worse, but, liberally laced with ginger ale or orange juice, it was usable. In the true bureaucratic tradition, the Department of Agriculture continued to distribute these pamphlets long after the Eighteenth Amendment had been adopted.

Almost immediately stores sprang up which were devoted exclusively to the sale of hops, yeast, malt, corn meal, grains, copper tubing, crocks, kettles, charred kegs, bottle tops and other supplies and apparatus for home-distilling and home-brewing. Specialty shops offered a vast array of gadgets aimed to assist in circumventing the law. The most popular item, for a while at least, was a flask designed to fit a man's hip pocket; in New York it caused quite a flurry. The prohibition authorities there proclaimed that pants were properly vehicles, and that any pair found with a flask of liquor in the hip pocket would be confiscated. The federal courts, they said, would be asked to sustain this view. However, this knotty question never reached the courts; the government finally decided to take the flask and let the pants go. In February 1920 a man was sent to jail in New York for carrying a pocket flask filled with whiskey, and there was a brief splash of indignation. However, it was really nothing; in Michigan a few years later a woman, the mother of ten children, was given a life sentence in prison for possessing a pint of gin.

Within a week portable stills of from one- to five-gallon capacity were on sale throughout the country, despite solemn warnings that they were illegal. In New York, James S. Shevlin, supervising prohibition agent, and a career man in the Internal Revenue Bureau who lasted eight months before the politicians got around to him, ruled that the purchaser of such a still must make an affidavit that it would not be used to manufacture potable liquor. This only served to increase sales, so Shevlin sternly ordered every citizen to surrender his whiskey-making machine to the government. Few did so, and Shevlin threatened to search every one of New York's 1,278,431 homes. Since only 178 agents were available for this task, nobody paid much attention. The government then adopted the sensible attitude that such things did not exist.

This was in late January 1920, and by that time thousands of homes everywhere in the United States were rapidly being transformed into miniature distilleries and breweries, and the pop of the home-brew bottle was heard in the land. The center of social activity was being transferred from the parlor and the living room to the kitchen, where the drinks were manufactured and served, and a large part of the population was reverting to the colonial practice of forcing a drink upon a visitor the moment he stepped across the threshold. At parties it soon became the custom for everyone to drink as much as he could hold as quickly as possible, and the popular host was one who circulated among his guests constantly replenishing or strengthening drinks. The lemonade pitcher was retired to the highest shelf of the pantry—or filled with gin.

3

Prohibition had scarcely gone into effect before women began to invade the speakeasies, to the unutterable horror of almost everyone but the women. For as long as anybody could remember, bellying up to a bar had been exclusively a masculine privilege, and the spectacle of a dainty female planting a foot on the brass rail and throwing a slug of raw hooch down her pretty throat without blinking was a spectacle that few could view with equanimity. However, everybody got used to it, and before the dry era ended, women had usurped even more of man's prerogatives, at least as far as the liquor business was concerned; many were operating big moonshine stills and alley breweries, others had become prosperous bootleggers, and there was at least one woman captain of a rum ship. Earl L. Douglass wrote in *Prohibition and Common Sense,* published in 1931 by the Alcohol Information Committee, a dry propaganda organization, "Since 1920 the changed attitude of women toward liquor has been one of the most influential factors in the encouragement of lawless drinking. Drinking in 1910 was a man's game, carried on in the saloon and club. . . . Drinking today . . . is a man-and-woman's game. . . . In all former times the man got drunk and came home to his disgusted and long-suffering wife. Today they sometimes get drunk together and try to slip into the house as quietly as possible, so as not to wake the children."

Some of America's greatest minds have struggled with the question of why the women of this country began drinking as soon as liquor became illegal, but none has yet formulated an acceptable explanation. Many have concluded that it was simply because the equal suffrage amendment was about to be adopted, and the ladies were feeling their oats. Perhaps part of the answer can be found in the fact that women are naturally outlaws. They'll do anything for love, and once in a while something for friendship; otherwise nobody can tell them what to do and get away with it. Law means little or nothing to them. Also, women had always drunk much more than was generally supposed, in their homes, in restaurants, and in the back rooms of saloons. The ordinary speakeasy had no back room, but it was supposedly a restaurant, so it was natural enough for the women to go there. And most of the great minds appear to have been under the impression that women could be found in *all* speakeasies. Actually there were thousands of such places, which did not pretend to be anything but saloons, where women were not admitted. A few, in some of the big cities, are even holding out today.

4

In the days before the Eighteenth Amendment a nice girl was horrified at the mere idea of taking a drink, and the boy who had the temerity to suggest such a thing was sent packing. The lad who appeared at a party with liquor on his breath, or who drank while he was there, was in grave danger of ostracism, unless he apologized to his hostess and thereafter watched his step. With the coming of prohibition, however, the attitude of thousands of young people changed. They began to carry flasks and to break out in whoopee parties at which a popular game was to see who could first get plastered. Since, despite their loud claims to independence and originality, the young are as imitative as monkeys, they could scarcely do anything else. They helped their elders handle the distilling and brewing apparatus in their homes, saw them guzzling liquor, making drunken passes at one another's wives and husbands, and nursing hangovers. They heard little conversation that didn't deal with the high cost of booze, the difficulty of controlling fermentation, the proper quantity of yeast, and the sterling qualities of "my bootlegger." Drinking became romantic and adventurous, the correct thing for all up-to-date young folks to do. The boy who took a girl out during the 1920s and didn't give her a few drinks, or went to a party without a flask of liquor, was considered a poor sport, a clod, a drip. In the younger set it became smart to drink, and smarter still to get drunk, while the boy who passed out was looked upon as a he-man of parts and something of a hero. He talked about it for weeks, preening like a little peacock, while the girls listened admiringly. About the manliest thing a lad could say was, "Boy! Did I tie one on last night!"

Speakeasies were opened near the schools to tap this new and promising market, and bootleggers appeared who catered exclusively to the youngsters, foisting upon them even worse liquor than their parents were buying. In Chicago more than a dozen booze joints ran for several years within a few blocks of three high schools. The prohibition administrator for the Pittsburgh district said in March 1925 that on a single residential street of that city there were seventeen places where liquor was sold to young boys, either by the drink or in flasks suitable for taking on skating and automobile parties. Half-drunk boys and girls brazenly necking in cars, and tipsy youths staggering along the streets, became common sights in many parts of the country. The Rev. Francis Kasackszul, a Catholic priest, testified before a congressional committee in 1926 that in his home town of

Sugar Notch, Pennsylvania, "the schoolteachers have been complaining about children coming to school under the influence of drink."

A special committee appointed by the Wickersham Commission reported in 1930 that welfare agencies in forty-one cities were greatly concerned with the effects of prohibition upon children, especially those whose families were engaged in bootlegging or illicit distilling. "They are involved in the conspiracy to outwit prohibition officials," the report said, "and become defiant, arrogant, hard to control in school and elsewhere. They show a tendency to vandalism and truancy, and to a disregard of other regulations, such as driving automobiles under age. . . . In some cases the results are excessive nervousness and fear. Ordinarily they learn to drink. . . . Instead of entering legitimate employment, they help in the family business and tend to acquire a distaste for work with less excitement and smaller returns." Colonel William L. Barker, head of the northern division of the Salvation Army, declared in 1925 that "prohibition has diverted the attention of the Salvation Army from the drunkard in the gutter to the boys and girls in their teens. . . . We have girls in our rescue homes who are fourteen and fifteen years old, while ten years ago the youngest was in the early twenties."

In Decatur, Indiana (population about five thousand), a typical "dry" town where the Volstead Act was supplemented by very stringent state laws, Alva Johnston, a reporter for the New York *Herald Tribune,* was told by a bank president in 1930 that heavy drinking by young people had the older generation very much worried. A prominent hardware merchant said, "Every high-school boy has a flask in his hip pocket and an automobile. The drinking among the younger people and the growing disrespect for law are the worst problems we have ever faced." It was the custom of the Adams County Grand Jury, which met twice a year, to summon groups of Decatur high-school boys and question them about their sources of supply. "A boy who has not been before the grand jury two or three times is not thought much of," wrote Johnston. "A boy who is suspected of having confided anything to the august body is a pariah. Contempt for the 'grand' is almost ingrained in the bright young Decaturite." A popular juvenile pastime in Decatur during prohibition was raiding cellars and stealing liquor which householders had laid away for their own use. "Some of the bolder home-town boys of Decatur," Johnston said, "have become very clever at picking locks and removing windows in order to get at these cellars. The bereaved cellar owner cannot complain, except privately, because it is a penal farm offense to possess liquor, home-brew, or otherwise, under the bone-dry law of Indiana."

Conditions in the colleges and universities, where the boys and girls were a little older, were about the same. By the spring of 1920 campuses swarmed with bootleggers, and most college towns supported a larger number of speakeasies than they ever had saloons. At many schools orders for liquor were taken by students who had made profitable connections with bootleggers; these young men, some of whom made a great deal of money, were generally considered dashing and romantic figures because of their association with the underworld. As one of the catch phrases of the 1920s put it, they were "living dangerously." At Syracuse University in 1921 the most-talked-about man was a former student, a star football player, who had graduated a year or two before. He was famous on the campus because he had joined a bootleg gang in New York and was reputed to have made one hundred thousand dollars in a single year in the liquor racket. Rivalry between two gangs of student bootleggers at Dartmouth College in 1920 resulted in a fight over a shipment of Canadian liquor in which one of the boys, a member of the junior class, was killed.

Dr. Samuel Harden Church, president of Carnegie Institute at Pittsburgh, testified before a congressional committee in 1926 that, "speaking of the students as a whole in Pittsburgh, I would say that conditions now are very much worse socially than they were before prohibition . . . it has become the fixed habit in the whole student body of Pittsburgh, or at least more or less so, to carry a hip flask and that which goes with it." Dr. Church also told the committee that the director of prohibition at Pittsburgh had published an advertisement inviting the students of the city's two great schools, the University of Pittsburgh and the Carnegie Institute of Technology, to spy upon their fellows and report to the government the name of any person who offered to sell or give them a drink. Dr. Church said that both the director of prohibition and the United States Attorney at Pittsburgh "are constantly urging upon this great student body to become spies and informers upon their own associates." This he described as "detrimental, undermining the sense of honor of these young men."

An article in the Yale University *Daily News* of April 21, 1926, placed in evidence before the committee, said that Yale undergraduates had voted by a majority of three to one that prohibition had not decreased drinking at the university. Russell Lee Post, chairman, and Greeley Sturdivant, Jr., managing editor of the paper, testified that students could buy all the liquor they wanted, although they had to leave the campus to get it. However, Dr. Irving Fisher, who had been a member of the Yale faculty for many years, testified that there was no more drinking at Yale than at any other large college, and that conditions were better than before prohibition. Matthew Woll, vice-president of the American Federation of Labor, told the committee that he had recently visited one of his sons, a student at the Massachusetts Institute of Technology at Boston. "Asking about the liquor situation," he said, "I was informed that every fraternity is solicited by liquor sellers once each week if not more often. I learned that there is never a party arranged at which liquor is not present." Woll's other son was at the University of Illinois, where "practically the same situation obtains."

5

It was increasingly clear that prohibition was engendering a spirit of lawlessness, and contempt not only for the Volstead Act but for all law, which was being fostered by a progressive breakdown in the machinery of enforcement. "That disregard of law and contempt for law have greatly increased and are still increasing in this country," said Dr. Nicholas Murray Butler, president of Columbia University, in 1923, "is not to be doubted." To many prominent Americans this attitude on the part of millions of people, which was soon reflected in an increase in all manner of crime, presented the most serious aspect of the entire situation, and was potentially the most damaging to American institutions. Following a survey of the five cities of Clinton, Dubuque, Davenport, Muscatine, and Burlington, the Anti-Saloon League of Iowa, on May 6, 1925, issued a statement describing conditions which were generally accepted as fairly typical. After speaking of "rampant lawlessness, increasing by leaps and bounds," the statement said, "the laws of the state and nation are now held in greater contempt in these cities than ever before." As early as October 1, 1920, a month before he was elected President, Warren G. Harding made a speech at Marion, Ohio, in which he pleaded for respect for the dry laws "as a fundamental principle of the American conscience." And Justice John H. Clarke of the Supreme Court, in an address before the alumni of the New York University Law School in 1923, declared that "respect not only for that law, but for all laws, has been put to an unprecedented and demoralizing strain in our country, the end of which it is difficult to see." The report of the Wickersham Commission, presented to Congress in January 1931, said that referenda among college students had shown "an attitude of hostility to or contempt for the law on the part of those who are not unlikely to be leaders in the next generation."

This attitude was not peculiar to the upper and middle classes; it was also prevalent among the so-called working people who, in the opinion of the drys, had been the chief sufferers from the evils of the old-time saloon, and were therefore the principal beneficiaries of prohibition. The report of the Wickersham Commission's special committee on welfare agencies said, ". . . the great mass of testimony is to the effect that the prohibition laws, as they are enforced, are not regarded in the same light as other laws; the prevailing attitude is one of defiance, resentment, or merely indifference. . . . A violation in itself does not involve a sense of guilt; the only shame is in getting caught, and successful violation is rather a matter of boasting. Fear of punishment does not act as a deterrent to manufacture for home use or to engage in the traffic . . . usually wife and children help in it and frequently it is the wife or a widowed mother who is the entrepreneur. . . . A story is told of a woman whose neighbors took up a contribution, when her husband died, to buy her a still and set her up in business."

Many wets ascribed part, if not all, of the wave of lawlessness and contempt for law which had suddenly swept the country to the insistence of the drys and government officials that the manufacture and sale of liquor be placed in the same category as murder, burglary, and the peddling of narcotics. They pointed out that the average American had no intention of killing, robbing, or selling drugs, and was not greatly concerned about the laws which aimed to prevent and punish such crimes. He was concerned about the Volstead Act, however, because it interfered with his personal habits and appetites and pleasures, and threatened to abolish the means of procuring them. To the number of millions, he resented such a law. Nor could he be convinced that his bootlegger was really a criminal; on the contrary, the man who sold him his liquor was "good old Joe, a fine fellow." Old Joe's masters, who manufactured or imported the booze, were shadowy figures with whom the average citizen had no contact; he vaguely believed that they were probably not as wicked as they had been painted.

Dry leaders in general were inclined to blame the rich and the well-to-do, who could afford to, and did, buy huge quantities of illicit booze, and therefore set a bad example to the rest of the population. "These so-called best people, who are doing so much to interfere with prohibition enforcement," said Dr. Charles W. Eliot, former president of Harvard University, on May 24, 1920, "are causing a great deal of trouble in nearly all parts of the country, and they are teaching lawlessness, especially to the young men of the country." Some who sought the answer concluded that the trouble was due entirely to the fact that Americans were still a pioneer people, resentful of authority and restraint, and therefore disinclined to obey any law of which they did not approve. This was a weak explanation, however, and was soon abandoned. In the September 1922 issue of *Current*

History, Judge William B. Swaney, chairman of the Special Committee on Law Enforcement of the American Bar Association, pointed out that the criminal element in this country comprised less than one third of 1 per cent of the population; and that careful comparisons with other countries, prior to prohibition, had shown that "the morals of the common people are better than those of any other great nation." His conclusion was that Americans, in the main, were honest and, until the Volstead Act came along, law-abiding.

6

At the end of the first year's attempt to enforce the dry laws, according to prohibition officials, one federal agent and one civilian had been killed. Thereafter the government men rapidly forged ahead. In April 1926 the Bureau of Internal Revenue said that eighty-nine civilians and forty-seven enforcement officers, including two members of the Coast Guard, had been killed since January 16, 1920. An official statement issued by the Treasury Department on April 5, 1929, said that up to that date prohibition agents had killed 135 civilians, while forty-five federal officers had been slain. The report of the Wickersham Commission said that by the beginning of 1931 sixty agents and 144 civilians had been killed, a total of 204. Senator Millard E. Tydings of Maryland accused the federal authorities of suppressing information about fifty-one killings of civilians, and his *Before and After Prohibition,* published in 1930, contained a list complete with names, dates, and places. A pamphlet called *Reforming America with a Shotgun,* issued in October 1930 by the Association Against the Prohibition Amendment, said that up to September 20 of that year eighty-six federal agents and two hundred civilians had been killed.

These figures, and those issued by various government bureaus, dealt only with the operations of federal officers—agents of the Prohibition Bureau, the Customs and Indian services, and members of the Coast Guard. They did not include killings by numerous non-federal groups—state enforcement agents, sheriffs, deputy sheriffs, town marshals, constables, undercover men, special squads appointed by local authorities, citizen volunteers employed by federal operatives; and state, municipal, and highway policemen. It was stated in *Reforming America with a Shotgun* that "we have found instances in which ardent prohibitionists, without any official standing whatsoever, have taken it upon themselves to enforce the law." The New York *World* of June 18, 1929, told the story of a clergyman who, representing himself to be the head of a civic league in the metropolis, had sent out a confidential circular soliciting money with which to organize and equip a corps of undercover agents to hunt down violators of the liquor laws. As far as the records show, no fanatics of this type had any killings to their credit. Approximately three fourths of the fatal shooting was done by local officers who were not responsible to, or under the control of, the federal government. Senator Tydings estimated that, if these killings were included, the total number of prohibition fatalities during the first ten years of the dry era was 1,365. In December 1929 the Washington *Herald,* after a survey of the entire country, said that 1,360 had been killed. At least one thousand more were wounded.

Many, perhaps a majority, of the killings were justified; it was clearly shown that the agents had used their guns in self-defense. But in a large number of cases it was equally clear that the enforcement officers had fired without provocation or reason. In others it was proved that the agents had handled their firearms with criminal recklessness. Some civilians were killed by officers who invaded their property without search warrants or other warrants. Others, stopped on a lonely road by armed men who wore no distinguishing uniform, were shot down when they became frightened and tried to escape. A few were innocent bystanders, struck by stray bullets. In many parts of the country, particularly along the Canadian and Mexican borders, there was so much indiscriminate shooting by prohibition officers that respectable citizens were afraid to drive their automobiles at night. Frequently squads of agents set up roadblocks and searched all cars, without warrant or authority; many citizens who resented such illegal and highhanded procedures were shot. Occasionally an agent who had killed a civilian was convicted in a local court and sent to jail or fined, but if a federal officer was involved, the government intervened and transferred the case to a federal court under a writ of habeas corpus. If brought to trial at all, the agent was generally acquitted; prosecution of a federal officer by a federal attorney was lackadaisical, to say the least. The Chicago *Tribune* of November 11, 1928, listed twenty-three civilian killings for which government agents had been indicted by local grand juries. All of these cases were transferred, with federal attorneys appearing for the defendants, and all of the agents escaped punishment.

Regardless of the circumstances in which they occurred, the frequent shooting of civilians aroused a great deal of public indignation, and provided propaganda material which was skillfully used by the wets. Many dry leaders heartily approved of the killings. Their sentiments were well expressed by Senator Smith W. Brookhart of Iowa during a debate in the Senate on June 19, 1929: "When we get senators in this chamber talking sense, instead of all this gush stuff about murders by men who make mistakes once in a while, we will have a better attitude toward the bootleg question." On another occasion dry congressmen broke into vociferous applause when it was announced on the floor of the House of Representatives that a young man driving a liquor truck in Washington had been killed by a policeman. Less fanatical drys, however, agreed with Miss Jane Addams, one of America's foremost sociologists and a lifetime worker for temperance. In the October 1929 issue of *Survey Graphic,* Miss Addams wrote, "What the prohibition situation needs, first of all, is disarmament . . . the federal agents should be taught some other methods than those of gunmen. It is their business to bring lawbreakers into court and not to punish them on the spot."

7

It was the duty of the agents of the Prohibition Bureau to arrest violators of the Volstead Act, but the Department of Justice made no special preparations to handle the cases of the malefactors after they had been caught. Dry leaders and members of Congress, firmly convinced that the country would greet the Eighteenth Amendment with joy and thanksgiving, were sublimely confident that the existing judicial machinery would easily be able to handle the few prosecutions that might be necessary. No additional courts were established, no increases made in the personnel of United States Attorneys, and no new jails built or authorized. The result was that within a few months federal courts throughout the United States were overwhelmed by the number of dry cases on their dockets, and government penitentiaries were running out of space in which to store the convicted bootleggers and other violators. By 1924 the population of federal prisons had almost doubled, and it was estimated by the American Prison Association that approximately sixty-five thousand federal prisoners whose sentences were less than one year each, were confined in local jails. According to the records of the Department of Justice, prohibition agents arrested 313,940 suspected violators during the first six years, while at least as many were arrested by state and municipal officers. The peak year was 1928, when federal agents arrested 75,307. Convictions in the federal courts ranged from 37,181 in the fiscal year 1921 to 58,813 in 1928. The cases pending at the end of each year averaged about twenty-five thousand, most of which were ultimately dismissed.

Two thirds of the cases brought into court were settled by pleas of guilty, and such cases were classed as convictions, a procedure to which many federal prosecutors objected. Emory R. Buckner, United States Attorney for the Southern District of New York, told a congressional committee in 1926 that in his judgment, "the proposition should be changed and the records read, 'escaped on payment of money.' Almost any violator," he said, "is willing to compound with the prosecutor and pay a small part of his earnings." Buckner further testified that when he assumed office on March 2, 1925, he found that violators of the Volstead Act were being brought into the Federal Building in New York City at the rate of about fifty thousand a year, and that the United States Attorney's office was five months behind in the preliminary steps of preparing cases. "I found the fifth floor of the Federal Building," he said, "a seething mob of bartenders, peddlers, waiters, bond runners, and fixers. Federal judges have told me that the whole atmosphere of the Federal Building was one of pollution, that the air of corruption had even descended into the civil parts of the court, and reports were made to the senior United States judge of attempts to bribe jurymen even in the toilets of the building." Buckner estimated that prohibition cases in the state of New York could be adequately prosecuted for about twenty million dollars a year, provided jury trials were abolished. If every case was heard before a jury, the annual cost would be seventy million dollars.

The situation may have been slightly worse in New York than elsewhere, because it was the largest and wettest city in the United States, but it was serious all over the country. In June 1920 the United States Attorney in Chicago reported that the courts there were already congested, with between five hundred and six hundred cases awaiting trial and more coming in all the time. During that same month the Department of Justice warned Congress that it lacked money to employ the large number of additional lawyers required, and mentioned "the mass of cases accumulating in the various districts." In 1924 the annual report of the department declared that "the United States courts today are staggering under the load imposed on them by prohibition legislation." A congressional committee reported in 1923 that an investigation had shown that United States Attorneys from Maine to California were devoting a minimum of 44 per cent of their time to dry-law cases. In some states the percentage was considerably higher. In the southern district of Alabama it was 90 per cent; in North Carolina, 70 per cent; in Minnesota, 60 per cent; in Kentucky, 75 per cent; in northern Florida, 60 per cent; in West Virginia, 70 per cent; in Arkansas, 50 per cent.

Congestion in the state courts was somewhat less, partly because the biggest cases were usually transferred to the federal authorities for prosecution. A more important reason, however, was the failure of the states to co-operate with the national government to the extent that had been envisaged by dry leaders, a fact which caused almost endless complaint by federal officials from the President down; their public utterances on prohibition always included urgent pleas for state help.

Enforcement laws were on the statute books of all states except five—New York, Montana, Maryland, Nevada, and Wisconsin—throughout prohibition, and some of them were extraordinarily drastic. In Indiana, for example, it was illegal to display pocket flasks or cocktail shakers in store windows, transportation of liquor by vehicle was punishable by one to two years in prison and fines up to a thousand dollars, and any person purchasing, selling, possessing, or carrying booze was liable to a jail sentence of thirty days to six months and a fine of one hundred to five hundred dollars. In Virginia a person arrested for intoxication could be sent to jail if he refused to disclose where he had obtained his liquor.

These laws were eagerly enacted by the legislatures at the behest of the Anti-Saloon League and other dry organizations, but almost no attempts were made to enforce them, even in the states which were under prohibition when the Eighteenth Amendment went into effect. In 1927, when the federal appropriation for enforcement was almost twelve million dollars, the total spent by the forty-eight states was less than seven hundred thousand. Utah's expenditure that year amounted to one hundred and sixty dollars; Missouri's and Nevada's to less than one thousand dollars each. Few states spent more than twenty-five thousand dollars. Ohio's appropriation of $146,577 was the largest. But even desultory activity of state and municipal law officers brought into the state courts more prohibition business than they could handle, and they creaked badly under the strain. Reporting on conditions throughout the country, *Liberty* magazine said in January 1926 that the courts of Kentucky were "cluttered with liquor cases," and that 75 per cent of the arrests in that state were for dry-law violations. In Georgia and West Virginia the courts were "clogged"; in Iowa more than 430 cases were awaiting trial; in Massachusetts arrests had increased more than twenty thousand a year since 1919; and in Maine there were "a great, great many liquor cases on the court dockets."

In New York a two-year experiment with a dry-enforcement statute —it was passed in 1921 and repealed in 1923—produced a situation which, if it had been carried to its logical conclusion, probably would have put a third of the state's population on trial and another third on jury duty. Less than two weeks after the law was passed ten times as many cases as could be handled were on the dockets of the courts in New York City, and the district attorney complained that he was having great difficulty finding citizens willing to serve as jurors. A little later the city chemist reported that the police had seized more liquor than his staff could analyze in a year. The grand jury of New York County, consisting of Manhattan Island, heard 6,902 liquor cases. Only twenty violators were tried and convicted. The charges against 6,074 were dismissed, and 496 pleaded guilty. What happened to the others is not shown by the record. After 1923 the New York police referred all complaints of violations of the Volstead Act to the Prohibition Bureau and the United States Attorney. In addition, the cops made occasional raids and arrests under the state's public-nuisance laws, and immediately turned their evidence and prisoners over to the government.

With the federal courts crowded to the suffocation point, and Congress resolutely refusing to enlarge the judiciary or appropriate additional funds, the Department of Justice finally managed to relieve the situation somewhat by establishing "bargain days," or "cafeteria courts." On certain days of each week large batches of violators, knowing in advance that no jail sentences would be imposed, pleaded guilty and paid fines, which seldom exceeded a hundred dollars. In thousands of cases it thus became cheaper to operate a saloon, or otherwise engage in the liquor traffic, under prohibition than under the old license system. The government also found it expedient to apply the bargain-day procedure to cases growing out of the injunction and padlock sections of the Volstead Act. A special padlock court held weekly sessions in New York and disposed of about one hundred cases a month. Each defendant, by prior negotiation, agreed to accept a "peace padlock" on his property for a certain term, rather than risk a much longer time which might be imposed by the court after trial. At first the set term was thirty days, but it was gradually lengthened to a year. Five hundred resorts in New York, including fourteen night clubs, were closed by this means in thirteen months.

The government began to use the padlock method in 1921, when the courts granted 446 injunctions, most of them in Illinois. The number of such cases increased each year until 1925, when they reached a high of 4,471. Of all the schemes devised by the federal authorities to enforce prohibition, this was, for a while at least, the most effective; but in the long run it failed as all the others did, and for the same reasons—lack of money and personnel. The Prohibition Bureau could never spare enough men from other duties to make inspections of padlocked premises, and places which had been closed by injunction usually reopened as soon as the excitement had subsided. Moreover, it was difficult to locate the real owners of property against which proceedings had been begun, and upon whom court orders must be served. A report of the Treasury Department in 1930 said that this was found to be impossible in some 50 per cent of the cases, and that in the country as a whole not more than 35 per cent of the padlock proceedings were successful.

Because of these and other difficulties, the padlock policy was gradually abandoned, and was used infrequently after 1926. For half a dozen years, however, the government enforced it with great vigor and severity. Many speakeasies were padlocked as the result of a single sale of liquor, and a large number of restaurants were closed for selling setups. Several hundred saloons were locked in San Francisco, Omaha, Chicago, and Detroit, and hotels were padlocked in Chicago; Albany, New York; San Jose, California; and Wichita Falls, Texas. In Chicago the front doors of two private residences were ceremoniously padlocked, and in New York prohibition agents obtained injunctions against seventy-five vats containing illegal beer. They were festooned with two hundred padlocks. Finally the Prohibition Bureau climaxed its campaign by padlocking a redwood tree, twenty-four feet in diameter, some six miles from Dyerville, California. Enterprising moonshiners were operating a fifty-gallon still in a cavity of the big tree, with the entrance hidden by a piece of canvas painted to resemble bark. To this canvas the United States Government affixed a sign, "Closed for One Year for Violation of the National Prohibition Act."

8

When the Volstead Act was pending in Congress the dry leadership committed two blunders which, together with the congestion in the courts, eventually brought enforcement to the edge of disaster—it permitted the lawmakers to set up the Prohibition Bureau in the Treasury Department, which didn't want it, instead of in the Department of Justice, where it belonged; and to exempt the field agents of the bureau from the Civil Service. Supposedly, this left all appointments in the hands of the Commissioner of Internal Revenue; actually, they were handled through the Prohibition Commissioner and the state and city directors and administrators. Afterward the Anti-Saloon League admitted that the exemption provision was "unfortunate," but pleaded political expediency. The secretary of the league was thus quoted in the New York *Times* of January 8, 1923: "When the Volstead Act was passed, neither the Anti-Saloon League nor any other agency could have gotten into that law a civil service provision, and for the League to have forced the issue would have been to jeopardize the passage of the bill." This brought forth a tart rejoinder from an officer of the National Civil Service Reform League, which had opposed the exemption. "The plain fact is," he said, "that the congressmen wanted this plunder and you let them have it." The Anti-Saloon League never attempted to justify, or even to explain, its action in allowing Congress to foist the Prohibition Bureau upon the Treasury Department despite the strenuous objections of Carter Glass, Secretary of the Treasury. In a letter to the Judiciary Committee of the House of Representatives, Secretary Glass pointed out that enforcement of the dry laws had nothing to do with the fiscal operations of the government, but would depend for effectiveness "principally upon the steps which will be taken in the courts throughout the country by the Department of Justice." Succeeding secretaries repeatedly requested that the bureau be transferred to Justice, but it was not done until July 1930, following the urgent recommendation of the Wickersham Commission.

As had been foreseen by the Civil Service Reform League, the politicians immediately enwrapped the enforcement machinery in the destructive tentacles of the spoils system. Field jobs in the Prohibition Bureau became so much political pap to be doled out to deserving members of whatever party happened to be in power. Since Woodrow Wilson was President when the Volstead Act became law, the service for the first year was loaded with Democrats. Nearly all were thrown out and replaced by Republicans when the Harding administration assumed control of the government early in 1921, and very few were able to fight their way back to the trough before the Eighteenth Amendment was repealed. In making appointments, honesty, ability, and experience were ignored; no applicant was even considered unless he had been endorsed by the Anti-Saloon League and a member of Congress, or by a political leader to whom the congressman had entrusted the task of handling his patronage. A typical recommendation was received in 1926 by Major Chester P. Mills, prohibition administrator for the New York City district, from Jacob A. Livingston, Republican boss of Brooklyn. It said, "This is to certify that Samuel Gross is an enrolled Republican." No other qualification was required. On another occasion Major Mills questioned the fitness of a man who had been recommended by a United States senator, pointing out that he had been a partner in an illegal sacramental wine store. The senator's campaign manager called on Major Mills and insisted that the applicant was a man of fine character who had made a great success in business. So Major Mills said:

"What does a high-class man want with a job that pays only twenty-four hundred dollars or three thousand dollars at most?"

"We're all over twenty-one," said the campaign manager. "He wants the job to get his the same as the rest of them in this prohibition racket."

While a few senators and representatives conscientiously tried to recommend good men, an appallingly large proportion of the bureau's field agents were men of thoroughly bad character—ignorant, incompetent, and venal. Many had criminal records, and some had even operated as bootleggers. Mrs. Mabel Walker Willebrandt, who in

August 1921 was appointed Assistant Attorney General in charge of all prohibition prosecutions, said, "I had not been in charge for more than a few months before I realized . . . that hundreds of prohibition agents had been appointed through political pull, and were as devoid of honesty and integrity as the bootlegging fraternity. I found that there were scores of prohibition agents no more fit to be trusted with a commission to enforce the laws of the United States and to carry a gun than the notorious bandit Jesse James."[2] Major Mills, after battling the politicians for almost two years, and losing, wrote in *Collier's* magazine for September 27, 1927, "Prohibition, as at present operative, is a party-spoils system. Three quarters of the twenty-five hundred dry agents are ward heelers and sycophants named by the politicians."

The attempt to administer the Volstead Act with an enforcement agency composed largely of incompetent political appointees, and containing a large core of actual or potential criminals, resulted in corruption on a scale unparalleled in American history. Stories of dry agents escorting liquor trucks, protecting smugglers and even helping them unload their cargoes, accepting bribes for information about raids, allowing real beer to be shipped as cereal beverages, dealing in withdrawal permits for alcohol and whiskey, and in general conniving with the illicit booze traffic, appeared in the newspapers day after day. On salaries averaging less than three thousand dollars a year, prohibition agents bought country homes, town houses, city and suburban real estate, speedboats, expensive automobiles, furs, and jewelry for their women, and fine horses; many reported for work in chauffeur-driven cars. "I don't know of anyone," said the superintendent of the New Jersey Anti-Saloon League, "who can make a dollar go further than policemen and dry agents. By frugality, after a year in the service, they acquire automobiles and diamonds." These prosperous agents were seldom asked by their superior officers to explain the sources of their sudden wealth, perhaps because so many of the Prohibition Bureau's high-ranking officials were themselves taking advantage of the opportunity to lay up treasure and provide for their old age.

Ten days after the Eighteenth Amendment went into effect three agents were indicted in Chicago for accepting bribes and selling seized liquor to bootleggers. Three weeks later two were arrested in Baltimore, charged with corruption. In May 1920 a deputy collector of Internal Revenue in New York was accused of conspiracy in connection with extensive bootlegging operations. In December 1921 the Prohibition Bureau dismissed one hundred agents in New York after an investigation of the illegal manipulation of withdrawal permits. In July 1923 the prohibition administrator of Chicago and his chief agent were indicted for conspiracy in a case involving two hundred thousand dollars' worth of whiskey. In April 1925 the prohibition director for Ohio was found guilty of conspiracy. In April 1925 a jury in the federal court at Cincinnati convicted fifty-eight agents and policemen; two Pullman cars were required to haul them to the United States Penitentiary at Atlanta. These were only a few of the many instances of corruption reported from official records. Hundreds of agents, of all ranks, were accused; scores were arrested and indicted, and many were convicted and sent to prison. During the first four years of prohibition, 141 agents were jailed. As William Dudley Foulke, president of the Civil Service Reform League, said in 1923, "Indictments and convictions have constantly followed each other for months and years in dreary succession."

General Lincoln C. Andrews, who became Assistant Secretary of the Treasury in charge of prohibition enforcement on April 1, 1925, testified before a congressional committee in 1926 that up to February of that year approximately ten thousand men had been appointed by the bureau to fill about twenty-two hundred jobs. Of this number, 875 had been dismissed for various reasons, including bribery, extortion, immoral conduct, intoxication, and falsification of records. From January 16, 1920, to June 30, 1930, according to the report of the Wickersham Commission, the bureau employed 17,816 agents, of whom 11,926 were separated from the service without prejudice and 1,587 were "dismissed for cause." The latter were the ones against whom the evidence of wrongdoing was not sufficient to justify court action. Proportionately, the turnover was about as great in the higher ranks of the enforcement service. There were four national commissioners during the first five years, the office of administrator for New York City was filled by four different men within thirteen months, and New York and Pennsylvania each had six different state directors in three and one half years. In each state one director was indicted for conspiracy.

The Pennsylvania case, involving State Senator William McConnell, a henchman of United States Senator Boies Penrose, provided an excellent illustration of the manner in which the politicians took care of their own. McConnell, the first state director for Pennsylvania, lost his job within a few months. In 1921 T. Henry Walnut, Assistant United States Attorney for the Philadelphia district, notified the Department of Justice in Washington that he had obtained proof of a conspiracy, on the part of McConnell and others, to withdraw seven hundred thousand gallons of alcohol and whiskey and to share a corruption fund of approximately four million dollars. He said he was prepared to go before the grand jury with his evidence. The Department of Justice ordered him to wait. At the next session of the grand jury he was again instructed to take no action. When for a third time Walnut asked permission to seek indictments, he received a letter from Attorney General Harry M. Daugherty peremptorily ordering him to resign. A committee of Philadelphia citizens protested, but Daugherty refused to discuss the case. He said simply that Walnut had been in office long enough.

Such an uproar was raised by the newspapers and various civic groups, however, that the United States Attorney in Philadelphia finally obtained indictments against McConnell and forty-eight others. The case was brought to trial a year after Walnut's "resignation." After the jury had been selected, three of the defendants suddenly pleaded guilty and asked the mercy of the court. Attorneys for the government then announced that fifty-six of the sixty pieces of documentary evidence upon which they had relied for conviction had disappeared, and that the government would be unable to proceed. Thereupon the judge directed the jury to return a verdict of acquittal, and the three men who had pleaded guilty were instructed to change their pleas. McConnell and all of his associates were discharged.

There has never been any way of estimating the amount of money that changed hands in bribes and other corruption during the fourteen golden years of prohibition, but on the basis of the vast sums reported by bureau officials as having been spurned by honest agents, the total must have been stupendous. The Wickersham Commission in 1931 published tables showing that in the first ten years of the dry era the personnel of the Prohibition Bureau received, and sternly rejected, 373 offers of bribes totaling $90,050.70. It was not revealed to whom, or by whom, the offer of seventy cents was made. In his *Prohibition Inside Out,* published in 1923 by Doubleday, Page and Company, Roy A. Haynes, who succeeded John F. Kramer as commissioner in 1921, gave the details of many bribes not included in the commission's statistics. Haynes said that the largest proffered bribe which came to his knowledge was a weekly retainer of three hundred thousand dollars. This, he said, was offered to a high-ranking agent by a group of brewers who wished to resume the manufacture of beer in five states. They planned to operate for one year, during which time the agent would receive $15,600,000. Needless to say, he refused to have any dealings with such unprincipled scoundrels, but reported the offer to Haynes. The agent's salary was six thousand dollars a year. Another dry agent told Haynes about a dicker with a distiller who wished to get possession of whiskey stored under federal guard in the distillery warehouse. The distiller offered to pay the agent ten dollars a case, with a starting bonus of fifty thousand dollars, and an additional fifty thousand dollars for each five thousand cases. Haynes's assertion that "few men in any line or calling are subject to the temptations which beset the prohibition enforcement agent at almost every turn" would appear to have been an understatement.

Less than three years after the beginning of the noble experiment, the political domination of the Prohibition Bureau, and the corruption for which it was mainly responsible, had become so notorious that some hint of the situation even reached the White House. President Warren G. Harding referred to it in his message to Congress on December 8, 1922. "There are conditions relating to enforcement," he said, "which savor of nation-wide scandal. It is the most demoralizing factor in public life." Neither then nor thereafter did the President castigate the politicians or suggest a remedy, although he repeatedly urged the people to respect and obey the dry laws. General Lincoln C. Andrews made a valiant attempt to rout the spoilsmen when he took charge of prohibition enforcement in 1925. He reorganized the bureau by dividing the country into twenty-four districts, without regard to state lines, to which there was no objection. Then he astonished everyone by announcing that he would purge the service by terminating all field jobs as of October 25, 1925. To fill the vacancies, he said, a selective system of reappointment would be used.

In a letter to all field officers, dated July 25, 1925, General Andrews said, "It is the intention of the department to select from those now in the service the men who will be retained and even promoted in the new organization. These men will be selected for merit only, and in accordance with personal fitness and qualifications . . . administrators will be given a free hand in the selection of personnel . . . the new organization will be a clean-cut business organization . . . promotion for merit assured . . . promotion will be based on personal performance only . . . appointment will be for merit only . . . the appointee will hold office so long, and only so long, as his services are satisfactory." These were bold words, and the politicians required a little time to recover from the shock of General Andrews's defiance. Then they attacked in force, and the general soon found that he was heavily outgunned; the few officials who had supported him scuttled away with shrieks of repudiation. Very few of the agents actually lost their jobs, and within a few months General Andrews was telephoning his district directors advising them to consult their local political leaders before making appointments or initiating any radical enforcement measures.

Charges of incompetence and worse were brought against the few directors who balked, and were generally sustained by evidence unearthed by the special espionage department which the government maintained to spy on all employees of the Prohibition Bureau. Many were hounded out of the service, or transferred to jobs where they wouldn't annoy the politicians. In New York City, for example, Major

Chester P. Mills was accused of trying to saturate his district with Democrats. He proved by his official roster that only twelve of these creatures were among the two hundred and forty agents who worked out of his office, but this was considered a weak defense, almost a confession. He was kicked upstairs to a harmless zone supervisorship, and promptly resigned. Later he learned that four Secret Service men, two operatives of the Treasury Department's intelligence unit, and a private detective agency had been busily investigating his past for several months. General Andrews hung on until September 1927, when he also resigned. Dr. James M. Doran, who had been the bureau's chief chemist, was appointed commissioner, and Seymour Lowman took over as assistant secretary of the treasury in charge of enforcement. Roy A. Haynes was dismissed. Since 1925, although he retained the title of commissioner and remained on the federal pay roll at seventy-five hundred dollars a year, Haynes had served as liaison officer between the Prohibition Bureau and the Anti-Saloon League.

Meanwhile the Civil Service Reform League and many sincere drys had continued their efforts to bring the bureau into the Civil Service. Several bills were introduced in Congress, but only one came to a vote. It was defeated by a majority of eight to one. In 1923 the Anti-Saloon League sponsored a civil-service measure which was introduced in the Senate. It was opposed by the Civil Service Reform League because it provided that all agents then in office be "continued as of their present rates and grades of compensation without further examination." Nothing was actually accomplished until early in 1927, when Congress finally passed a law establishing the Prohibition Bureau—up to that time the official title had been Prohibition Unit—and placing all employees under civil-service regulations. This statute went into effect on April 1, 1927.

Great difficulty was experienced in finding applicants who could pass the examinations. In January 1928 the Prohibition Commissioner announced that almost three fourths of the old employees had failed, although some were later qualified as a result of appeals and regrading. By November 1928 only two thirds of the available jobs had been filled by the Civil Service, and new and easier examinations were prepared. As late as March 2, 1929, however, according to a report of the Secretary of the Treasury, only 1,282 agents, inspectors, investigators, and chemists had been given civil-service status. Temporary appointments were held by 604 employees in these grades, which meant that most of them, at least, were beholden to politicians for their jobs. As far as corruption was concerned, conditions improved somewhat after the victory of the civil-service advocates, but they remained far from perfect throughout the remainder of the dry era. Seymour Lowman declared in the fall of 1927 that there were still crooks in the service and that bribery was rampant. "Some days," he said, "my arm gets tired signing orders of dismissal."

Although enforcement agents received more than their share of unfavorable publicity, corruption was not confined to the Prohibition Bureau. It spread to every department of the government that had anything to do with the dry laws. Not even congressmen were immune. Several were suspected at various times of too-close connection with the illicit liquor trade, though not actually accused, and one served a term in prison for accepting a bribe of five thousand dollars in a case involving the withdrawal of four thousand cases of whiskey in Pittsburgh. When he was released he ran for re-election and was supported by the Anti-Saloon League; he had always voted dry. One of the great scandals of the times was the boldness with which liquor was sold in the Capitol at Washington. "Bootleggers infest the halls and corridors of Congress and ply their trade there," wrote Mrs. Mabel Walker Willebrandt in *The Inside of Prohibition.* "I have found a curious impression or state of mind among members of Congress and other government officials, to wit: that they are above and beyond the inhibitions of the prohibition law."[3] Several liquor dealers were reported to keep large stocks of booze in the basement of the Capitol, and in the Senate and House office buildings, in order that congressmen might be given prompt and efficient service. Prohibition agents were not permitted to molest the so-called government bootleggers, and were advised by their superior officers that search warrants for federal buildings would not be issued.

With considerable fanfare, and much proud talk of its historic traditions and record of unselfish service, the Coast Guard steamed out to disperse the booze ships of Rum Row. The corruption of the service began as soon as contact had been made. Within two years seven temporary warrant officers and thirty-six enlisted men had been convicted of conniving with bootleggers and smugglers, while many others were dishonorably discharged. Still others were arrested by the civil authorities, but were not convicted. At the trial of Big Bill Dwyer and members of his rumrunning gang, in 1925, it was shown that a large number of coastguardmen were on Dwyer's regular pay roll. On many occasions Dwyer's motorboats, loaded with liquor, were escorted into port by Coast Guard patrol ships, and coastguardmen helped unload the cargoes. Similar helpful service was given, or sold, to other rum syndicates on both the Atlantic and Pacific coasts, on the Gulf shore, and on the Great Lakes. In December 1925 the entire crews of two Coast Guard patrol boats were court-martialed for protecting and assisting smugglers. In February 1926 a boatswain's mate was dishonorably discharged, and in March of the same year the commandant of an important Coast Guard station off Rhode Island was indicted on two counts in connection with smuggling operations. Both the commandant and the boatswain's mate were among the Coast Guard's famous heroes—the former had taken part in five hundred rescues at sea, and the latter had once walked barefoot through ice and snow to bring help to his comrades, whom he had left unconscious from the cold on a patrol boat.

Many instances of bribery and connivance among the agents of the Customs Service and the border patrol were reported on the Canadian and Mexican borders, on the Gulf Coast, and at almost every other point where these officers were stationed. At New Orleans, in August 1925, the intelligence unit of the Treasury Department exposed "one of the largest liquor conspiracies as yet uncovered in this country." A federal grand jury indicted the Controller of the Customs, a police captain, a sheriff, a state senator's brother, and twenty-seven others. At Buffalo in 1928 a grand jury investigation disclosed that a gigantic rum ring, with a working capital of some ten million dollars, had corrupted agents of the Customs Service and other government employees. Many were suspended during the inquiry, including the chief immigration inspector of a station near Buffalo, but none was indicted and tried. The most extensive corruption in the Customs Service was at Detroit, the principal port of entry for smuggled liquor. In 1928 and 1929 a grand jury there revealed that bootleggers and smugglers disbursed annually a corruption fund of approximately two million dollars. About one hundred agents were involved in the "graft trust," and their individual monthly take was said to average seventeen hundred dollars. This graft was paid by the rumrunners at the basic rate of 29½ cents a case for beer and $1.87 cents for whiskey. In addition the customs men received lump sums for "free nights" on the border, when the smugglers were permitted to run in as much liquor as they could handle. A curious feature of the Detroit case was that the customs agents bribed rumrunners to give them information leading to the seizure of liquor shipments on which the graft toll had not been paid.

The federal government kept fairly accurate records of the indictment and conviction of its own agents, but no reliable statistics concerning the extent of corruption among state, county, and municipal officials were ever compiled. It is not the custom of politicians to record their misdeeds for posterity. It is abundantly clear, however, that such crimes as bribery, extortion, and conspiracy to violate the Volstead Act and other dry laws occurred all over the country. In every large city it was common knowledge that the police were in collusion with bootleggers and speakeasy operators. For fourteen years the newspapers published, almost every day, accounts of arrests, investigations, trials, and convictions which disclosed incredible conditions everywhere. Hundreds, even thousands, of local officials and policemen were heavily fined or sent to prison; sometimes large numbers were involved in a single case. In May 1921 twenty-three justices, ex-justices, sheriffs, and aldermen were accused of extortion and conspiracy in Fayette County, Pennsylvania. In March 1923 a grand jury indicted seventy-five citizens of Gary, Indiana, among them the mayor, a judge of the city court, the chairman of the board of public works, a former sheriff, a former prosecuting attorney, and a motley group of policemen, deputy sheriffs, bootleggers, and speakeasy proprietors. Fifty-five of the defendants, including the mayor, were convicted. They were sentenced to jail terms ranging from one day to one year, and fined from one hundred to five hundred dollars each. In September 1924 two state officials and seventy-seven citizens of Little Rock, Arkansas, were arrested on warrants charging conspiracy. At Columbus the state treasurer of Ohio was convicted of bribery, and of conspiring to protect Cincinnati breweries which were manufacturing real beer.

In Pittsburgh, in 1928, a federal grand jury returned more than a hundred indictments for bribery and conspiracy. Among those named were two police magistrates, two members of the state legislature, five Republican ward chairmen, the superintendent of police, fourteen police inspectors, five patrolmen, and a constable. A grand jury investigation in Philadelphia disclosed a liquor conspiracy in which about ninety-five police officers, in addition to several city officials, were involved. Evidence presented to the grand jury showed that Maxie Hoff, known in Philadelphia as "king of the bootleggers," had a corruption pay roll of three thousand dollars a week, most of which went to important officers of the police department. The lower ranks were taken care of by a similar fund to which bootleggers and speakeasy operators contributed, and by a third into which moonshine distillers paid considerable sums. Salaries of police inspectors were from three thousand dollars to four thousand dollars a year, and police captains were paid from twenty-five hundred dollars to three thousand dollars. On this modest pay, however, many had done well. One inspector had $193,533.22 in his bank account, another had $102,829.45, and a third had $40,412.75. One police captain had accumulated a nest egg of $133,845.86, and nine had bank accounts ranging from $14,607.44 to $68,905.89. Experienced journalists estimated that the liquor graft in Philadelphia in less than three years amounted to almost twenty million dollars.

By the fall of 1923 conditions in Philadelphia had become so frightening that Mayor W. Freeland Kendrick called upon President

Harding at the White House and requested the President to lend the city the services of Brigadier General Smedley D. Butler of the Marine Corps, a famous soldier of the first World War. Early in January 1924, preceded by a barrage of threats and predictions, General Butler arrived in Philadelphia and was sworn in as Director of Public Safety. He imposed a measure of military discipline upon the police department, organized the cops into special raiding squads, announced that he would enforce the law "impartially and without fear," and began a war of extermination against the speakeasies and the bootleggers. In the first five days of the campaign the police closed almost six hundred booze joints, and in a week had made two thousand arrests. The crash of police axes and the rumble of the patrol wagons resounded throughout the city, and it began to look as if General Butler might fulfill his promise to transform Philadelphia into a law-abiding community. A great wave of praise swept over the country; he received thousands of congratulatory messages and a movement began in Washington to have him appointed Prohibition Commissioner.

But the general's whirlwind campaign gradually petered out; the politicians became alarmed, and after his first successes he began to have trouble. His cops continued to make raids and arrests, but nothing seemed to happen afterward; nobody went to jail. General Butler remarked that enforcement after arrests had been made didn't seem to amount to "a row of pins." He found himself hampered and thwarted at every turn. High police officials warned speakeasies of impending raids, politicians and city officials interceded for the violators, and the magistrates discharged them as rapidly as Butler brought them into court. In many cases liquor held as evidence mysteriously disappeared; immediately following these losses policemen resigned from the force and opened speakeasies. General Butler stuck it out for two years, but after the first few months accomplished almost nothing. When he returned to the Marine Corps he declared that the job had been a waste of time. "Trying to enforce the law in Philadelphia," he said, "was worse than any battle I was ever in."

The Association Against the Prohibition Amendment examined

the New York *Times* Index from January 1, 1927, to October 1, 1928, selected a large number of typical cases of corruption, and published them in a pamphlet called *Scandals of Prohibition Enforcement,* which later became a part of the record of the Wickersham Commission. Here are a few of them:

Chicago—Indictments were returned against the Mayor of Special-ville, a suburb, and twenty-four other persons.

South Jacksonville, Florida—Practically the entire city administration, including the mayor, the chief of police, the president of the city council, the county commissioner, and the fire chief, were indicted by a federal grand jury.

St. Louis—A former Missouri State Labor Commissioner was sentenced to serve eighteen months in jail, and to pay a fine of two thousand dollars, for conspiracy to violate the Volstead Act.

Fort Lauderdale, Florida—The sheriff, the assistant chief of police, and seventeen others, including policemen and deputy sheriffs, were arrested on charges of conspiracy.

Morris County, New Jersey—The former county prosecutor was found guilty of accepting bribes from liquor-law violators.

Philadelphia—A city magistrate was sentenced to six years in prison for accepting $87,993 in liquor graft during his ten months in office.

Pittsburgh—The president of the borough council of Homestead, four other councilmen, and four bootleggers were found guilty of violating the Volstead Act.

Edgewater, New Jersey—The mayor, the chief of police, two local detectives, a United States customs inspector, a New York police sergeant, and eight others were found guilty of conspiracy. A rum-runner confessed that he had paid them sixty-one thousand dollars to help land liquor worth one million dollars.

Monessen, Pennsylvania—The chief of police, four constables, and two former police officers were convicted of conspiracy.

9

None of these problems was ever solved; on the contrary, all of them grew progressively worse as prohibition staggered toward its destined end. Nevertheless, Commissioner Roy A. Haynes announced on January 14, 1922, two years after the Eighteenth Amendment became effective, that the era of clear thinking and clean living had got off to a wonderfully fine start. "The results," he said, "are nothing short of remarkable. The amendment is being enforced to an even greater extent than many devoted friends anticipated. . . . People generally, both foreign and otherwise, have quietly acquiesced in the new law, and those now engaged in the illicit traffic constitute a negligible minority. . . . From various sources it is estimated there were twenty million drinkers in the United States before the country went dry. . . . If there were twenty million drinkers when liquor was accessible—and it is doubtful—and if there are 2,500,000 drinkers now—more doubtful—then 17,500,000 former drinkers have quit— a wonderful record. Only 15 per cent of the former drinkers are drinking now, and these are drinking but 5 per cent of the quantity of liquor that was formerly consumed, while the entire drink bill of the nation has been decreased two billion dollars a year." The source of these startling statistics was never revealed.

As time went on, Commissioner Haynes became even more optimistic. In a series of speeches and interviews during the next eighteen months, he informed the country that "the home-brew fad is taking its final gasp," that "bootleg patronage has fallen off more than 50 per cent," that "the redistillation of denatured alcohol is now impossible," that "moonshining in the cities is on the wane," that the bootleggers "are in a desperate plight," and, finally, in August 1923, that "the death rattle has begun." The wets promptly produced facts and figures to disprove these statements, and it was suggested that what Haynes thought was the death rattle was actually the chatter of submachine guns in Chicago. Dry leaders in and out of Congress, however, accepted the commissioner's pronouncements at their face value, and concluded that nothing more needed to be done to make the United States completely arid. When wet senators proposed early in 1924 that every phase of enforcement be investigated, the drys rejected the idea as nonsense. Senator Morris Sheppard, of Texas, author of the Eighteenth Amendment, said, "In view of the marvelous achievements of the prohibition enforcement unit, a general investigation would be worse than useless—a waste of funds and energy and time. Instead of a resolution of investigation, the unit should have a vote of thanks."

CHAPTER TEN

A New Moral Tone for Broadway

In pre-Volstead times New York City, especially the amusement district of which Broadway was the center, was celebrated throughout the world for its fine hotels, restaurants, and barrooms, and for its lively cabarets and elegant lobster palaces. Prohibition drastically reduced the revenue of these resorts; the barrooms had nothing to sell, and the restaurants and cabarets couldn't operate profitably on the sale of food alone. Most of the best-known eating and drinking places, and many famous hotels, were compelled to close their doors. Some of the latter were old and out-of-date, and probably would have surrendered to the expanding demands of business during the booming 1920s, which brought about a shortage of office space and enormous increases in rentals. The outlawing of liquor, however, was an important factor in their destruction; to many the proceeds of the bar meant the difference between profit and loss.

Within half a dozen years after the Eighteenth Amendment went into effect, virtually everything that had made Broadway famous was gone, and the amusement area had been transformed into a raucous jungle of chop-suey restaurants, hot-dog and hamburger shops, garish night clubs, radio and phonograph stores equipped with blaring loud-speakers, cheap haberdasheries, fruit-juice stands, dime museums, candy and drug stores, speakeasies, gaudy movie houses, flea circuses, penny arcades, and lunch counters which advertised EATS! Many of these places added to the noise and confusion by employing barkers and pullers-in. As Wilson Mizner, playwright and noted Broadway *bon vivant,* said a few years before his death in 1933, "The once great Broadway has become something of a heel, definitely run down."

From the viewpoint of the drys, however, the change was a glorious one, very much for the better. Their conception of what the Eighteenth Amendment had done for Broadway and the amusement district was expressed in an extensive report compiled by Robert E. Corradini, research secretary of the World League Against Alcoholism, and presented as part of his testimony before a congressional committee in 1926. He said:

> Prohibition has infused a new moral tone into Broadway . . . has taken a lot of the coarseness and vulgarity out of the "roaring forties." Nor has prohibition killed the gaiety of Broadway. Whiskey and booze are not the *sine qua non* of merriment on Broadway. The amusement district seems to be able to have oodles of fun even with the new national drink—water. The only difference between then and now is that Broadway is more sober—that's all. A few years ago drunkenness was common. Intoxicated men and women could be seen every night staggering through the streets or being helped into taxis. Today one can walk up and down the district without seeing these scenes of the old days.

The first of the celebrated hotels to feel the withering effects of the dry victory was the Holland House on Fifth Avenue; it was turned into an office building in January 1920. Later in the same year a similar fate befell the Hotel Knickerbocker at Broadway and Forty-second Street. The Knickerbocker Bar, widely known as the Forty-second Street Country Club, was frequented by literary and theatrical people; it served the finest free lunch in town, and was the home of Maxfield Parrish's famous painting of Old King Cole, which hung above the back bar. During the celebration of Armistice Day on

November 11, 1918, Enrico Caruso stepped from his room onto a balcony of the Knickerbocker and sang "The Star-Spangled Banner" to a huge crowd in Times Square. His great voice is said to have been audible as far north as Fifty-ninth Street. In the middle 1920s so many of the Knickerbocker's offices were occupied by liquor dealers that the building was popularly known as "Bootleggers' Curb."

In 1921 the Manhattan Hotel at Madison Avenue and Forty-second Street, where the Manhattan cocktail is said to have been invented, went out of business. A year later the long career of the Buckingham at Fifth Avenue and Fiftieth Street came to an end; it was immortalized by Edith Wharton in *The Age of Innocence,* and was the refuge of Dom Pedro, the last Emperor of Brazil. The Hotel Marlborough at Broadway and Thirty-sixth Street, where Anna Held took her famous milk bath in the presence of reporters who were chagrined to learn that milk is not transparent, gave up the struggle in 1923. Three famous houses closed in 1925—the Savoy and the Netherland, on Fifth Avenue near Fifty-ninth Street; and the Park Avenue, which was built in the 1870s by A. T. Stewart, the famous merchant, as a home for his salesladies. However, they refused to live there because of the stringent regulations. In 1927 the Normandie, at Broadway and Thirty-ninth Street, closed, and soon afterward was torn down. Although never really first-class, the Normandie had three claims to fame—it had housed Kid McCoy's popular Rathskeller, it was the favorite stopping place of Samuel Gompers, the labor leader, and for some time around 1910 it was the headquarters of the woman-suffrage movement. The Majestic Hotel at Central Park West and Seventy-second Street, where O. O. McIntyre, perhaps the most renowned of all newspaper columnists, began his career as a lowly press agent, closed in the fall of 1929. That same year also saw the end of the greatest of all New York hotels, the Waldorf-Astoria at Fifth Avenue and Thirty-fourth Street; the site is now occupied by the Empire State Building. The name of the hotel, however, was perpetuated by an even grander house, built a few years later farther uptown, on Park Avenue. Among its many distinctions, the old Waldorf-Astoria was the first thousand-room hotel ever built.

Of the fine hotels which were actually located on Broadway, only the McAlpin, the Astor, and the Claridge survived, and the latter, never a large house but in its day very swank, deteriorated rapidly; by the middle 1920s it was no longer first-class. These and other well-known hotels which weathered the dry spell, among them the Biltmore, the Imperial, the Martinique, the Vanderbilt, the Commodore, and the Murray Hill, closed their barrooms and leased the space for candy stores, soda fountains, and other businesses. The bar of the Astor, at Forty-fourth Street and Broadway, famous for its Christmas eggnog and Tom and Jerry and for a fine punch called simply, "Hotel Astor No. 1," was remodeled to house a drugstore and a shirt shop. Prior to prohibition there were many good second-class hotels in the side streets, particularly in the West Forties between Fifth Avenue and Broadway. Nearly all operated small but profitable restaurants and barrooms. Some of these houses were closed, while others were filled with prostitutes, pimps, dope peddlers, gamblers, small-time gangsters, bootleggers, and other riffraff of the underworld, and their bars were turned into speakeasies. The big hotels which continued to operate kept their dining rooms open, but most were run at a loss, and neither food nor service equaled those of the good old days. A few well-known restaurants, notably Luchow's in East Fourteenth Street, also managed to keep going, but they suffered similar deterioration. For a long time dining in New York was a grim business.

The theater in general prospered during the years of the great blight, but some of New York's best-known playhouses were put out of business by the ravages of prohibition and the competition of the movies, especially after the latter had learned to talk. Another contributing factor was the northward movement of the amusement district, which was intensified after the closing of such night spots as Maxim's, the Pré Catelan, and the Café des Beaux Arts, all of which were south of Times Square. At the end of the dry era only three important theaters, the Empire, the National, and the Maxine Elliott, remained below Forty-second Street. Several noted houses on that thoroughfare, and above it on Broadway, had been turned over to burlesque, while others had been taken over by the movies. Thus passed the George M. Cohan, the Gaiety, the Globe, the Broadway, the Apollo, the New Amsterdam, where Florenz Ziegfeld produced the *Follies;* the Eltinge, named for a famous female impersonator; the Republic, where *Abie's Irish Rose* made theatrical history, and many others.

2

Delmonico's restaurant was founded in 1830, and for more than half a century after the Civil War was one of the great eating places of the world. Many famous dishes were invented at Delmonico's; perhaps the best known is lobster à la Newburg. According to legend, this toothsome delicacy was first concocted in a chafing dish in a Delmonico dining room by Captain Ben Wenberg, shipowner and a noted gourmet, sometime in the middle 1880s. It immediately became popular, and for several years appeared on Delmonico's menu as lobster à la Wenberg. The name was changed when Charles Delmonico put Captain Wenberg's name on the restaurant's black list after the captain had quarreled loudly with another diner and, in Delmonico's opinion, thus became an objectionable character. The only change that Delmonico's made in the original Wenberg recipe was to substitute sherry for rum.

International prestige and fine food were not enough to save Delmonico's, and by the beginning of 1924 its doors had closed forever. Rector's, one of the best in the days of George Rector, was also gone, and so were the original Shanley's, where the Paramount Theater now stands, and a later Shanley's on West Forty-second Street. Hearty eaters of the pre-prohibition days claimed that the old Shanley's served the best corned beef and cabbage on earth. Another regular attraction at Shanley's was Bat Masterson, the famous western law officer and gun fighter. During his final years Masterson wrote prize-fight news for the *Morning Telegraph,* and every night he sat in a corner of Shanley's grill and demolished a huge steak— a big man with a big appetite. Oblivion had also claimed the Ted

Lewis Club, the Boardwalk, the Little Club, the Monte Carlo Club, Murray's Roman Gardens, the two places operated by the Bustanoby brothers, Captain Jim Churchill's noted restaurant at Broadway and Forty-eighth Street, Thomas Healey's Golden Glades; Reisenweber's at Eighth Avenue and Fifty-eighth Street, Jack's at Sixth Avenue and Forty-third Street; Sherry's, a Fifth Avenue place of great distinction; Mouquin's, probably the best French restaurant in New York; Brown's Chop House; and Joel Rinaldo's chile con carne house in West Forty-first Street, where a balcony overlooked the dressing rooms of the New Amsterdam Theater.

There were better restaurants in New York than Reisenweber's and Jack's, as far as food and liquor were concerned, but none was more widely known or more popular. Jack's was especially renowned for Irish bacon and Irish whiskey, and for a "flying wedge" of tough waiters who were extraordinarily efficient at the task of ejecting obstreperous customers. Every year the waiters of Jack's issued a formal challenge to the Harvard and Yale football teams, offering to play both on the same afternoon. Jack's, which never closed, was at its best from midnight to dawn, when its habitués, principally theatrical people, journalists, politicians, and sporting figures, scurried home to avoid the debilitating effects of daylight. Reisenweber's was founded as a suburban tavern in 1856, and was operated by the Reisenweber family for sixty-seven years. It was New York's first modern cabaret, and the first important resort to provide a dance floor; and John Reisenweber always claimed that it introduced jazz music to the metropolis. It was also the scene of Sophie Tucker's greatest triumphs. In its heyday Reisenweber's was a big place; it extended half a block down Eighth Avenue and some three hundred feet on Fifty-eighth Street. It employed one thousand persons, and maintained more than a dozen dining rooms in which five thousand customers could be, and often were, seated and served at one time. When it was finally closed it had dwindled to two rooms and had been renamed the Paradise.

Many of these places attempted to sell liquor—the prices ranged from two to four dollars for a one-ounce drink and from seven to ten dollars for a pint—and were frequently raided by enforcement agents. The owners, or the managers and waiters who made the actual sales, were fined and the liquor found was confiscated. Jack's and Reisenweber's were each raided half a dozen times; in one assault upon Jack's the agents discovered a secret room in which—so they said—more than one hundred thousand dollars' worth of fine liquors had been hidden. Since the fines imposed were usually trivial, and the quantity of liquor seized generally small, some of the resorts were able to keep going for a few years despite the raids. They succumbed quickly, however, to the injunction and padlock provisions of the Volstead Act. Some closed their doors as soon as proceedings were started against them in federal court; others fought and were eventually padlocked for from six to twelve months. Reisenweber's, after a legal battle that lasted for more than eight months, was padlocked in January 1923 for a year, and never reopened.

3

When New York's great eating places disappeared, there vanished also one of the city's most ancient traditions—the art of leisurely dining. There were plenty of places where food was sold—the number of restaurants in New York increased from fifty-two hundred in 1918 to about twelve thousand in 1921—but almost without exception they were hole-in-the-wall lunchrooms or dismal little eateries of the gobble-and-run variety. All were distinguished by poor food and worse service, and none offered anything calculated to induce a customer to linger over his dinner. A few speakeasies served acceptable meals, but it was not until half a dozen years after the Eighteenth Amendment had been repealed that New York could boast of restaurants worthy of being mentioned in the same breath with Delmonico's, Jack's, Sherry's, Mouquin's, Churchill's, Rector's, or the dining rooms of the Park Avenue, the Waldorf-Astoria, the Buckingham, and other famous hotels. Nor, for that matter, with the unpretentious little French and Italian restaurants with which New

York abounded in pre-prohibition days, and where a good dinner, with wine, could be obtained for from forty cents to one dollar.

4

Soon after the Eighteenth Amendment went into effect the Brooklyn *Eagle* said editorially that "the knell of the cabaret was sounded when the specter of total abstinence stalked through the front door." Prohibition not only destroyed the cabaret as New York had known it for many years; the word itself disappeared from the popular vocabulary and was replaced by "night club." The cabaret and the night club were alike in some respects—both provided dancing and entertainment to attract customers, and both depended for profit upon the sale of a little food and a lot of liquor. But there the similarity ended. The entertainment in an old-time cabaret was usually more formal than that in a night club, and of a higher caliber; in the latter, noise and gaudy decorations, to say nothing of the deadening effects of prohibition booze, covered up the short-comings of the orchestra and the performers. Operating a cabaret before prohibition was a legitimate business, while running a night club during the dry era was, in general, a racket. As long as he obeyed the closing law and other laws and paid his license fees, with perhaps a reasonable donation to the Tammany district leader, the cabaret operator had nothing to fear from the authorities. For the man who ran a night club, life was not so simple. Although he may have made proper arrangements with the politicians, the police, and the pro-hibition agents, and had taken care of the inspectors of the health and fire departments and the other city services, he never knew whether he would be allowed to keep his place open one day or one year; the double cross was one of the great indoor sports of the period. Moreover, he was constantly exposed to the possibility that a disappointed business rival might attempt to equalize matters with a pistol, a bomb, or a submachine gun. Consequently he got what he could while the getting was good. His motto was, "A short life and a thievish one."

There were literally hundreds of night-club operators during prohibition, and many of them made a great deal of money, for customers were plentiful and prices high. The cover charge in a place rated first-class ranged from two dollars to whatever could be extracted from the customer, or sucker, without evoking too many squawks. The price of a dinner varied, but was seldom less than four or five dollars, and in most of the resorts the food was terrible. It was not uncommon for a man who only a few years before had been accustomed to dining at Delmonico's or Churchill's or Mouquin's to burst into tears at the mere sight of a night-club meal. If a sucker ordered champagne, he got aerated cider and a bill for twenty-five dollars. For a split of ginger ale, or a small glass of orange juice, which were generally used to kill the taste and smell of bootleg hooch, he paid a dollar and a half and sometimes two dollars. A setup, consisting of ice and soda or plain water, into which the customer poured his own liquor, cost from one to two dollars. A fifth of whiskey, so called, which might contain anything from wood alcohol to embalming fluid, was twenty dollars. As soon as the sucker got drunk, which was usually after the second slug of raw booze had ripped down his throat, the official schedule of prices went out the window; thereafter the waiters used their own judgment and charged whatever the traffic would bear.

One of the most profitable branches of the night-club business was the "clip joint," which for downright viciousness was equaled only by the worst of the old-time saloons. These fragrant dives were usually hidden away in a side street, although occasionally the police found one in a Broadway basement. The typical clip joint was staffed by a bartender, two or three waiters who doubled as strong-arm men, a tough floor manager, a singer and a piano player, a half-naked cigarette girl, and from two to ten hostesses, depending upon the size of the place. The sucker was usually brought to the clip joint by a taxi driver or sent there by a hotel clerk; he was assured that he would find girls galore and lots of good liquor "right off the boat."

When he arrived he was immediately importuned to buy drinks for one or more of the hostesses, who intimated that they would be

available for more interesting activities "after we get through work."
The girls usually drank "gin highballs," which were compounded of
water and a little orange juice or ginger ale, and for which the
sucker was charged from one to two dollars. The sucker himself, for
his initial drink, was given a double slug of raw alcohol doctored to
resemble whiskey. If he got helplessly drunk, he was simply robbed
and dumped into the gutter a block or so away from the clip joint.
If through some miracle he remained fairly sober and showed a
disposition to quit spending, the usual procedure was for one of the
hostesses to accuse him of insulting her. Thereupon the floor manager
would indignantly tell him to leave and present him with a bill, an
outrageous compilation which included a large cover charge, a dozen
drinks he hadn't ordered, all those he had already paid for, a bottle
or two of liquor, a half dozen packs of cigarettes at a dollar each, and
extras. If he paid, he was permitted to depart, although he was lucky
if a sympathetic hostess didn't pick his pocket before he reached
the door. If he protested, he was kicked and slugged until he was
groggy or unconscious, after which he was robbed and thrown out.
The police seldom raided a politically protected night club—that
unpopular chore was generally performed by the federal agents—
but when they did, the assignment was carried out in a very genteel
and considerate manner. But the clip joints had few friends, and the
police were pretty rough with them. When a victim complained about
one of these dives, and could remember the address, the cops simply
wrecked the joint and beat up every member of the staff they could
catch. They sent a lot of clip-joint operators and strong-arm men to
the hospitals, but brought very few into court.

5

The restaurant and cabaret operators who dominated New York's
night life before prohibition—George Rector, the Delmonicos, Louis
Sherry, the Bustanoby brothers, Captain James Churchill, the Shan-
leys, Thomas Healey, Jack Dunstan, Joel Rinaldo, John Reisenweber, and others—were men of standing and integrity. The night-

club and clip-joint entrepreneurs who succeeded them, and whose operations invested Broadway with its "new moral tone," were of an entirely different stamp. Occasionally an honest but misguided promoter would attempt to open a night club, but since it was impossible to operate profitably without liquor, he had to begin by making an illegal connection with a bootleg ring. That meant paying off the politicians, the police, and all the others, and he soon found himself deeply involved in a situation which he couldn't handle. Invariably he either went bankrupt or was frozen out, which is a way of saying that gangsters muscled in, if he had a good location, and told him to get out or get killed.

Throughout the fourteen years of prohibition, which the Anti-Saloon League had hailed joyfully as "an era of clear thinking and clean living," and for several years afterward, virtually all of New York's best-known drinking and dancing resorts were dominated by big-shot criminals. These men controlled the flow of liquor into the metropolis and managed its distribution and sale; they operated or financed night clubs partly to provide good outlets for their booze and partly for reasons of vanity. They were the real top-drawer crooks of the period; they ran the whole criminal setup in New York, and their alliances, especially in liquor, extended northward to Chicago and Detroit, southward to New Orleans and Miami, and westward to Los Angeles and San Francisco. Among other things, they planned and directed the New York liquor wars in which a thousand gangsters and bootleggers were killed. The gunmen who handled these murders, which to them were just so many jobs, never received as much publicity as their colleagues in Chicago, nor did they reach the heights of cruelty achieved by the killers who followed the banners of Johnny Torrio, Al Capone, and Dion O'Banion. Nevertheless they frequently displayed considerable imagination, and are said to have invented many of the methods used with such spectacular success in Chicago, Detroit, and elsewhere.

Nearly all of the underworld luminaries who looked upon such murders as legitimate ways to handle competition owed their eminence to the Eighteenth Amendment. They included some of the most vicious thugs and racketeers that New York has ever produced. The most powerful of the lot was Arnold Rothstein, a sure-thing gambler, and, reputedly, a fixer of prize fights, horse races, and other sporting events. His greatest achievement in this field, the details of which didn't become generally known until after his death, was rigging the 1919 World Series, which resulted in baseball's greatest scandal. Rothstein was pre-eminent in such undertakings, but actually they were just the frosting on the cake. The real source of his power was his huge bank roll. He was the underworld's big money man and backer of shady enterprises. Rothstein had money in more than a score of New York night clubs, including such famed resorts as the Cotton Club, the Silver Slipper, the Rendezvous, and Les Ambassadeurs, as well as in a considerable number of clip joints and ordinary speak-easies. He also backed an occasional musical show in the legitimate theater, and invested large sums in race horses, gambling houses, hotels, judges, politicians, policemen, and other properties which appealed to his sense of possession or were useful to him in his business. When Rothstein financed an underworld project he always received a high rate of interest, his money back, and an exorbitant share of the profits. And whoever owed Rothstein paid him, in one way or another. He retained half a dozen skilled and unscrupulous lawyers to handle the legal aspects of his transactions—he frequently operated under cover of a corporate organization. Rothstein was at the peak of his career when he was shot in the Park Central Hotel on November 5, 1928. He lived for two days, but failed to disclose the name of his murderer, who was never found, or, at least, never arrested.

Jack Diamond, Dutch Schultz, Charley Luciano, Lepke Buchalter, Bugsy Siegel, Jake Gurrah Shapiro, and Meyer Lansky, together with many others whose names were less familiar, all helped finance night clubs at various times, and provided gunmen to protect the resorts in which they were interested and to discourage rivals with whom they were at war. (A classic example of discouragement occurred on July 13, 1929, when Jack Diamond put the Hotsy Totsy Club out of business by shooting down two of its owners on a crowded dance floor.) Their main interests, however, were in rumrunning and boot-legging, and in the related fields of murder, hijacking, narcotics, prostitution, crooked gambling, racketeering, robbery, and extortion. The only one of this group who invested heavily in the night-club business was Arthur Flegenheimer, better known as Dutch Schultz, who was the beer baron of the Bronx and boss of the numbers or policy racket. His principal partner and protector in the latter enter-prise was James J. Hines, a well-known Tammany politician who was sent to prison in 1939.

During the final years of prohibition Schultz owned the Embassy Club, a very plush night spot which catered to the high-class, or Park Avenue, trade. In return for paying exorbitant prices for poor food and bad liquor, which did them little harm, the Park Avenuers rubbed elbows with top-flight gangsters, which thrilled them, and listened to the singing of Helen Morgan, Morton Downey, and the Yacht Club Boys, which amused them. Dutch Schultz was also dis-tinguished in the underworld as the first employer of Vincent Coll, the so-called "mad dog of gangland," who was probably the most brutal killer of his time, at least in New York. Coll loved to kill, and did so on the slightest provocation. He put several notches on his gun during a war with the Jack Diamond gang, but later broke with Schultz, organized his own mob, and began hijacking his former boss's liquor trucks. Schultz immediately offered to pay fifty thousand dollars to any man who would kill Coll, and every free-lance gunman in New York went on the prowl, eager to earn the money. On the night of February 7, 1932, one of Schultz's own killers trapped Coll in a telephone booth in a drugstore on West Twenty-third Street, near Ninth Avenue, and poured fifty bullets from a submachine gun through the glass doors. Most of the slugs lodged in Coll's body be-tween the head and the knees. The mad dog had just passed his twenty-third birthday.

In the night-club business, the biggest of the big shots, besides Rothstein, were Owney Madden, Larry Fay; Frankie Marlow, whose real name was Gandolfo Civito; and Waxey Gordon, born Irving Wexler. The second to retire from New York's night life, after Rothstein, was Marlow, his departure being effected by the usual burst of gunfire. Marlow started as a gunman on the staff of Francesco Uale, better known as Frankie Yale, the big liquor and racketeering boss of Brooklyn, whose activities were centered in the Gowanus and Coney Island sections. One of Yale's properties at Coney Island was the Harvard Inn, which he had opened several years before prohibition, and where a young man named Alphonse Capone began his career as a dishwasher. Yale was one of the first to bring liquor into New York from the rum fleet off the coast, and in these operations Marlow was his right-hand man and chief killer. Within two or three years Marlow's share of the proceeds amounted to a fair-sized fortune, so he left Brooklyn and moved to Manhattan, where for several years he was a prominent figure in Broadway and sporting circles as well as in the liquor racket. During the middle 1920s he controlled the sale of all beer sold in Manhattan between Harlem and Forty-second Street. He also owned race horses and prize fighters, a gambling house or two, and had shares in the Silver Slipper, the Rendezvous, and other night clubs, including a vicious dive called the Club La Vie. He also owned a sizable interest in Les Ambassadeurs, and once threatened to sell out unless the name was changed to something he could spell, or at least pronounce.

It was common gossip in the underworld that Frankie Yale had provided the money for some of Marlow's night-club ventures, although as far as was publicly known Yale confined his operations to Brooklyn, with an occasional trip to Chicago to do a job of killing for his old friends Johnny Torrio and Al Capone. When Yale was murdered in 1928, Marlow owed him forty thousand dollars, and when pressed for payment by Yale's successor, Little Augie Carfano, insisted that Yale's death had canceled the debt. Less than a year later, on June 24, 1929, Marlow was lured from a New York night club by several of his old Brooklyn pals, and taken for the customary ride, with death at the end of the journey. His body, full of bullets, was found by motorists under a bush near a graveyard in Queens Borough, on Long Island. In his pockets were seventeen dollars in cash, a pawn ticket for a diamond ring, and a pistol permit signed by a justice of the New York Supreme Court.

Owney Madden became captain of the Old Gopher gang in 1910, when he was eighteen years old, and as such was lord of the Hell's Kitchen section of New York's lower west side. Four years later, proudly bearing the sobriquet of "Owney the Killer," and suspected by the police of five murders, Madden was convicted of complicity in a gang killing and sent to Sing Sing to serve from ten to twenty years. He was released in 1923, and so missed some three years of the golden era. He came along rapidly, however, and within a year or two had made a big name for himself as a gunman, a bootlegger, a hijacker, and as a strong-arm man in clip joints. In common with many other big shots, he was interested in the Silver Slipper, and was also associated with Rothstein in the Cotton Club and other resorts. Before he retired in the middle 1930s, Madden had been arrested fifty-seven times, on charges ranging from homicide to stealing. His record, however, shows only two convictions—the one in 1914 and another for violating a traffic ordinance. He always managed to know the right people.

And so did Waxey Gordon until 1933, when the government, unable to do anything about his more serious crimes, sent him to prison for income-tax evasion. Before the Eighteenth Amendment gave him his big chance, Gordon was a pickpocket, a sneak thief, and a small-time peddler of narcotics. He immediately went into the liquor business, and within half a dozen years was head of a big bootleg ring which imported fine whiskeys from Nova Scotia and the Bahamas. Gordon sold a little of this good liquor to selected customers at from two to four times the usual price, but most of it was cut and recut and doctored and colored until by the time it reached the ultimate consumer it was the same terrible stuff that was available everywhere. Gordon was a very rich man during the late 1920s and the early 1930s. He owned several hotels in midtown Manhattan, including the popular Piccadilly; a brewery, a distillery, a line of seagoing rum ships, a luxurious summer home in New Jersey, half a dozen expensive automobiles, handfuls of diamonds and other jewelry, a wardrobe that had cost him many thousands of dollars—he was a noted dandy—and, of course, shares in half a dozen night clubs.

Larry Fay was a gangster and rumrunner, and a partner of James J. Hines, in a profitable racket by which small milk producers were shaken down for protection money. His police record, as published in the New York *Herald Tribune,* filled half a column of small type. Aside from all this, he possessed three distinctions—he named some of his night clubs after himself, he financed most of them with his own money, and he was the first of the big shots to become an important figure in the business. He was a little man, long-jawed and decidedly unhandsome, and he had an abiding passion for flashy clothing; he is said to have started the fashion of wearing solid-color shirts—his favorite was a violent indigo blue—with loud neckties and expensive suits. Fay's habiliments were always the best that money could buy, and many of his topcoats, suits, shoes, and shirts were made in England. When he returned from a trip to Europe in 1923 he brought twelve trunks filled with Bond Street creations made especially for him by London's most fashionable tailors. He knocked Broadway's eye out for months. He was always grateful for any flattering reference to his appearance; a newspaper reporter who called him the "Beau Brummel of Broadway" received a case of liquor and an invitation to eat and drink on the cuff for six months at one of Fay's clubs. However, the great man was practical; beneath his gaudy raiment he wore a bulletproof vest. Fay also disliked the term "racketeer"; he always insisted that he was a businessman, and to prove it he maintained an ornate suite of offices near Columbus Circle, where he employed an extraordinarily large number of handsome secretaries and stenographers.

Until he hit a hundred-to-one shot at Belmont Park in 1918, when he was twenty-nine years old, Fay was a taxi driver and an unimportant punk-about-town. He sometimes ran with the old Hudson Duster gang on Manhattan's west side, and became friendly with a Duster chieftain called Big Frenchy de Mange, who was afterward his partner in several night-club ventures. With the money won at the race track Fay bought several taxicabs; eventually he operated a large fleet and became so powerful in the industry that he controlled the two most profitable stands in New York—the Grand Central Terminal and the Pennsylvania Station. When prohibition changed the complexion of New York's underworld, Fay began running liquor down from Canada, using his taxicabs and several trucks which he was soon able to purchase. He was also associated, for a few years, with Big Bill Dwyer and others whose speedboats brought liquor into New York from Rum Row.

In less than two years Fay had accumulated about five hundred thousand dollars in cash, according to underworld report, and huge sums were rolling in from his taxi and liquor enterprises. His initial venture into the night-club field was early in 1921, when he financed several clip joints, said to have been the first dives of this type ever opened in New York, although they had already become fairly common in Chicago, Philadelphia, and Detroit. Also in 1921, Fay started the first of his big night clubs, Fay's Follies at Eighth Avenue and Fifty-fourth Street, the decorations of which are said to have cost seventy-five thousand dollars. The new resort was a big success, and took up so much of Fay's time and attention that in 1923, when Owney Madden got out of Sing Sing, Fay hired the ex-Gopher captain to supervise his clip-joint interests and act as a sort of foreman over the strong-arm boys and pullers-in. In 1924 Fay opened the most celebrated of his night spots, the El Fey at 107 West Forty-fifth Street, and when that was padlocked by the government he started another which he called the Del Fey. During the next several years he opened four or five others, and was one of the many partners in the Silver Slipper, the Rendezvous, the Cotton Club, Les Ambassadeurs, and the Casablanca. Fay was murdered while standing in front of the Casablanca on January 1, 1933, the first day in six months on which he had not worn his bulletproof vest.

Fay's greatest contribution to the night life of the prohibition era was his sponsorship of one of Broadway's most celebrated figures—Mary Louise Cecelia Guinan, better known as Texas, a Waco girl who came to New York in 1922 to make her fortune. She made it, too, but apparently was unable to keep it. During a period of ten months in the middle 1920s Texas Guinan is said to have banked seven hundred thousand dollars, but when she died on November 5, 1933, at Vancouver, B.C., where she had been appearing with a troupe of dancing girls, she left a net estate of $28,173. She was forty-nine years old. Texas Guinan's first appearance in New York was as a substitute singer at the Café des Beaux Arts, which had been reopened as a night club after the retirement of André Bustanoby. Her singing voice never amounted to much, and she was a very poor actress, as she afterward proved when she played several parts in the legitimate theater, but she had a remarkable personality that was made to order for the noise and excitement of a night club. She was such a big hit that the operator of the Beaux Arts immediately hired her as mistress of ceremonies. Larry Fay engaged her for El Fey soon after that resort opened, and later she appeared at the Rendezvous. During the next half dozen years she operated several clubs of her own, among them the 300 Club, the Argonaut, the Century, the Salon Royal, the Club Intime, and two or three Texas Guinan Clubs, some of which were believed to have been backed by Arnold Rothstein. All of her places were frequently raided, and several were padlocked. Texas Guinan herself was often arrested, but she never went to jail, and she was never even in court for more than a few hours. Chester P. Mills, who was prohibition administrator of the New York district during the middle 1920s, wrote in *Collier's Weekly* for September 17, 1927, "I spent many wakeful hours trying to bring into camp such persons as Texas Guinan . . . who finally eluded our men with the aid of shrewd lawyers."

At the peak of her career Texas Guinan was by far the loudest noise on Broadway, and with the possible exception of Helen Morgan was the most popular night-club attraction New York had ever seen; the crowds loved her brashness and the atmosphere of excitement which surrounded her everywhere she went. Only one rival ever tried to usurp her title as Queen of the Night Clubs—an aging dame named Belle Livingston, who away back in the early 1890s was a Broadway show girl known as the Kansas Sunshine Baby. Belle

Livingston opened three clubs in the late 1920s and the early 1930s, but was not very successful; she talked too much and was inclined to fight the prohibition agents instead of appealing to their better natures. Her best-known resort was the Fifty-eighth Street Country Club, a big place of five floors with bars, grills, private rooms, ping-pong games, and a miniature golf course. Belle Livingston was a big woman, some six feet tall and weighing about one hundred seventy-five pounds, and usually acted as her own bouncer. She tried to bounce a squad of enforcement agents who raided one of her clubs in 1931, and was herself bounced into jail for thirty days.

Belle Livingston has long been forgotten, but as long as there is a Broadway, Texas Guinan will be remembered for the famous wise-crack, "Hello, Sucker," with which she greeted visitors to her clubs; and for half a dozen other phrases which are still part of the night-club and underworld argot. One night at the Rendezvous an enthusiastic sucker paid the cover charge for everybody present and grandly presented to each performer a fifty-dollar bill, whereupon Texas Guinan hauled him under a spotlight and introduced him as "a big butter-and-egg man." The name of this character has not been preserved, but as a type he was immortalized in a successful play by George S. Kaufman. On another occasion, when a singer had given her best to scattering applause, Texas Guinan shouted, "Give this little girl a great big hand." This cry is still used by masters of cere-monies to stimulate enthusiasm for their favorites, and the injunction is nearly always obeyed by docile night-clubbers. Once, however, it boomeranged, and the usually jovial Texas Guinan became furiously angry. During a raid a prohibition agent placed a paternal hand on her shoulder and called to a colleague: "Give this little girl a great big handcuff!"

6

Robert E. Corradini, the discoverer of Broadway's new moral tone, reported equally remarkable findings when he turned his investigative talents upon the speakeasies which had succeeded the saloons in New

York. He made two "saloon surveys" of the metropolis. He found 881 saloons in 1922, and 463 in 1924, as compared to 8,168 licensed places in 1918, the last full year before prohibition went into effect. He reported that in 1924 there were no saloons whatever in the amusement district, from Thirty-fourth to Fifty-third streets, and only fifteen on the whole of Broadway from the Battery to Yonkers. These surveys were bolstered by a vast array of charts and statistical tables, which purported to prove many things. One chart showed that arrests for profanity in New York had declined 80 per cent because of the benign influence of the Eighteenth Amendment. "Along with it," said the legend under the chart, "have disappeared the mud and filth and slums that formerly distinguished the metropolis."

To stop 80 per cent of the cussing in a city of more than five million people in less than four years was in itself a mighty accomplishment, but to rid New York of its slums in such a short period of time was in every way extraordinary, the more so because it was apparently done in complete secrecy and without the expenditure of a nickel! At any rate, there is no record that any money was ever appropriated, or that the newspapers, the city officials, or even the people who lived in the slums possessed any knowledge of the gigantic project. According to another of Corradini's charts, the number of disorderly houses in New York, and the arrests for operating such places, declined 97 per cent between 1920 and 1924, "chiefly due, in all probability, to national prohibition." This achievement likewise escaped the attention of the press, the police, and the welfare organizations which had been fighting prostitution in New York for many years. The Committee of Fourteen, an anti-vice agency of many years' experience, said in its annual report for 1927 that the Volstead Act had been responsible for an increase in commercial vice, and that immorality thrived in night clubs and speakeasies and cabarets, because the conditions in those establishments were more inviting than they were in the old saloons.

The results of Corradini's surveys were published by the World League Against Alcoholism, and were widely used as dry propaganda throughout the prohibition era. They were not, however, accepted by the wets or by neutral observers, whose estimates of the number of speakeasies in New York were far higher. In 1926, two years after Corradini had been able to find but 463 saloons, Izzy Einstein, most celebrated of prohibition agents, estimated that there were a hundred thousand speakeasies in the metropolis; he and his partner, Moe Smith, had raided more than six hundred in less than five years. Dr. Charles Norris, chief medical examiner, said in his report to the mayor for 1925–26 that the "speakeasies greatly outnumber the licensed saloons of former days." In 1929 the police reported that they had counted thirty-two thousand, but admitted they may have missed a few. In 1930 Representative F. H. La Guardia, later mayor of New York, estimated the number at twenty-two thousand; he also said that to enforce the Volstead Act in the metropolis would require two hundred and fifty thousand policemen, and an additional force of two hundred thousand to police the police. That same year Representative William P. Sirovich said there were a hundred thousand places in New York where liquor could be purchased; an Assistant United States Attorney estimated that there were ten thousand speakeasies on Manhattan Island alone; and Maurice Campbell, former chief enforcement agent for the New York district, agreed with the police that the correct number was thirty-two thousand.

All of these estimates received considerable publicity, but the truth is that, in common with Corradini's conclusions, they possessed little or no value; it was probably impossible to determine, accurately, how many speakeasies New York harbored. As Grover Whalen, the police commissioner, pointed out, "All you need is two bottles and a room and you have a speakeasy." Moreover, the speakeasy as an institution was in a state of constant flux; new ones were opening all the time, and old ones were shifting to new locations. It is clear, however, that liquor was being sold all over New York, and that the number of places where it was available ran well into the tens of thousands. During the middle 1920s complaints of Volstead Act violations were being referred to the federal authorities, by the police, at the rate of fifteen thousand a month; while in one year, from July 1, 1928, to June 30, 1929, the police made 18,589 arrests, most of them of bartenders and waiters in speakeasies, night clubs, and restaurants. And the police never pretended to catch more than a small fraction of those who, under the law, deserved arrest. The best answer to the question of where the speakeasies could be found was given by the New York *Telegram,* which said in 1929:

> Where on Manhattan Island can you buy liquor?
> ANSWER: In open saloons, restaurants, night clubs, bars behind a peephole, dancing academies, drugstores, delicatessens, cigar stores, confectioneries, soda fountains, behind partitions of shoeshine parlors, back rooms of barbershops, from hotel bellhops, from hotel headwaiters, from hotel day clerks, night clerks, in express offices, in motorcycle delivery agencies, paint stores, malt shops, cider stubes, fruit stands, vegetable markets, taxi drivers, groceries, smoke shops, athletic clubs, grillrooms, taverns, chophouses, importing firms, tearooms, moving-van companies, spaghetti houses, boardinghouses, Republican clubs, Democratic clubs, laundries, social clubs, newspapermen's associations . . .

Liquor joints in New York probably would have been much fewer in number if the Prohibition Bureau had been able to recruit more agents like Izzy Einstein and Moe Smith. Nobody ever looked less like sleuths than Izzy and Moe—Izzy was five feet five inches tall and weighed two hundred twenty-five pounds, while Moe stood two inches higher and tipped the scales at ten pounds more—and nobody ever proved to be better ones in their particular field. They became the terrors of the speakeasies; many booze emporiums posted Izzy's picture over the bar, framed in black crepe and bearing such signs as "Look out for this man!" and "This man is poison!" There was good reason for the fear and respect with which the booze sellers regarded Izzy and Moe, for they were incredibly efficient, both at planning and executing raids and in preparing their cases for trial. In less than five years they seized fifteen million dollars' worth of liquor and many moonshine stills and breweries, and destroyed thousands of dollars' worth of saloon fixtures and liquor-making equipment. They made 4,392 arrests, 95 per cent of which resulted in convictions; officials of the Prohibition

Bureau once admitted that they were responsible for 20 per cent of the successful liquor prosecutions in the New York district. All this was accomplished without benefit of shooting. Izzy had a horror of firearms, and wouldn't even touch a gun. Moe carried a revolver occasionally, but fired it only twice, once at a padlock and once at a barrel of whiskey. However, Moe was a mighty man with his fists.

Both Izzy and Moe were products of New York's lower east side, and possessed plenty of the ingenuity and self-reliance which was essential to survival in those dismal purlieus. When prohibition began, Izzy was a minor clerk in a branch post office, supporting a wife and four sons, all of whom afterward became successful lawyers, on a meager salary. Moe was running a small tobacco and stationery store. Izzy became a prohibition agent early in 1920, getting the job principally because of his linguistic gifts—he could speak English, German, Hungarian, Yiddish, Polish, French, Italian, and Russian, and had a smattering of Chinese. Also, he knew all the east-side politicians. Moe joined the prohibition forces a few weeks later, at Izzy's behest, and thereafter the two men usually worked together, although Izzy often attacked the speakeasies singlehanded.

An actor at heart, Izzy loved to dress up; he once said that he had used at least a hundred different disguises during his career as an agent. He wangled his way into speakeasies as an Irishman festooned with shamrocks; as a collegian, in which guise he wrecked the liquor business at Cornell University; as a delivery boy lugging a box of groceries; as a shirt-sleeved family man carrying a pitcher of milk; as a fisherman with his catch slung over his shoulder; as a grimy coal-wagon driver; as a violin player, which he was; as a society dude splendidly arrayed in a "full-dress evening suit" and twirling a gold-headed cane; as a football player with his face smeared with mud; as a pickle peddler with a big jar of that popular East Side dainty; as a lawyer in a frock coat and horn-rimmed glasses, with lawbooks under his arm; as a longshoreman, and as a gravedigger. He and Moe once dug graves for hours in a New York cemetery before they could attract the attention of the moonshiner they were after. Izzy even got into one closely guarded speakeasy by announcing that he was a prohibition agent. The bartender laughed heartily at the gag until Izzy arrested him.

The zany exploits of Izzy and Moe attracted the attention of the newspapermen, and since they were really charming characters and very co-operative, they were soon the darlings of the press. Sometimes they notified the journalists in advance of raids, and were accompanied by swarms of reporters and photographers. They could always be counted upon to do something spectacular and apparently absurd— actually, they knew exactly what they were doing and had carefully planned every move—so by common consent the story of Izzy and Moe was reserved for the funny men. They received more publicity than the rest of the prohibition agents combined, a fact which eventually brought about their downfall. The higher-ups in the Prohibition Bureau couldn't stand seeing so much newspaper space, which might have been filled with their own pompous misstatements, devoted to the activities of "a couple of clowns," even though the clowns were doing a far better job than anybody else in the enforcement business. Early in 1925 a high official of the bureau called Izzy to Washington and said, "You get your name in the newspapers all the time, whereas mine is hardly ever mentioned. I must ask you to remember that you are merely a subordinate and not the whole show." But Izzy and Moe were helpless. When they refused to talk, the reporters simply used their imaginations, and the stories published about the pair became wilder and funnier than ever. Finally, on November 13, 1925, Izzy and Moe were dismissed "for the good of the service," and turned in their badges. "The service must be dignified," said an official of the Prohibition Bureau. And didn't crack a smile.

7

It is the fashion in these times, especially among our aging literati, to heave nostalgic sighs over the speakeasy, where brains were addled and kidneys and digestions wrecked by concoctions which resembled whiskey and tasted like nothing in this world. Actually, there was little to choose between the speakeasy and the old-time saloon. There were good speakeasies and there were bad speakeasies. Down on the Bowery and the lower east side, across town in Hell's Kitchen, and uptown in Little Italy, were the dingy dumps where "smoke," a mixture of alcohol and water, was sold for ten cents a slug. In midtown were the fancy places, with subdued lights, soft seats, tablecloths, excellent service, hostesses and other conveniences, and sometimes free lunch, where fine liquors were dispensed with considerable ceremony at $1.50 a drink. At least the bottles bore the labels of fine liquors. Some of the speakeasies of this type were incorporated, and many were operated as chains, with central purchasing and efficient management.

There was even a speakeasy operated by the United States Government, one of several entrapment schemes evolved by the thinkers of the Prohibition Bureau in Washington. In the late fall of 1925 the bureau's undercover operatives leased the premises at 14 East Forty-fourth Street, a few doors from Delmonico's last stand, and opened a plush booze joint which they called the Bridge Whist Club. There they sold liquor to all comers, and, as A. Bruce Bielaski, head of the bureau's undercover corps, said in an article for *Collier's Weekly* of August 13, 1927, "did a roaring business at all hours of the day and night with thirsty souls who relished the tidbits of free lunch and its old-time atmosphere." Bielaski said that although the speakeasy was not his idea, he believed in its utility "as a means of enabling us to make direct contacts with the wholesale importers." In this, however, the government was disappointed. "We found," Bielaski wrote, "that the bootlegging business was so well organized that even a pretentious blind pig like the Bridge Whist Club could have no direct dealings with the wholesale smugglers. Our orders for liquor had to be placed with middlemen." One of the booths in the Bridge Whist Club was equipped with a dictograph, with wires leading from a lamp shade to a back room where stenographers recorded all conversations. Samuel Senate, a wholesale bootlegger, was caught by this means; he was heard offering a prohibition agent five thousand dollars to help him land a cargo of alcohol from a Belgian schooner. Another big-shot liquor dealer, however, gave the stenographers and their superiors something to think about. Knowing that the place was a federal joint, and being very suspicious, he refused to discuss his own business; instead he described in great detail the drinking habits and personal peculiarities of important government officials, top men of the Anti-Saloon League, and other prominent personages. "His irreverent statements," Bielaski said, "would have made sensational reading."

The Bridge Whist Club flourished until wet members of Congress heard about it. Already in a tizzy over the revelation that prohibition agents had spent $279 entertaining suspected bootleggers at dinner in the Hotel Mayflower in Washington, they raised such a fuss that on May 1, 1926, the Prohibition Bureau formally announced its withdrawal from the enterprise. "The strange sequel," wrote Bielaski, "is that when the government quit dram selling the Bridge Whist Club ran on, apparently undisturbed." The bureau was also compelled to close a similar establishment in Norfolk, Virginia, where enforcement agents were busily trapping policemen and small-time bootleggers; to dismantle stills which had been set up in the mountains of North Carolina and Virginia to supply the federal speakeasies; and to abandon an ambitious scheme to smuggle liquor into the United States from Canada, sell it to American bootleggers, and then arrest the bootleggers. After the government had closed its speakeasy in Norfolk, the enforcement agents complained bitterly that the Norfolk policemen refused to co-operate with them in their campaigns to hunt down liquor-law violators. The Virginia cops seemed to be suspicious.

CHAPTER ELEVEN

Where the Booze Came From

No one ever knew how much good liquor was in the United States when the country went constitutionally dry on the early morning of January 17, 1920. An unknown quantity was in the hands of private citizens and farsighted bootleggers who had bought it before the prohibition era began and stored it away for future use or sale, and the saloonkeepers and wholesale dealers had some. The largest supplies were in some eight hundred warehouses, both free and bonded, many of which were attached to distilleries. Information given out by the government about this liquor was always vague and contradictory. On January 30, 1920, the New York *Times* said that it amounted to sixty-nine million gallons, figures obviously obtained from federal sources. William G. Shepherd, a well-known journalist of the period, said in *Collier's Weekly* for March 21, 1925, that liquor stocks at the beginning of prohibition included fifty million gallons of rye and bourbon whiskey alone. Other guesses ranged from forty millions to seventy millions. Early in 1923 Roy A. Haynes, Prohibition Commissioner, made the most positive statement that any federal official had ever issued on the subject. He said that on July 1, 1922, the government held thirty-eight million gallons of pre-prohibition liquors.

This liquor was taken over by the government, but it wasn't exactly confiscated. The distillers who had put it in the warehouses still owned it, and under the law were responsible for it, but they couldn't touch it or dispose of it. As Representative James R. Mann said in a speech in Congress on January 30, 1920, "The man who owns liquor in a bonded warehouse is between the devil and deep sea. He cannot sell it for beverage purposes. He cannot withdraw it for beverage purposes. He cannot destroy it without paying the government tax upon it. If somebody steals it from him, he is required to pay the beverage tax upon it. He cannot make use of it in any way except to let it remain in the warehouse at his own risk, not the risk of the government. . . . Eventually there must be some disposition by Congress of this liquor." Congress appropriated one million dollars in 1921, and other large sums in later years, to pay for guarding the booze, but the ultimate disposition of most of it was determined by the bootleggers.

These stocks were augmented, from time to time, by confiscated liquor, and by legally manufactured whiskey, brandy, and rum. It was not true, as Wayne B. Wheeler of the Anti-Saloon League wrote in the New York *Times* of March 30, 1926, that when the liquor provisions of the Food Control Bill became effective on September 8, 1917, "the distilling of beverage liquor in the United States was ended and was never legally resumed." The production of distilled liquors continued throughout 1918; whiskey, according to government records, to the extent of 17,383,511.3 gallons. No gin was manufactured after 1918, and in 1919 no legal whiskey was distilled. In the fiscal years 1920, 1921, and 1922, however, selected distilleries—it was never explained how or why these selections were made—were permitted to operate. They produced in those yars 1,303,879.49 gallons of whiskey.

The distillation of rum and brandy was never stopped, although the manufacture of both liquors was considerably curtailed after 1918. The production of rum ranged from 534,507.5 gallons in 1921 to 953,350.8 in 1928; of brandy, from 1,802,422.3 gallons in 1919 to 338,430.7 in 1927. A considerable number of wineries maintained full production throughout the dry era, and as late as 1926 four breweries were being legally operated. (The excuse given by the government for permitting the distillation of whiskey was that it was needed to replenish existing supplies, which dwindled rapidly after the Eighteenth Amendment went into effect.) Rum was required, principally, in the manufacture of tobacco products, and brandy was needed to fortify sacramental wines. It was solemnly explained that although millions of gallons of wine were on hand, a great deal more was needed for religious purposes and for the manufacture of vinegar. Inquisitive journalists who tried to find out why the breweries were running were ignored or brushed off, for not even a federal official with all his double talk could get around the fact that there were no legal uses for beer.

2

A small quantity of the liquor impounded by the government was used by industry, mostly in the manufacture of a few food products, but the great bulk of it was held for medicinal purposes and was released to wholesalers who in turn sold it to the drugstores. Both required permits, but none was issued to retailers in nineteen states because of local laws. Under the regulations as first promulgated by the Prohibition Bureau, a physician, who also had to obtain a permit, could prescribe one quart of whiskey per patient per month, on numbered blanks furnished by the government. This seemed to be a simple enough procedure, but it was so entangled in what the New York *Times* called "onerous and burdensome red tape" that many druggists and doctors announced that they would not sell or prescribe liquor because the law made it too easy for an innocent man to get into trouble. Nevertheless, by June 1920, less than five months after the Eighteenth Amendment went into effect, some fifteen thousand physicians and fifty-seven thousand druggists had applied for permits. Most of the latter were retailers.

The Prohibition Bureau announced after a few months that the new system was working perfectly; it ignored the fact, as shown by its own records, that medicinal liquor was moving out of the warehouses in enormous quantities. In 1921 well over eight million gallons of whiskey were withdrawn, probably twenty times as much as was used in any pre-prohibition year. In March 1921 the bureaucratic machinery was suddenly jammed by a ruling of the Attorney General, A. Mitchell Palmer, who said that the Volstead Act placed no restrictions upon the prescribing of beer and wine. Immediately thousands of Americans complained of ailments which could be relieved only by copious draughts of these beverages. There was a tremendous uproar from the drys, and meetings of protest were held throughout the country. The Anti-Saloon League rushed into action, and in November 1921 Congress passed the Willis-Campbell Law, which forbade a physician to prescribe beer for any purpose, or wine containing more than 24 per cent of alcohol by volume. The wine provision was a phony, as very few wines contained that much alcohol. The new law also limited a physician to a hundred prescriptions in ninety days, and no more than one half pint could be prescribed for any one person within ten days. This made legal whiskey very expensive; the doctor usually received two dollars for the prescription, and the druggist charged from three to six dollars for the half pint. And it was apt to be adulterated.

Before prohibition medicinal liquors were handled by approximately four hundred wholesale drug houses. It was a profitable business, for most doctors who prescribed booze specified drugstore whiskey, which, in those days, was almost certain to be of good quality. By the latter part of 1920 some thirty-three hundred such firms, supposedly carrying ten thousand dollars' worth of drugs each, were withdrawing medicinal liquor on permit. Most were fronts for bootleg gangs. So were many retail druggists; they cut their stocks and diverted half to the illicit liquor trade. Federal inspectors, on the rare occasions when they appeared, were concerned only with the quantity of whiskey on hand and not its strength. Much of the drugstore liquor was 25 per cent whiskey and 75 per cent water. In addition to the wholesale druggists there were a great many dealers who didn't pretend to be anything but liquor sellers; they were likewise granted permits. Mannie Kessler, who became one of the country's biggest bootleggers, was in the liquor business for fifteen years before the United States went dry, and late in 1919 he bought a thousand cases of whiskey and stored it in one of his private warehouses. The Prohibition Bureau gave him permission to sell it to drugstores, and issued another permit which enabled him to withdraw as much more as he wanted. It is very doubtful if he ever sold an ounce legitimately.

During the first six years of prohibition the Prohibition Bureau gave permits to an average of 63,891 doctors annually, and revoked 169. By 1929 the number of permits in force had risen to more than a hundred thousand. These physicians were writing about eleven million prescriptions for whiskey every year. Theoretically, all were carefully checked by agents of the bureau after they had been filled by druggists, who were also subject to rigid controls. Actually, the Prohibition Bureau never had enough agents to make even token inspections. In New York, for example, the bureau in 1925 assigned seventeen agents to watch the city's twelve hundred drugstores and check the one million prescriptions issued every year by fifty-one hundred doctors. These figures did not include the forged and counterfeit prescriptions which were circulated all over the country; on June 2, 1920, the prohibition administrator for Illinois said that three hundred thousand had been issued in Chicago alone. In 1922 federal agents in New York uncovered a counterfeiting ring which was selling prescription blanks at from twenty-five to fifty dollars a hundred to bootleggers who in turn sold them to consumers for two dollars each. All the buyers had to do was take them to drugstores; they were properly filled out and signed, supposedly by reputable doctors. Prohibition officials said the bootleggers had forged the name of almost every physician listed in the New York telephone directory.

Some of the big bootleg syndicates used more direct methods to get the liquor out of the warehouses. The largest operator in this field was George Remus, a Chicago lawyer who abandoned a lucrative practice in the latter part of 1919 to become one of the most successful illicit liquor dealers in the country. Handling nothing but medicinal whiskey, Remus made more than five million dollars in less than five years; in one period of eleven months he deposited $2,800,000 in a single Cincinnati bank. Remus's system was simple but effective—he bought distilleries; eventually he owned at least a dozen in Kentucky, Ohio, and Missouri. He thus became the legal owner of whatever whiskey was stored in the distillery warehouses. These transactions were legitimate, and Remus and his associates would have made a reasonable profit if they had continued to sell the liquor on permit under government control. But no bootlegger was ever satisfied with less than 100 per cent return on his investment, and the big syndicates made far more. For example, Remus paid $125,000 for 891 barrels of whiskey in the Jack Daniel distillery in St. Louis, or approximately fifteen dollars a barrel. He removed 890 barrels, and sold the liquor at from twenty-five to thirty dollars a gallon. The total was well over a million dollars.

Once he had obtained title to a distillery, Remus bribed everybody who might conceivably interfere with his schemes. In October 1920, when he was planning to remove liquor from a Cincinnati distillery, federal agents planted a microphone in his hotel room. In one day they heard him paying off forty-four persons, including policemen, prohibition agents, warehouse guards, politicians, officers of the Internal Revenue Bureau, and other government officials. When these matters had been arranged, Remus moved into the distillery at night with his trucks and other equipment. Occasionally the barrels of liquor were boldly loaded into the trucks and then shipped by railroad. On one occasion a single train pulled into Cincinnati with eighteen freight cars carrying Remus booze.

Usually, however, Remus was more careful. Inside the distillery he built a large wooden trough, from which a rubber hose led through a window into a shed or other outbuilding. There an electric pump was installed. The liquor was poured into the trough and then pumped through the hose into barrels waiting on Remus's trucks, which sped away to hiding places in Ohio, Kentucky, Missouri, Indiana, and Illinois. It was in these states that Remus and his associates sold most of their stolen whiskey; a great deal wound up in Chicago cutting plants, and some was sent to New York and Philadelphia. To cover up the withdrawals, Remus sometimes refilled the empty whiskey barrels with water, and enough alcohol to bring up the proof. At other times all the barrels were emptied of liquor except one, which was left near the warehouse door for the convenience of any honest government gauger—there were such—who might visit the distillery on an inspection tour. It was usually from two to four months before the theft was discovered.

The government obtained twenty-six indictments after an investigation of the Jack Daniel conspiracy, which was probably Remus's best-known adventure, and twenty-three of the defendants were convicted, including a Missouri state senator, a former Internal Revenue collector, a former circuit-court judge, and one member each of the St. Louis Democratic and Republican city committees. Remus himself turned state's evidence and was not prosecuted. However, he served five short jail sentences during his career as a rum king, and paid fines totaling eleven thousand dollars. He was released from the county jail at Portsmouth, Ohio, on April 26, 1927, and after spending a few days in New York went to his home in Cincinnati. He immediately accused his wife of having been unfaithful while he was in prison, and on October 6, 1927, shot her to death in a Cincinnati park. He conducted his own defense, and although the verdict was guilty, the jury found him insane, and the court committed him to an asylum. A few months later he convinced the Ohio Court of Appeals that he was sane, and was released. He was never resentenced or tried again.

Early in 1925 the Prohibition Bureau began to gain at least a measure of control over the medicinal liquor situation. The number of permits to wholesalers was reduced to 446, and the privilege of selling the liquor was restricted to drug houses, which were required to carry at least twenty-five thousand dollars' worth of drugs in stock and to prove that the liquor business was not more than 10 per cent of their total volume. The regulations dealing with retail drugstores were also tightened, but were never strictly enforced. By 1930 legal withdrawals from the warehouses had been reduced to about 1,500,000 gallons a year, which was still considerably more than was actually needed but was only a small fraction of the total consumption. Armed robbery of warehouses declined when the bureau, acting under laws passed by Congress in 1923, began to concentrate the booze in a smaller number of storage places. This was a slow process, but in 1928 all the legal whiskey in the country was stored in thirty-seven warehouses. By that time, however, probably two thirds of the original supply was gone; it was officially admitted in Washington that one half had been withdrawn, in one way or another, by 1926.

3

Approximately a hundred million gallons of alcohol a year were manufactured during the prohibition era by licensed distilleries in nineteen states, Hawaii, and the District of Columbia. Most of it was made from cane- and beet-sugar molasses, although in the Middle West corn and other grains were used. All of this alcohol, except a small proportion kept for use in its pure state, passed through denaturing plants, where it was made unfit to drink by the addition of various substances, many of them poisonous. It was then concentrated in bonded warehouses, and released for sale by the government under three main classifications—pure, specially denatured, and completely denatured. The pure variety could be withdrawn only on permits issued by the Prohibition Bureau, and upon payment of a tax of about six dollars a gallon. It was used for medicinal and scientific purposes, and in the production of pharmaceuticals, candy, spices, extracts, and other preparations intended for human consumption. Permits were also required for specially denatured alcohol, but it was tax-free. It was necessary in the manufacture of cosmetics, insecticides, soap, photographic supplies, remedies for external use, and many other products. Completely denatured alcohol was also tax-free, but there were no restrictions upon its sale, purchase, or use. Anybody could buy it, and the government had no interest in what the purchaser did with it, although of course as a good American he was supposed to obey the law and not try to drink it. The principal use for this alcohol was in the manufacture of anti-freeze solutions for automobile radiators, but it was also needed in making paints and varnishes.

Several factors combined to make the problem of controlling the flow of industrial alcohol very difficult of solution, and for a good many years almost impossible. The attempt to enforce the Volstead Act and the Eighteenth Amendment paralleled an enormous expansion of the American chemical industry, and it was the established policy of the United States Government to foster and encourage this growth. In 1906, when the laws making denatured alcohol tax-free were passed by Congress, the legitimate demand was satisfied by a production of one million gallons. By 1910 this had increased to a little less than seven million gallons, and in 1920 it jumped to almost thirty million. The increase was even greater every year thereafter. At the beginning of prohibition, because of the large and uncertain demand, no restrictions were placed upon the quantity of alcohol a manufacturer might produce. The result, of course, was a tremendous overproduction of which the government knew little or nothing, and for which there was no outlet except the illicit liquor business.

For the usual reasons of incompetence, corruption, shortage of personnel, and, particularly, political meddling, the administration of the permit system was lax and slipshod. Mrs. Mabel Walker Willebrandt, Assistant Attorney General, wrote in *The Inside of Prohibition* in 1929 that "the policy of granting permit privileges has always been subject to so much political pressure that it has been marked by vacillation and puerility."[1] She might also have said pusillanimity and plain crookedness. In general an applicant had only to say that he was engaged, or about to engage, in the manufacture of products requiring the use of alcohol; keep silent about his criminal record, if any, and present the endorsement of a powerful politician. After 1921 it was helpful to be an enrolled Republican. If the application was refused, pressure could be brought to bear or recourse to the courts could be had; but as Mrs. Willebrandt pointed out, the Prohibition Bureau said no so seldom that few such suits were filed. In ten years only one reached the Supreme Court, where the government was upheld. In addition to the vast number of permits officially issued by the bureau, which Mrs. Willebrandt said "reached into higher mathematics" during the regime of General Lincoln C. Andrews, there was always a brisk business in forged and stolen permits, all of which were usually honored without investigation. Occasionally a permit was revoked, and the holder had to pay the politicians as high as twenty thousand dollars to get it restored.

Thousands of new companies appeared in the chemical industry; they far outnumbered the "wholesale" drug houses which were making such heavy inroads in the stocks of medicinal liquor. They were prepared and eager, they said, to manufacture anything in the chemical line, provided they were given enough alcohol. The financial backing of these concerns was usually provided by big bootleggers or gang chieftains, but as front men they frequently used politicians and federal and state officials; often they were granted permits when their political big shots solemnly asserted that they intended to manufacture something but wished to have supplies of alcohol on hand before they equipped their factories and sought customers. The vast majority of these companies never manufactured anything. They simply withdrew alcohol up to the limit of their permits, stored it awhile in warehouses, and then sent it along to the bootleggers, protecting themselves by means of fake corporations and partnerships known as "cover houses." These houses, supposedly wholesalers and jobbers, seldom possessed any more facilities for doing business than a desk, a fountain pen, and a supply of receipts.

The cover house was one of the safest and easiest methods of beating the prohibition laws ever devised, because the power of the Prohibition Bureau to investigate didn't extend beyond the original purchase of the alcohol. The holder of a permit would withdraw a certain quantity of denatured alcohol and turn it over to his bootleg principals, but his records would show that it had been used to manufacture, say, toilet water, which had been shipped to a cover house. A prohibition agent could make inquiries about the transaction between the permittee and the manufacturer of the alcohol, but the former could stop the investigation by simply producing a receipt from the cover house. If the agent called upon the cover house and asked what had become of the toilet water, he was told that it was none of his business. And under the law it wasn't. The only chance the authorities had of exposing a cover house was to intercept a shipment and find that it was alcohol and not the preparation it was supposed to be, or trace it and prove that the cover house never received it. Similar methods were used to get alcohol out of denaturing plants, which could always produce receipts for shipments of alcohol to manufacturers of cosmetics and other products. Sometimes they offered forged receipts from legitimate houses.

Diversion of industrial alcohol to the bootleggers was considerably reduced in the late 1920s by a determined attack upon the source, although it was never entirely stopped. For almost ten years no attempt was made to ascertain the actual alcohol requirements of the legitimate chemical industry, although such a survey was frequently urged by officials of the Department of Commerce. It was finally done, however, and regulations imposing production quotas were put into effect on January 1, 1928. As a further precaution against surpluses, no distillery was permitted to produce more than 40 per cent of its quota during the first six months of any year. Changes were also made in the system of handling permits; thereafter they were issued by state administrators instead of in Washington, which somewhat reduced, or at least distributed, the political pressure.

How much alcohol was diverted into the illicit liquor trade was anybody's guess, and estimates varied widely. Chester P. Mills, prohibition administrator for the New York City area, said that in 1926 sixteen denaturing plants in the metropolis turned out eleven million gallons, of which about ten million went into the manufacture of bootleg hooch. Emory R. Buckner, United States Attorney for the southern district of New York, declared that the total diversion in 1926 was sixty million gallons. He estimated the value of the booze made from industrial alcohol, in New York and Pennsylvania alone, at $3,600,-000,000 a year. General Lincoln C. Andrews told a congressional committee that one million gallons a month was being diverted in Philadelphia in 1926, and that the country-wide total was enough to make 150,000,000 quarts of booze annually.

Dr. James M. Doran, then chief chemist of the Prohibition Bureau, disputed General Andrews's statement: he estimated that in 1926 the bootleggers' share of a total production of 105,000,000 gallons of alcohol was only thirteen million gallons. Dr. Doran was Prohibition Commissioner in 1928, when the quota system was established; he testified later in the year that industrial alcohol presented "only a minor enforcement problem. It has to be watched all the time," he said, "but the leakages are comparatively small." Late in 1930 the bureau estimated that in that year the booze boys managed to get hold of five million gallons, a little more than 4 per cent of the total production. During the remaining years of the dry era, according to government records, the diversion was even less.

4

The government eventually managed to reduce the diversion of medicinal liquor and industrial alcohol, and to make life fairly miserable for the smugglers, but it was never able to do much about the moonshiners. During the first few years of prohibition the illicit distillers made whiskey, or at least they called it whiskey, and some continued to do so, especially in isolated areas. After about 1925, however, the great majority concentrated on alcohol, which was easier to make, required no storage, and netted a larger profit. In time they became more important than all other sources combined. As General Lincoln C. Andrews gloomily put it in 1926, "When we cut off one source of supply, moonshine wells up to fill the gap." Two years later the Prohibition Commissioner said that the moonshiners were producing eight times as much alcohol as was being diverted to bootleggers from government warehouses. Many observers thought this estimate was too low.

Stills were everywhere—in the mountains, on the farms, in the small towns and villages, and in the cities. In New York, Chicago, Detroit, Pittsburgh, and other cities with large foreign populations, the pungent odor of fermenting mash and alcoholic distillate hung over whole sections twenty-four hours a day. West Madison Street in Chicago, from the edge of the Loop to Halsted Street and beyond, smelled like a distillery throughout the dry era; in 1928 the Chicago police estimated that at least a hundred stills were running full blast in every block.

In many places the operations of the moonshiners created problems of waste disposal, as in North Tarrytown, New York, where the sewer inspector officially asked them not to flush the refuse from their stills down the drains. Prune pits, potato peelings, grain, and other discards were clogging the sewers.

The Rev. Francis Kasackszul, a Catholic priest of Sugar Notch, a coal-mining town in Luzerne County, Pennsylvania, told a congressional committee in 1926 that since prohibition began liquor had been manufactured in "practically every other home" in his community. "They make it, they drink it, they sell it," he said. A survey published in 1925 by the Federal Council of Churches of Christ in America said, "The illicit liquor traffic has become a means of comparative opulence to many families that formerly were on the records of relief agencies. In one New England industrial town a row of somber tenements has been adorned with Stutz and Packard cars purchased with the profits of a new-found illicit livelihood." In many foreign families the children were taught to mind the still, while Mama bought the ingredients and prepared the mash, and Papa sold the product, after liberal samplings by all members of the family.

An enormous mass of similar testimony was accumulated by congressional committees, the Wickersham Commission, and other investigating agencies. Mrs. Viola M. Anglin, deputy chief probation officer for New York City, assigned to the family court in Manhattan, quoted the sixteen deputies under her supervision. "They tell me," she said, "that in each one of their districts you can find from one hundred to one hundred and fifty, and in some of them two hundred, stills. And these stills are not operated alone in cigar stores, delicatessen stores, and all sorts of places, but they are operated also in the homes of the people who live in the tenements. You open the door of a tenement and walk in, and the first thing you get is a whiff of liquor, or some kind of alcohol. . . ." Mrs. Anglin told of a case of nonsupport in which the father of a family had been sent to jail. A week or so later a probation officer called at the family's tenement home, intending to refer the mother and her three children to a relief agency. She found that they had moved into a larger apartment and were doing splendidly.

The mother was operating a still in her living room, and the liquor she made was sold by her brother and brother-in-law. The children were happy, well-dressed, and much interested in the new business.

Moonshining or alky cooking in the big cities was a highly organized racket controlled by the gang leaders in association with their political henchmen, although of course there were many little independents whose operations were too small to interest the big shots. As a rule the gangsters provided the stills and the raw materials, and employed the tenement dwellers to handle the details of manufacturing, to barrel or bottle the alcohol, and to have it ready for shipment when the collecting trucks made their periodic calls. Sometimes the men who actually made the moonshine were given a small percentage of the profits, sometimes they worked on a straight wage basis, and sometimes they were simply told that they and their families would be murdered unless they ran the stills, obeyed orders, and kept their mouths shut. The gang captains sold the alcohol to wholesale bootleggers or ran it through their own cutting plants and themselves supplied the speakeasies and the retail dealers. A great deal was sold to consumers without further treatment—raw, fiery stuff that could scarcely be drunk without the addition of ginger ale or orange juice. Most people turned it into the beverage known in prohibition times as gin.

Virtually all of the Italian moonshiners, who formed the largest racial group engaged in the business, worked for the Unione Siciliana, or for the gang leaders who controlled the Unione's loosely connected branches. This organization, which was more or less an offshoot of the Mafia, was founded in the early 1900s by Ignazio Saietta, a Sicilian counterfeiter and professional murderer who was also known as Ignazio Lupo and Lupo the Wolf. Under Lupo's leadership the Unione engaged in a criminal business in women, narcotics, extortion, kidnaping, burglary, bank robbery, counterfeiting, and murder. In less than half a dozen years Unione gunmen committed sixty homicides, the details of which were known to the United States Secret Service, which investigated Lupo and his followers because of their counterfeiting operations. About half of these killings occurred in the Little Italy section of New York, in the vicinity of East 125th Street. In

1920 the current leader, Joe (The Boss) Masseria, reorganized the Unione for bootlegging and moonshining, although other activities were continued and the gang also worked in the field of industrial and labor-union racketeering. The branches that Lupo the Wolf had formed in Chicago, Detroit, and other cities with large Italian districts were strengthened, but not until several bloody gang wars had been fought for control. Largely because of the protection afforded by Frankie Yale of Brooklyn and Al Capone and the murderous Genna brothers of Chicago, Joe the Boss managed to retain his national leadership until 1931, when he was shot down. Lucky Luciano, the notorious pander who was later convicted and deported, was with Masseria at the time, and succeeded Joe the Boss as the big shot of the Unione.

Criminal gangs, generally with big-city connections, also controlled moonshining in many country areas, especially in the Middle West and the South; they induced farmers, by money payments or threats, to run their stills. Typical of these outfits were the Traum gang of St. Louis and Terre Haute, Indiana, and the Stephens gang of San Antonio, Texas. The latter, protected by state and county officials and political leaders, handled the production of twenty-three large stills which had been set up on farms in the vicinity of San Antonio. Extensive aging and cutting plants were maintained, and the gang supplied most of that part of Texas with liquor. When the gang was exposed, following a pistol battle in which a prohibition agent was killed, indictments were obtained against seventy-six persons, including the assistant district attorney of Bexar County and the chief investigator for the state of Texas.

The Traum gang was a group of about a dozen St. Louis hoodlums, most of whom had served prison sentences for bank robbery in Illinois and Missouri. In 1928 these ruffians invaded Terre Haute, Indiana, where they opened offices and made the usual arrangements with state and county officials and prohibition agents. The gang handled the output of thirty-seven big stills, some of which could produce a thousand gallons of alcohol a day. All the liquor-making plants were on farms in two adjacent Indiana counties, and with their combined production the Traums supplied that part of the state and ran convoys of alcohol-laden trucks to St. Louis, East St. Louis, and Louisville. The gang owned only a few of the stills; the operators of the others, in addition to turning over their entire output, were compelled to pay a tribute of $1.50 on every barrel of mash and fifty cents on each one-hundred-pound sack of sugar. From these sources the gang collected about thirteen thousand dollars a week.

A government report on the operations of the Traums, prepared by the Department of Justice for the Wickersham Commission, said that two murders were committed by the gang. "This combine," the report continued, "owned a number of Thompson machine guns and terrorized the community, in some instances, by going to the homes of farmers, placing guns in their backs, and forcing them to put stills on their farms. . . . The deputy administrator at Indianapolis raided one of these stills, and secured a confession from the farmer on whose property the still in question was located. On the following day the farmer was killed by machine-gun fire as he drove through one of the main streets of Terre Haute." The government investigated the Traum gang early in 1930, and thirty-five members of the outfit were indicted. Of these, twenty-nine were convicted, and sentenced to serve a total of thirty-six years in prison and to pay fines aggregating twenty-five thousand dollars. This seems to be a long time and a lot of money; actually, it averaged considerably less than a year in jail and a fine of one thousand dollars for each defendant.

The hundreds of thousands of moonshine stills which operated day and night from the Atlantic to the Pacific and from the Gulf of Mexico to the Canadian border were of all sizes and types. They ranged from crude homemade contraptions with a capacity of five gallons or less to huge, well-equipped distilleries capable of producing two thousand gallons of high-proof alcohol a day. Many of the big plants were in Chicago, where the political protection was unexcelled, and some were in New York, Detroit, and other cities where politicians and gangsters were playfellows. In 1927 federal agents captured a moonshine plant in Detroit which occupied an acre of space in a Twelfth Street warehouse and had cost at least $250,000 to equip. It contained, among other things, thirty-four vats, each holding two thousand gallons of mash, and a still which could turn out fifteen hundred gallons of alcohol in twenty-four hours. This plant was discovered because, despite their huge investment and the obvious necessity for undercover operation, the moonshiners stole electric current from other tenants of the warehouse, thus saving at the most a few hundred dollars a year.

Prohibition agents seized an enormous number of stills in the course of the noble experiment; according to the records of the bureau, a total of 696,933 were captured in the five years from 1921 to 1925. Of these, 172,537 were found in 1925. General Lincoln C. Andrews presented these figures to a congressional committee in 1926 and remarked, "This means that a great many people are distilling." He estimated that five hundred thousand persons were engaged in the moonshine business, and expressed the opinion that for every still seized nine remained undiscovered. This would seem to be a very poor record, but when everything is considered, it is much better than it sounds. The Prohibition Bureau never had more than twenty-three hundred field agents, and if the entire force had done nothing but search for moonshine stills, which were widely scattered all over the United States, each man would have had to patrol 1,316 square miles of territory. State, county, and city authorities were never of much help in the never-ending quest for illicit liquor-makers; by and large, the moonshiners and the gangsters were their pals.

5

The Volstead Act outlawed beer, which had long been the favorite tipple of the American people, but permitted the manufacture of "cereal beverage" with an alcoholic content of not more than one half of 1 per cent, a concoction which became widely, but not favorably, known as near beer. All breweries were supposed to close when the Eighteenth Amendment went into effect, and to reopen only if granted permits to operate as cereal-beverage plants. The system under which these permits were issued was similar to that used for the withdrawal of alcohol and medicinal liquor, and was administered in the same irresponsible manner and subject to the same corruption and political pressure. When the regulations dealing with beer were being prepared by the experts of the Treasury Department, several forward-looking federal officials suggested that permits be restricted to large, long-established breweries, which had millions of dollars invested in plant and equipment, and would be more apt to obey the law than smaller concerns with little or nothing to lose. It was also proposed that permits be issued slowly until it had been determined how much near beer the country would consume. Such a policy would have greatly simplified the problem of policing the beer industry. But the politicians opposed it with great vehemence; they screamed indignantly that this was a free country and that every man should have a chance to get into the near-beer racket if he so desired. Consequently, permits were granted, as Mrs. Mabel Walker Willebrandt put it, to "any person with a nice clean face and no guns sticking out of his pockets"; he merely had to fill out an application form and present it with the endorsement of a congressman or other politician. On the rare occasions when an investigation was made, it was confined to inquiries addressed to the persons whom the applicant had named as references. Government records show that a minimum of five hundred plants made near beer throughout the dry era, forty in New York City alone. And there were many special and temporary permits which were not listed. Ten or a dozen big breweries, such as Anheuser-Busch in St. Louis, Pabst in Milwaukee, and Ruppert in New York, could have supplied all the cereal beverages needed; except in one year, 1921, the production never exceeded two hundred million gallons. This was a very small percentage of the consumption of real beer before prohibition; and, for that matter, a not much larger percentage of the consumption of real beer *during* prohibition.

The control of beer production was hopeless from the beginning, partly because of the chronic shortage of prohibition agents and partly because of a simple fact of manufacturing which nullified any serious attempt to enforce the law. In order to make near beer it was necessary first to manufacture real beer containing from 3 to 8 per cent alcohol. The excess alcohol was then drawn off until it had been reduced to the legal limit of one half of 1 per cent. The alcohol thus removed was supposed to be shipped to government warehouses for denaturing, but a great deal was diverted to bootleggers and cutting plants. There was nothing to compel the brewer to lower the alcoholic content of his beer except his conscience—and almost everybody's conscience seems to have been on vacation during the fourteen years of the Eighteenth Amendment. "If a brewer is disposed to violate the law," said the Prohibition Commissioner in 1930, "it is just a question of putting a hose in a high-powered beer tank and filling near-beer kegs with the high-powered beer and running it out as near beer. So it is a rather difficult thing to get at."

Prohibition agents were seldom able to make a case against a brewery suspected of sending out real beer unless they captured a shipment in transit; beer away from the brewery was evidence. It was comparatively easy to escape the few men assigned to watch the breweries, and enormous quantities of real beer were shipped as cereal beverage. Some of the breweries, when caught, were found to have no sales departments to handle near beer, and no customers. Many brewers honestly tried to obey the law and to build up a legitimate business in real beer, but they couldn't control all of their employees; there were always some who would accept bribes from the bootleggers and run real beer out at night. The big beer rings employed expert "beer shooters" to handle such operations. Scores of brewers sent near beer openly to the speakeasies, but followed it with secret shipments of alcohol to bring the stuff up to full strength. Sometimes this was done in speakeasy cellars by forcing the alcohol into a barrel of beer with a compression pump. In many places, however, the bartender squirted a little alcohol into each glass as it was served. This was the famous needled beer which caused so many stomach-aches and so much unpleasant drunkenness; it contained anywhere from 3 to 20 per cent alcohol, depending upon the generosity of the bartender or the speakeasy proprietor. There was a big profit in beer; a half keg cost about one dollar to make, and the brewer sold it for twenty-five to thirty dollars. At twenty-five to fifty cents a glass, over the bar, it brought from seventy-five to one hundred and twenty-five dollars.

The beer situation was further complicated by the introduction of "wort," which was first manufactured in Chicago, spread quickly to Wisconsin and thence throughout the country. Wort was simply beer in which the manufacturing processes had been halted before the addition of yeast. To make beer, the purchaser simply dropped a cake of yeast into the wort, let the mixture ferment, and then filtered it. Since wort contained no alcohol, it was a perfectly legal commodity, and was sold openly everywhere. Many breweries abandoned the production of near beer and concentrated on wort. It gave a tremendous impetus to home-brewing, and was a great help to the wildcat, or moonshine, breweries. Many of these were "alley breweries," which were really large home-brew units. They were operated by the thousands in tenement cellars, abandoned buildings, caves, and wherever else they could find concealment. In the aggregate they manufactured a great deal of bad beer, which was always sold green. The usual reaction to a few glasses of alley beer was described by a Detroit businessman to a Detroit *News* reporter in 1928: "The beer tastes wonderful, but after I've had a couple of glasses I'm terribly sleepy. Sometimes my eyes don't seem to focus and my head aches. I'm not intoxicated, understand, merely feel as if I've been drawn through a knothole."

In theory, all breweries to which near-beer permits had been refused were immediately dismantled, in such a manner as to make the manufacture of beer impossible. In practice, the dismantling usually consisted of the formal removal, by a prohibition agent, of a section of pipe. Since the government men seldom inspected a "dismantled" brewery, hundreds of brewers immediately replaced the pipe, or substituted a piece of rubber hose, and resumed the production of beer. When General Smedley D. Butler, of the Marine Corps, was assigned to clean up Philadelphia, he was told before he left Washington that he must confine his activities to alcohol and whiskey, as the federal authorities were taking care of the breweries. They were indeed. General Butler found thirteen, all supposedly dismantled, running full blast. He immediately wrote to the prohibition administrator for the

Philadelphia district, describing the situation and asking what action the administrator's office intended to take. Several months later he received a letter from the assistant administrator, who wrote that little could be done because "suspicion is attached to a majority of the employees on whom we have to depend for results." General Butler then publicly threatened to raid the breweries, and was promptly notified by the United States Marshal's office that any policeman who entered a Philadelphia brewery would be shot. That angered the old war horse, and he sent cops into the breweries. They performed the operation without casualties, and brought the operators of the plants into the city courts. The cases against twelve were immediately dismissed, and a small fine was imposed upon the thirteenth.

Roy A. Haynes, Prohibition Administrator, said in 1923 that the great beer centers of the country were Chicago, New York, Detroit, Atlantic City, Philadelphia, St. Louis, Baltimore, New Orleans, and Buffalo. There were many others, however, just as important; breweries operated, either as wildcats or in the guise of near-beer manufacturers, in every state and in almost every city. One of the largest producing areas was northern Illinois; it "teemed with breweries" which made huge quantities of beer for Chicago, Detroit, and other midwestern cities. It also produced Lawrence Crowley of Joliet, Illinois, better known as Butch, who called himself King of the Beer Runners and who was one of the fantastic characters of the early years of the dry era. Crowley was the son of a Joliet dogcatcher, and when prohibition began he was working in a garage as a mechanic's helper and occasionally driving a taxicab. He started bootlegging in a small way, and as business increased spent a large part of his profits making political connections.

About the middle of 1921 Crowley suddenly bloomed as the big shot of a beer ring which controlled more than twenty breweries, scattered from Joliet to the Wisconsin line. He made an enormous lot of money—and loved to spend it. He was married early in 1922, and gave the priest one thousand dollars. He wore a four-carat diamond ring, and two platinum wrist watches, one set with diamonds. He carried a roll of fifty thousand dollars in a pants pocket, and displayed it at every opportunity. He drove a different car every day in the week; he owned eight, one a spare. He bought a fourteen-room house in an exclusive residential section of Joliet and equipped it from cellar to attic with gold doorknobs. He bought the garage where he had worked. When the Commercial Club blackballed him, he bought the business block in which the club was located and ordered it to move. He bought the Joliet *Times* and assigned the paper's best writer to turn out editorials signed "Lawrence Crowley." He buried his mother in a fifteen-hundred-dollar casket and erected a twenty-five-thousand-dollar monument over her grave.

He was a notable spender and put a great deal of money into circulation, but he made one big mistake—he did all of his splurging in his home town. Everybody talked about Butch, and eventually the gossip reached the ears of Mrs. Mabel Reineke, a go-getting young woman who was serving her first term as Collector of Internal Revenue for the Chicago district, of which Joliet was a part. She ordered an investigation, and it was found that Crowley had never even heard of the income tax. The government thereupon unlimbered its arsenal of liens, writs, and other lethal weapons, and demanded back income taxes amounting to several hundred thousand dollars, with penalties. Within a year the federal tax hounds had stripped Crowley of his wealth, and he started all over again in the bootleg business. But he was never able to regain his former eminence.

6

Although wine was somewhat harder to come by than in pre-prohibition times, those who liked to tarry at the wine cup never lacked supplies for their bibbing. The framers of the Volstead Act gave them a head start in the race for booze by including a provision permitting a householder to possess two hundred gallons of grape juice or cider a year, strictly for the use of himself and his family. It was assumed that of course nature would co-operate and not let the grape juice ferment or the cider get hard. This was intended to placate the farmers, but everybody took advantage of it. The winegrowers, much

gratified and anticipating a further demand, greatly increased their production of grapes; in California alone the acreage devoted to vini-
culture jumped from ninety-seven thousand acres in 1919 to 680,796
in 1926. Grape juice was sold in stores which specialized in materials
and equipment for home liquor-making, and in grocery stores and other
establishments, and by door-to-door salesmen in five- to twenty-gallon
kegs. Each keg was accompanied by a printed notice warning the
purchaser not to do so-and-so. "If you do," the notice said, "this grape
juice will ferment and turn into wine. That would be illegal." In every
home where wine was liked, the cellar, garage, or a closet usually
held a keg of grape juice quietly obeying the call of nature and violating the Volstead Act. However, there was a dearth of really good
wine, even though almost any bootlegger would gladly supply the
finest French champagnes and still wines; that is, the bottles looked
authentic and bore the labels of famous foreign producers. Actually,
99 per cent of the still wines came from tenement cellars, and almost
all of the champagne was cider pumped full of air and needled with a
little alcohol. Prohibition agents in New York raided forty night clubs
in 1926 and seized some eight thousand cases of champagne, all of
which was analyzed. Not one drop was genuine.

The most important source of professionally made wines was the
large stocks stored in government warehouses and intended for the
manufacture of vinegar and for religious purposes. As soon as prohibition began, new vinegar-manufacturing plants appeared all over the
country, and of course had no trouble getting permits to withdraw
wine. Before the dry era twenty vinegar factories supplied the needs
of New York and Connecticut; by the middle of 1922 more than a
hundred had received permits in these states, and were withdrawing
nine hundred thousand gallons of wine a year. The government finally
solved this problem by loading the wine with acetic acid before it was
shipped to the plants, so that it was vinegar when the vinegar men
got it. This didn't hamper the operations of those who were really
making vinegar, but it was a serious blow to the fakes. They tried
various reagents, but found none that was effective for more than ten
days or two weeks, after which the wine became vinegar again. They

lost their customers, and after struggling for a year most of them quit in disgust.

Far more serious was the leakage of sacramental wines, of which the Jews were the largest legitimate consumers. The Protestants and the Catholics caused very little trouble; they use no sacramental wines in their homes, and not very much in their church services. Most of the Protestant denominations, in fact, use unfermented grape juice. Moreover, the Protestant ministers and the Catholic priests are under the control of their bishops and can be disciplined. The Jews, on the other hand, use a great deal of sacramental wine in both their homes and synagogues. And since the Jewish faith is not organized, in the sense that the hierarchal churches are, the rabbi is under no control. Under the regulations of the Prohibition Bureau a Jewish family was permitted one gallon of wine a year for each adult member, up to a total of five gallons. They purchased the wine from the rabbi, who received a withdrawal permit upon presentation of a list of the members of his congregation and an approximate estimate of their needs.

A few real rabbis went crooked, withdrew more wine than was required, and trafficked with bootleggers, but the proportion was small. The trouble was that anyone could become a rabbi upon being certified as such by a senior rabbi, and the senior rabbis were gentle, unsuspicious old men with an abiding faith in the goodness of humanity, and easily imposed upon. Even a proper certification was not always necessary; to the Prohibition Bureau any man who dressed in solemn black, possessed a Jewish cast of countenance, and wore a beard was automatically a rabbi. Many of the membership lists were later found to have been copied from telephone directories, and contained names of Christian ministers, Irishmen, business houses, and factories. Some applicants didn't even bother to prepare lists, but bought them from the clerks in the various prohibition offices, paying ten to twenty-five cents a name. One young woman in New York did a prosperous business in lists for more than two years; she came to work in a two-thousand-dollar automobile, wore diamonds and fur coats, and lived in a big apartment. Her salary was forty dollars a week.

The result of these goings on was that the big cities swarmed with fake rabbis busily diverting wine to bootleggers. Many opened wine stores; they were supposed to sell only to members of their own congregations and to Jews certified by other rabbis. Actually, they sold to everyone. In some the stocks included such unusual sacramental items as champagne, vermouth, cordials, and even gin. Izzy Einstein, the celebrated dry sleuth, investigated almost two hundred rabbis during his five years as a prohibition agent, and found some curious things. One rabbi's synagogue consisted of a tiny hall bedroom in a tenement flat; his congregation was a mailing list for which he had paid ten dollars. Another rabbi ran a butcher shop, a second a pork store, and a third a pool parlor with dice games in the back room. Izzy bought wine from a score of stores, and was asked for no identification. Only one refused to sell, on the ground that Izzy didn't look Jewish enough. So Izzy sent another agent around to make the purchase, which he did. His name was Dennis J. Donovan.

After a series of conferences with prominent rabbis, General Lincoln C. Andrews in 1926 put in effect a new set of rules for the issuance and renewal of permits. All lists were carefully checked, and all applicants were required to submit letters from their bishops, or, in the case of Jews, from leading laymen of their congregations. Within one year withdrawals of sacramental wine had been reduced from well over two million gallons to a little more than six hundred thousand. In 1928 the Prohibition Commissioner said, "There is no troublesome situation in sacramental wine as it affects law enforcement."

CHAPTER TWELVE

Smugglers Afloat and Ashore

American drinkers first heard the good news about Rum Row in July 1921, when some of the New York newspapers reported briefly that several strange ships lying offshore were believed to be selling liquor. All doubt was soon dispelled. Within a few months rum ships were strung out along the Atlantic coast from Maine to Florida, busily dodging the Coast Guard and discharging their cargoes of booze. The number varied, for they were constantly coming and going, but at times as many as a hundred vessels were in line. Another, but much smaller, Row was operating in the Gulf of Mexico, principally off Tampa, Mobile, New Orleans, Galveston, and other Gulf ports. A third was beginning to form on the Pacific coast, bringing liquor down from Vancouver and up from Mexico and Lower California; eventually it extended from Seattle to San Diego. The western rum fleet, however, was never as large or as important as the one on the Atlantic coast; it was too far from the main sources of supply and the big eastern markets.

Segments of the fleet lay off Savannah, Norfolk, Baltimore, Boston, and other eastern seaboard cities, but the greatest concentrations were off Long Island and the coast of New

Jersey. There was also a large group of ships off Florida, but it is doubtful if they brought in as much liquor as the swarm of speedboats and other small craft which scurried back and forth between the Florida coast and the little Bahama islands of Bimini and Gun Cay. Most of the larger ships were New England fishing schooners, with a carrying capacity of from one thousand to three thousand cases, and were manned by American seamen, with a sprinkling of Canadians and sponge fishermen from the West Indies. Converted yachts and a few boats from Lunenburg and Halifax also appeared in the fleet, and occasionally a rusty old tramp steamer or an ancient windjammer wallowed across the Atlantic with a cargo of French wines and brandies, Belgian alcohol, and other European liquors. One ship which was seen frequently during the early days of Rum Row was identified as a former light cruiser of the Spanish Navy, which had been abandoned in Cuban waters during the Spanish-American War. The rum fleet loaded most of its liquor at Nassau, in the Bahamas, but the ports of Cuba and Bermuda also furnished many cargoes. In fact, the whole West Indies was dripping with booze, most of which was eventually smuggled into the United States.

For the first year or so, while American officials floundered about wondering what to do about it, the rum ships anchored well within the three-mile limit, sometimes so close that the Manhattan skyline was visible from their decks. They sold to all comers, and the buyers came out from shore in every imaginable type of boat, from rowboats to fast speedboats and skiffs kicked along by outboard motors. Some of the power boats not only carried loads but towed light barges piled high with liquor. There is a record of one small-time bootlegger who rowed out to the rum fleet half a dozen times every night for a month, hauling three or four cases on each trip. As the big booze syndicates ashore perfected their organization, however, and the Coast Guard pushed the rum ships farther out to sea, the small independents gradually disappeared. The business of bringing the liquor ashore was in the hands of big shots who sent their own buyers to the West Indies, and even to England, chartered the ships, and loaded their own cargoes. They also built their own speedboats, and put larger vessels into the ocean-going trade, some of them big enough to carrry from thirty thousand to fifty thousand cases. Mannie Kessler, a New York wholesale bootlegger who had connections with several syndicates, once brought in a cargo of scotch and brandy worth $850,000 before cutting. His personal profit from this and a few smaller ventures was said to have amounted to more than two-hundred-thousand dollars in three months.

For the ship-to-shore run the syndicates used big boats, some of which could handle a thousand cases. Some of these craft were seventy-five-footers powered by three Liberty engines, with speeds up to fifty miles an hour. On a trial spin one ran circles around the French liner *Ile de France* while the big ship was outward bound at full speed. It was not until the late 1920s that the Coast Guard had boats fast enough to get within hailing distance of these craft. Even then the bootleggers kept one jump ahead. Specifications of the government boats were always published, and the syndicates simply took them to a shipyard and said, "Make us something ten knots faster than this." Some of the rumrunners installed armor plate around the driving cockpits of their boats, and a few experimented with suits of armor for the crews. These innovations were soon abandoned, however, because of the additional weight. What the smugglers wanted most was speed. The fast boats began operating in the late summer of 1922, but didn't get into the news very much until December 1923, when they landed liquor worth $250,000 on a beach near Atlantic City in a few hours. It was common knowledge in New York that this shipment was coming, and a great sigh of relief arose when the newspapers announced that the landing had been successful. A bountiful supply of booze for the holiday needs of the metropolis was assured.

The Coast Guard cutters and patrol boats captured many small craft, but caught very few of the big, fast boats. Their most effective method was to cruise in the vicinity of a rum ship, which, being under foreign registry, was safe while anchored outside the American territorial limit, and seize the speedboat when it came up to load. The rumrunners tried many tricks to lure the Coast Guard boats away.

Sometimes they faked engine breakdowns; again, they sent other boats, apparently loaded, laboring past. If the cutters succumbed to the latter ruse, the laden craft led them for a while, then threw a lot of empty boxes overboard, put on speed, and vanished. One night two speedboats approached a rum ship carrying several thousand cases of liquor, and found it attended by three Coast Guard cutters, all armed with machine guns and three-inch cannon. The rum boats went farther up the Row, and located an old tub with only a few hundred cases on board. They bought both cargo and ship, the latter for two thousand dollars, and then sent the vessel some two or three miles out to sea, where it was set on fire. When the Coast Guard rushed to the rescue, as it was bound to do, the speedboats came alongside the rum ship and took her liquor aboard.

Despite the slowness of the government craft, the Coast Guard optimistically tried to overhaul every rum boat sighted, and some of the chases were very spectacular, with much shooting and casualties on both sides—eighteen rumrunners killed and wounded and eight coastguardmen killed up to November 2, 1929, according to government records. Some curious things happened during these pursuits. Once on a dark night in 1923 a speedboat was slipping in to unload a rum ship from Nassau when a cutter loomed up ahead. The captain of the rum boat immediately put on power and threw his wheel over, but his clutch jammed and he made four complete circuits of the Coast Guard boat at full speed, with the crews of both crafts yelling and shooting. On the third time around, one of the men on the speedboat fell overboard. When the boat came by again, it was slowed a trifle while crewmen scooped the unfortunate out of the water. By that time the clutch had been repaired, and the speedboat scooted away in the darkness. Later the captain of the rum ship congratulated the speedboat skipper on the daring rescue.

"Hell!" said the rumrunner. "That bastard's our buyer. He had forty thousand dollars in his pocket!"

More than once the pursuit of a speedboat led through the maze of water-borne traffic in New York Harbor and in the East and Hudson rivers. These chases aroused great excitement, with guns roaring and ferryboats and other craft dodging bullets and shells and voicing their fear and indignation with wild whistle tooting and bell clanging. As far as is known, nobody was killed or hurt in these runs, but many narrow escapes were reported, and there were several minor collisions. The most spectacular chase of this sort occurred on a hot Sunday afternoon in July 1924, when a Coast Guard cutter pursued two fifty-foot speedboats along the Coney Island beach front in full view of a hundred thousand bathers in the water and lolling on the sand. The three boats raced at full speed, with the smugglers firing pistols and submachine guns and the cutter trying to hit the rumrunners with three-inch shells, none of which fell within a hundred yards of the targets. Two policemen, excited by the yelling and screaming of the crowd, ran to the end of the Steeplechase Pier and began shouting, "Stop! Stop!" When the rumrunners waved at them, but kept going, the cops fired their revolvers into the air until they ran out of ammunition.

The establishment of Rum Row caused considerable rejoicing, for everybody was sure that the ships were bringing in good liquor. Most of them were, but the ultimate consumer saw very little of it until it had gone through the cutting plants. And all of the liquor brought ashore from the Row was not good; some of the ships were nothing more than floating booze factories. They carried cargoes of cheap, low-grade Cuban alcohol and a few cases of real whiskey, and manufactured hooch while anchored off the coast. It was then sent ashore and sold as smuggled liquor at an enormous profit to everybody concerned. Whatever supplies they lacked were sent out from shore; in 1923 the Coast Guard seized a large lighter loaded with bottles, labels, revenue stamps, flavoring extracts, and other things necessary to the production of fake whiskey. It was also not uncommon for a bootleg gang to unload the good liquor from a ship and replace it with booze from its own cutting plant. The vessel would then move to another point on the Row and sell the cargo as genuine stuff.

Rum Row was a great thing for the retail bootlegger; he sold ten times as much "smuggled" liquor as the ships ever brought to American shores. It was also productive of many scandals, what with coastguardmen brooding protectively over the fleet, while ashore cops and prohibition agents helped the bootleggers unload their cargoes, and the politicians stood by to pull wires if anybody got into trouble. Newspaper and magazine writers hailed the advent of the rum fleet with delight. There had been a few spectacular raids, but the gang wars hadn't begun, and as far as exciting copy was concerned, the pickings had been pretty slim. Here at last was something they could really get their teeth into. They sailed into the story of the rumrunners with rhetoric flying and adjectives falling like rain. The volume of romantic gush written about Rum Row compared very favorably, both in quality and quantity, with the enormous output during the journalistic beatification of the great gang chieftains a few years later.

The run from the West Indies to the American coast, probably the safest and simplest sea voyage in the world, became an epic adventure in which the bold rumrunners were beset by more perils than Ulysses or the Argonauts. They battled their way northward against gales, earthquakes, battleships, destroyers, submarines, trigger-happy coastguardmen, pirates, hordes of flying W.C.T.U.s, and under-water battalions of vicious Anti-Saloon Leaguers. All this was very exciting to the journalists who managed to wangle places in speed-boats operating from shore, or who made the run from Nassau, but to the crewmen of these vessels life appears to have been pretty hum-drum. One man who worked on a small boat did a lot of talking before a federal grand jury in New York in 1927. "It wasn't exciting," he said. "That's only newspaper talk. It was just hard work—running the boat, dodging the destroyers and picket boats, loading those hundreds of cases off the schooner, loading them on the speedboat, unloading again at a dock." However, the pay was good. The men who brought the ships in from the West Indies received as high as one hundred dollars a week, while those who ran the small boats were paid an average of about fifty dollars for each trip. The captain of a speedboat got about two hundred dollars.

Not unnaturally, many of the rum-ship captains believed what was written about them and began to fancy themselves as throwbacks to earlier times when pirates and freebooters ravaged the western seas. They swaggered and swashbuckled afloat and ashore, and were righteously indignant when the Coast Guard laid them by the heels. Several of the rum ships were owned by women, a few of whom went to sea; they tried earnestly to conform to the tradition of Anne Bonney and Mary Read. One of the most illustrious of these ladies was a Florida woman known as Spanish Marie, who took over her husband's ship when he fell overboard in 1926 after excessive sampling of his cargo. She strutted about with a revolver strapped to her waist and a big knife stuck in her belt and a red bandanna tied about her head. Legend has it that she was about as tough as she looked. Spanish Marie enlarged her activities in 1927, and began smuggling narcotics and aliens as well as liquor, and also bought a few small boats to land her cargoes and a fleet of trucks to handle them after they were ashore. She was captured in March 1928, while unloading liquor on the beach at Coconut Grove, near Miami, and was released on five hundred dollars' bail on the plea that she must take care of her babies. The bail was increased to thirty-five hundred dollars when investigators found the children at home with a nurse and Spanish Marie at a speakeasy. However, the record doesn't show that she was ever tried.

The founder of Rum Row and the King of the Rum Runners, according to his autobiography,[1] was Captain Bill McCoy, widely known as "the real McCoy," who often compared himself to John Hancock and other patriotic smugglers of colonial times. In his own account of his exploits, McCoy suggested that Hancock, who ran cargoes of liquor and other illicit commodities into the American colonies, "might stand as the patron saint of rum runners." Whether McCoy actually invented the phrase "the real McCoy" is unknown, but he certainly popularized it. He bought and sold his own booze, sometimes in partnership with wholesalers in Nassau and in this country, but he had no tie-ups with the big bootleg syndicates and was notorious along Rum Row for selling good liquor and dealing fairly with the purchasers. He often boasted that he handled nothing but "the real McCoy." The expression spread through the liquor industry and soon found a place in the body of American slang. Even today anything that is strictly as advertised and on the level is referred to as "the real McCoy." The doughty captain also claimed to have been the first to run liquor out of St. Pierre et Miquelon, French islands off the coast of Newfoundland, which for various reasons became the principal base for smuggling operations after about 1924. McCoy is generally credited with the invention of the "burlock," which revolutionized methods of loading and stowing liquor cargoes. The burlock was a package containing six straw-jacketed bottles, three on the bottom layer, two in the middle, and one on top. The bottles were sewed tightly in burlap. Liquor packed in burlocks required a third less space in the hold of a vessel than when shipped in the ordinary bulky, wooden boxes.

McCoy was an upstate New Yorker who went to Florida with his brother in 1898. When prohibition began he was struggling with a small line of pleasure boats and coastwise freighters. In the spring of 1921 he sailed for Nassau in command of the schooner *Marshall,* with a guaranteed salary of one hundred dollars a day and a contract to carry fifteen hundred cases of liquor to Savannah. He found plenty of liquor in Nassau, with a few rumrunners already dickering with local dealers over cargoes. During the year or so that preceded prohibition many American distillers shipped large quantities of rye and bourbon whiskey to the West Indies, intending to bring it back to this country and sell it for high prices after the collapse of the Eighteenth Amendment, which they regarded as inevitable. Most of this liquor went to Nassau, which was conveniently located, had a fairly good harbor, and was the capital island of the Bahamas. Canny British producers, foreseeing a profitable market, had increased their shipments of scotch and other liquors, and ships were constantly arriving with more. In 1917 the Bahamas imported only about fifty thousand quarts of liquor, enough for domestic consumption, and total revenues from all sources amounted to less than four hundred thousand pounds. By 1923 the islands were bringing in ten million quarts annually, and government receipts from liquor alone were well over a million pounds. A great deal of this money was spent on roads, schools, and other public improvements, but the British authorities neglected to improve the harbor to handle the larger ships which the rum syndicates were putting into the trade. The lack of facilities, together with increases in export duties and several treaties between Great Britain and the United States, caused the rumrunners to transfer most of their activities to St. Pierre et Miquelon.

The rumrunners brought great prosperity to the Bahamas, but there were also some drawbacks. By the beginning of 1922 Nassau had been transformed from a somnolent tropical village into a replica of an American mining camp at the height of a gold rush. The harbor was crowded with rum ships, and the town swarmed with tough characters from the United States—important liquor buyers with their retinues of thugs and gunmen, spotters for hijacking gangs seeking information about cargoes and destinations, lone gorillas and crooks of every description on the prowl for anything that might help them turn a dishonest penny, and roistering sailors with more money that they had ever seen before. Their presence created many problems, most of which the natives solved by ignoring them. They sold the Americans all the liquor they wanted, for cash, and helped them load their ships and make arrangements for sailing, but to the slugging and knifing in dark alleys, to the carousing and fighting in the bars and hotels, and to the occasional killings, the Nassau authorities paid no attention unless a native was involved. The American gunmen disposed of their own dead, if any, handled their feuds and quarrels in their own way, and nursed their own wounds. Nassau counted its gold and called it even.

When McCoy's mission to Savannah had been accomplished, he turned the *Marshall* over to another captain and bought the fast New England fishing schooner *Arethusa,* which he later rechristened the *Tomoka.* It became the most celebrated ship on Rum Row. The *Marshall* was captured by the Coast Guard cutter *Seneca* in August 1921, the first seizure of a booze boat in American waters. On his second trip to Nassau, McCoy transferred the *Tomoka* to British registry, a procedure which most of the rumrunners followed as a measure of protection against the United States Coast Guard. It was one thing for the Guard to seize an American boat, but it was quite another to interfere with a vessel sailing under a foreign flag. It was apt to cause international complications even within the three-mile limit. The rum ships cleared from Nassau with a cargo of liquor for a British port, but through connivance and the expenditure of a little money they usually carried a second set of clearance papers which showed that they were bound for an American port in ballast. With these papers they could dispose of their cargoes and then put in anywhere for repairs or recreation.

In the latter part of May 1921 McCoy anchored the *Tomoka,* loaded with fifteen hundred cases of whiskey, off the coast of Long Island, and got in touch with bootleggers whose representatives he had seen in Nassau. The word quickly got around, and the *Tomoka's* cargo was sold within a few days. Other rum ships soon appeared off the coast, but it was not until July that they became numerous enough to attract attention. Thereafter McCoy made one voyage a month, and in four years brought to Rum Row some 175,000 cases of liquor worth three million dollars. He began operating out of St. Pierre et Miquelon in the late summer of 1923, but had made only a few trips when he was arrested. He was indicted by a federal grand jury, but remained free on bail until the middle of 1925, when he was sentenced to nine months in the federal prison at Atlanta. When he was released he found that the competition of the big syndicates was too great to overcome, so he sold the *Tomoka,* and his interests in two or three other ships, and retired, with comparatively little money to show for his smuggling activities. He lived in Florida until his death on December 30, 1948.

Most of the rum ships which sailed out of Nassau and other ports were armed with machine guns and rifles, and revolvers were usually served out to the crew when the vessel came within easy running distance of the American coast. Very few of the ship captains were foolish enough to exchange shots with the coastguardmen, and since their vessels were even slower than the Guard's cutters and patrol boats, they seldom disobeyed an order to heave to, especially if it was followed by a shot across their bows. But the weapons were needed for protection against the pirates, known along Rum Row as "go-through men." These seagoing hijackers, in fast boats, swarmed along the Row and robbed everybody they could catch and over-power. They preyed principally on the small craft, some of which carried huge sums of money, jumping them if possible on their way out to the Row. Sometimes the crews of these boats, if they resisted, were killed and their bodies thrown overboard. Some of the pirates hijacked cargoes of liquor inbound from the booze fleet, and nearly always freely sampled their loot. This brought on rows which usually ended in somebody being shot. It was not at all uncommon for the hijackers to return to shore with fewer men in their boats than had started on the adventure. Many killings occurred on Rum Row which never came to the attention of the police or federal authorities; in gangland such affairs were regarded as strictly private matters. Occa-sionally one of the schooners from Nassau or St. Pierre et Miquelon was attacked, but the crews of these ships were watchful and well armed, and as a rule the captains were careful. It was McCoy's practice, when approached by an unidentified speedboat, to train his machine guns and rifles on it, and to permit only the leader of the gang to come aboard. When Rum Row moved far out to sea the problem of piracy, as far as the rum ships were concerned, pretty well solved itself. Most of the hijackers were landlubbers, and by the time they got thirty or forty miles offshore they were so seasick as to be interested in nothing except a bit of dry land. Sometimes the ship captain gave the helpless pirates slugs of liquor and sent their own men to run the boat back to shore. On at least one reported occasion the hijackers revived sufficiently to rob the crewman of his money and pistol.

Some of the most spectacular piratical exploits were said to have been planned by a mysterious genius called Big Eddie. Little was ever known of Big Eddie, although the New York police said that he and his gang hijacked many truckloads of liquor on the roads of Nassau and Suffolk counties, the principal highways into New York from the lower end of Long Island. Generally, however, he seems to have operated as a consultant and a planner. He was believed to have organized the biggest piracy in the history of Rum Row, the taking of the French steamer *Mulhouse* with thirty-three thousand cases of liquor, although Captain Bill McCoy always insisted that the job was directed by an American rumrunner who resented the intrusion of foreign ships into the trade. The *Mulhouse* was under charter to a French syndicate, which had also sent an agent to New York to arrange the sale of the cargo. Some of Big Eddie's gangsters called upon this innocent, representing themselves as wholesale bootleggers and owners of a large fleet of speedboats, and began negotiations, which they supplemented with lavish entertainment in Broadway speakeasies and night clubs. Meanwhile, on a dark night, a score of hijackers sailed out of Sheepshead Bay in a black schooner, came alongside the *Mulhouse,* and swarmed aboard before the French captain realized what was happening. Some seven thousand cases were sent back to New York on the schooner, and for three days the pirates held the steamer's crew below decks, under heavy guard, while they sold the remainder of the cargo at cut prices. McCoy said that while the thugs were on their way to shore, having drunk freely of the *Mulhouse's* liquor, a quarrel broke out in which the leader of the expedition was shot and his body thrown overboard.

The profits of some of the smugglers who sailed the rum ships into American waters from the Bahamas and St. Pierre et Miquelon were very large, but the really big money was made by the syndicates which hauled the liquor ashore and handled the cutting, distribution, and sale. In time they controlled the seagoing end of the business as well. There were hundreds of these combinations, big and little, operating in every American seaport, with their tentacles stretching far inland. The biggest were elaborately organized, maintaining large offices, keeping complete files and records in the manner of legitimate businesses, and frequently paying large income taxes, thus escaping the investigations which proved disastrous to many prosperous bootleggers. Many employed from one hundred to two hundred persons, and special departments were organized to handle the various phases of the operation—sales and distribution, transportation, purchasing, et cetera. A political department kept in close touch with the politicians, whose good offices were often necessary, and a corruption department took care of payments to policemen, prohibition agents, coastguardmen, customs officers, and federal, state, and city officials. Most of the syndicates operated their own cutting plants, and owned garages, drops, trucks, and speedboats. The purchasing department sent agents to Canada, England, the Bahamas, and St. Pierre et Miquelon, to buy liquor and to oversee the loading of the ships. These vessels served as mother or station ships for the fast speedboats which visited them every night to take off cargo. A few of the syndicates brought in from twenty thousand to forty thousand cases a month, usually in the dark of the moon. The movements of the station ships, which shifted about to avoid the Coast Guard, were directed by short-wave radio, which also gave sailing instructions, and information about landing places, to the speedboats before they cast off for the run to shore. Some of the syndicates maintained two radio stations, with a third in reserve for emergencies.

Nearly all of the combinations were controlled by gangsters and racketeers, although many had been started by men who, prior to prohibition, were not criminals. The ramifications of these organizations have never been fully explored, but it is clear that for a few years, until the inevitable rivalries and territorial encroachments brought on the gang wars, they more or less worked together in a series of complicated alliances. For example, Mannie Kessler owned a couple of rum ships and several speedboats, and was also a minor partner in the syndicate headed by William Vincent Dwyer, better known as Big Bill. In addition, Kessler had a tie-up with Maxie Boo Boo Hoff's outfit in Philadelphia, and with Frankie Yale, the underworld boss of Brooklyn whose headquarters were in his cabaret, the Harvard Inn, on Coney Island. Yale in turn was connected with Vannie Higgins, who operated a few speedboats and captained a gang of hijackers which dominated the highways of Long Island. There was a tie-up between Yale and the Manhattan night-club impresarios and bootleggers, Larry Fay and Frankie Marlow; and Yale was, for some years, an intimate personal and business friend of Johnny Torrio and Al Capone in Chicago.

Big Bill Dwyer apparently had some sort of working agreements with almost all of the big syndicates. He is known to have dealt with Yale, and through Yale with the Capone gang and its various affiliates, and had other connections in New Orleans and in Florida. He did business occasionally with George Remus of Cincinnati and St. Louis, the biggest bootlegger in the Middle West; and had a vague tie-up in Kansas City with a three-hundred-pound thug named Solly Weissman but better known as Slicey and Cutcher-Head-Off. Dwyer's operations required a big spread; his syndicate was probably the largest and most powerful in the United States. In the middle 1920s Dwyer's enterprises, including race tracks, hotels, restaurants, and other properties bought with the proceeds of illicit liquor, were estimated to be worth at least forty million dollars. He owned a dozen seagoing rum ships and a score or more of fast speedboats; his fleet would have made a respectable Rum Row in itself. He maintained offices in several Manhattan office buildings, operated big fleets of trucks, and had a large number of drops or storage warehouses, with shops and expert mechanics to repair his various machines. On his pay roll, which was enormous, were scores of policemen, including captains and inspectors; coastguardmen, prohibition agents as well as higher-ranking figures in the bureau; city, state, and federal officials; and the usual politicians and lawyers, in addition to truck drivers, seamen, garage operators, mechanics, thugs, gunmen, and assorted riffraff. Dwyer was arrested in 1925, together with thirteen men of the Coast Guard and a large number of other accomplices, and in 1926 was convicted and sentenced to prison for two years. Appeals kept him free on bail until July 1927, and he was released on parole about a year later. When he returned to New York he said he was broke, but he was able to buy interests in several race tracks, professional hockey and football teams, and other properties. He became a prominent figure in the sporting world. In 1934 the federal government started proceedings against him for evasion of income taxes, and years later, after a ten-minute trial, obtained a judgment for $3,715,907, covering taxes and penalties since 1922. The claim was settled for an undisclosed sum. Dwyer died at his home on Long Island on December 10, 1948.

While Dwyer was in prison his syndicate was run by Frank Costello, who continued to be the big shot after Big Bill was released. Costello had been associated with Dwyer in the rum business since 1921, and reputedly was the syndicate's pay-off man and head of the corruption department. Many observers, however, believed that he was the real brains of the syndicate and that the popular Big Bill was little more than a front. Costello was also arrested in 1926, but was not tried until 1927, when the jury disagreed. In 1933 the indictment was dismissed. Costello has been the great mystery man of the American underworld for more than twenty-five years. He has often admitted his bootlegging activities and his interest in slot machines and gambling houses, and has made no secret of his association with and friendship for Arnold Rothstein, Al Capone, Lucky Luciano, and virtually every other big-shot criminal and gangster. He has been accused of a great variety of misdeeds, and the government has charged him with cheating on his income taxes. But he has been convicted of nothing since 1915, when he was sent to prison for carrying concealed weapons. Today Costello is supposed to be the big boss of American bookmaking and other forms of illegal gambling, and to have a finger in many underworld pies, but the occasional flare-ups of investigation haven't produced sufficient evidence to justify his arrest. For several years he possessed such power in Tammany Hall, the New York Democratic organization, that he was able to dictate the nomination of judges and other officials. He still exerts considerable political influence.

2

Rum Row was the most spectacular smuggling operation carried on during prohibition, but as a source of liquor for dry American throats it was far less important than Canada. Roy C. Haynes, Prohibition Commissioner, estimated that in 1922, one of Rum Row's big years, the booze fleet accounted for 1,500,000 gallons. The Department of Commerce reported to a committee of the House of Representatives that in 1924 the total value of smuggled liquor, from all sources and of all types, and including beer and wine, was forty million dollars. At forty dollars a case delivered in this country, this would mean approximately a million cases, considerably less than twenty million gallons after cutting. These figures were absurdly low, but even if multiplied by ten, the quantity would still have been little more than a trickle compared to the more than two billion gallons consumed by American drinkers in 1917, the last full year of production before prohibition.

Whatever the actual quantity may have been, at least two thirds came from Canada, and most of the remainder from Rum Row. Importations from Mexico never amounted to very much. The ships of the rum fleet were dependent upon the liquor available in the West Indies, at a few Canadian ports, and at St. Pierre et Miquelon—and about one fourth of the booze shipped from St. Pierre was smuggled into Canada, where high taxes in some provinces made bootlegging a profitable business. On the other hand, American bootleg syndicates operating out of Canada could draw upon the legal production of Canadian distilleries and breweries, which was enormously increased, and the additional large output of several American whiskey-making plants which were dismantled before the Eighteenth Amendment went into effect and shipped to the Dominion, where they were put into operation. A few distilleries were also sent to Mexico, and since they could operate with little regulation or supervision, they produced a great deal of bad whiskey. The normal Mexican production of American-type liquors had always been small, but there was a large border trade in mescal and tequila, which boomed after prohibition began.

Smugglers bringing booze in from Canada or Mexico possessed other advantages. In the first place, liquor was a legal commodity in both countries, and didn't become contraband until it had actually crossed the American border, whereas during the final years of the dry era a ship loaded with booze was liable to seizure almost anywhere on the high seas. And while the rum ships had to approach the American coast by a limited number of routes, the smugglers on the continent had a choice of many, both by land and by water, along the six-thousand-mile boundary lines, including some thirty-five hundred miles of water frontage. From Canada into the United States there were four hundred roads classed as good or fair, one hundred and fifty that were passable, and one hundred known trails, while probably one fourth as many in each category led into this country from Mexico. In addition the smugglers could run boats into the United States by way of the Great Lakes, the Detroit and St. Lawrence rivers, and Lake Champlain, while coming from Mexico they could use the Rio Grande, although in most places it was too shallow for heavily laden craft. It was impossible for the Customs Service and the Coast Guard to maintain stations at more than a comparatively few strategic points, even with the aid of the prohibition agents. There were never one tenth as many of the latter as were needed to do their job. During the first few years only thirty-five agents were available to watch the Mexican border and catch bootleggers and moonshiners in Texas, New Mexico, and Arizona. Not more than three times as many were assigned to the Canadian border. General Lincoln C. Andrews told a congressional committee in 1926 that at least fifteen thousand men would be required to properly police the borders.

It was almost two years before Rum Row was in full operation, but smuggling across the Canadian and Mexican borders began immediately. On January 31, 1920, eleven days after the start of the noble experiment, the Director of the Customs notified the Appropriations Committee of the House of Representatives that large supplies of liquor were being brought across, and that only "an infinitesimal quantity" was being intercepted. Naturally, he wanted an additional appropriation; two million dollars, immediately. Just as naturally, Congress refused the request; the lawmakers were ready to pass any law the drys wanted, but were inclined to accept the assurance of Wayne B. Wheeler and the Anti-Saloon League that enforcement would not be expensive. The director thereupon predicted that the flow of liquor across the borders would soon become a flood. He was right. By the early spring of 1920 smugglers were operating with great success everywhere. The first fatality had occurred—

Candide Dumais of Van Buren, Maine, was killed on March 10, 1921, by a customs guard who had caught him trying to transport thirty gallons of alcohol from New Brunswick into Aroostook County.

With little to stop them, trucks and automobiles roared over the border roads, fast boats sped across the lakes and rivers, and horses, mules, and burros carried liquor along the trails. All were usually met on the American side by escorts of gunmen who were ready to fight either hijackers or customs guards. And there was considerable shooting; up to November 2, 1929, according to government reports, the score stood at eight guards killed and twenty-three civilians slain by the customs men. Most of the latter were smugglers, but the number also included a woman and two men who were said to have been shot accidentally. Many of the automobiles used were equipped with special bodies, hollowed out to hold sacks filled with bottles, and with extra springs to carry the load. Bottles were also hidden in the hood, and, well wrapped, snuggled cozily against the engine. Seat springs were removed and the space filled with bottles; they were stuffed into the spare tire in place of an inner tube, and tied to the under part of the chassis.

In October 1921 the first airplane loaded with liquor was reported to have left Winnipeg; ten years later, in the single month of April 1930, sixty-two planes cleared from Ontario landing fields for points in Ohio, Michigan, Indiana, and Wisconsin. The pilots were usually paid five dollars a case, and many smuggled liquor by air for several years. However, the risks were very great and most of them were eventually caught. The railroads were used with considerable success; in 1928 the Detroit *News* estimated the value of liquor annually smuggled into this country in freight cars, billed as hay, cleaning fluid, machinery, and other commodities, at fifteen million dollars. The usual procedure was to ship a carload of, say, baled hay from Buffalo to Detroit via Canada. On the American side the car was inspected and sealed by American customs authorities. In Canada it was switched to a sidetrack, the hay removed, and whiskey or beer substituted. The car was then resealed with counterfeit seals, picked up by a train, and generally hauled into the United States without further inspection. This trick required co-operation on the part of railroad employees, who were well paid by smugglers. Throughout the dry era rumors persisted that a rich rum syndicate had constructed a pipe line across the Detroit River through which beer was pumped into Detroit from Windsor, Ontario. Several investigations were made, but American and Canadian agents were never able to locate the line. Nor could they find the electric torpedoes which, filled with liquor, were said to swish across the river every night.

American tourists and Canadians visiting the United States, and small-time smugglers, devised ingenious schemes by which many managed to bring in small quantities of liquor. They wore special suits with many pockets filled with pint bottles. Beneath their clothing they wore carpenters' aprons with wide, deep pockets; they carried booze in inner tubes and garden hose wound around their bodies next to the skin, in hot-water bags dangling from the neck, in oversize shoes with little bottles tucked into the toes, in baby carriages, with infants perching atop the loads. One man hurried over the International Bridge at Buffalo, carefully carrying two dozen eggs, which had been emptied and refilled with whiskey. Another lugged two tin life preservers; he said they were souvenirs stolen from a ferryboat, but the customs guards found them filled with liquor. This stunt was also tried several times in New York harbor; one afternoon the harbor police picked up half a dozen such preservers which a passenger on a British liner had thrown overboard to a friend in a small boat. Unfortunately, one struck the friend and broke his arm. Bottles were brought in by both passengers and crewmen of transatlantic ships. The latter usually sold their loot at the water-front speakeasies for whatever it would bring; at times these joints were the best places in New York to get good liquor. Members of Congress and government officials were persistent smugglers when they returned from overseas junkets. Since most of them could demand the privilege of free entry at the port, they generally got away with it. Sometimes, however, their baggage leaked and they were caught. One congressman, an ardent dry, brought in nine trunks, which were passed by the customs and were being hauled away when one began to drip brandy. All nine were then seized and examined. Several yielded varying quantities of French liquors, and one contained nothing but a barrel of rum, well packed.

Along the Mexican border there were a few variations. Mexican women waddled over the bridge between Juarez and El Paso, wearing voluminous skirts and bulging in all directions because of the goat bladders and stomachs filled with mescal and tequila and tied about their waists. Smugglers waded the shallow Rio Grande pushing ahead of them barrels filled with bottles of liquor. Others tied a rope to a dog and sent the animal swimming across the stream; a confederate on the American side then pulled across barrels of liquor. Rafts were used occasionally on the Rio Grande, but a discouragingly large proportion grounded on sand bars or mud banks and were captured.

Most of the liquor smuggled into the United States from Canada was brought in by boats of all sizes and speeds, but generally faster than the government craft, which carried from five to one thousand cases each. They ran across the Detroit River to Detroit, the St. Lawrence to the small towns of upper New York, and the Niagara to Buffalo; through the Great Lakes to Duluth, Toledo, Cleveland, Sandusky, Erie, Buffalo, and other ports; down Lake Champlain to Plattsburg, New York, and Burlington, Vermont; and to isolated docks and beaches in both states; where trucks picked up the liquor for the haul to the cutting plants in the cities. In the middle 1920s federal officials said eight hundred rum boats were in service on the Great Lakes, and there were at least as many more operating on the rivers and Lake Champlain. Detroit was the principal port of entry for the illicit cargoes; it is probable that as much liquor was landed at the docks of the Michigan metropolis as at all other border cities combined. The Detroit *News* said on May 1, 1928, "At least thirty-five millon dollars' worth of liquor comes to Detroit annually through a huge funnel neck—the seventy miles of river and lake front stretching from the village of St. Clair to South Rockwood. On the Canadian side of the waterway lie the liquor docks of the exporters, drawing their stores from a potential source of eighty-three breweries and twenty-three distilleries throughout the Dominion."

In many respects the adventures of the rumrunners who carried liquor on the rivers and lakes of the Canadian border paralleled those of their colleagues of Rum Row—they had to cope with pirates and dodge or outrun the boats of the Customs Service and the Coast Guard, and the little operators were eventually frozen out, to a large extent, by the big, powerful syndicates, generally known in Detroit and other border cities as "combines." The largest concentration of pirates appears to have been in the vicinity of Detroit, which was a gangster-ridden city throughout the 1920s. Things were a little tougher for the Detroit pirates—they had less space in which to maneuver than their brethren off the seacoast, their victims seldom carried really large sums of money, the cargoes they hijacked were comparatively small, and they had to keep their eyes open for gunmen hired by the bootleggers to cut them down. Professional killers ended the career of the Gray Ghost, a melodramatic figure who dressed in gray from head to foot, drove a fast gray boat, and, according to legend, had his machine gun and pistols painted gray. He was noted for the cleverness of his jobs, and for his cruelty. He shot at the slightest provocation, usually slugged his victims unconscious after robbing them, and once put a rumrunner adrift in an open boat in early December because the fellow had hidden his money in his shoe. In time, however, the Ghost went too far; he began buying liquor from the combines and Canadian exporters and paying in counterfeit money. So five wholesalers contributed one thousand dollars each and made a deal with a gang leader. A few days later the Gray Ghost was shot down on a Detroit street by three men in an automobile.

The principal differences between the border combines and the big syndicates of the East were that the former used no seagoing ships and usually brought in smaller cargoes at a time. Most of them were controlled by gangsters, but the initial backing was often furnished by Canadian distillers and brewers, who also set up offices and organized distribution facilities. Canadians financed a big Detroit outfit identified by the American government as "the Pascuzzi combine," which maintained a fleet of speedboats and imported some six hundred cases a day for several years. The operation of these boats was directed by lookouts posted atop wooden towers erected on islands on the Canadian side of the international boundary. Another syndicate, called "the Miller smuggling combine," shipped four hundred cases of liquor every night, by freight car and truck, to Chicago and other cities. A majority of the Detroit River smugglers made their runs at night, but many, under the protection of American customs guards, prohibition agents, and state and city police officers, brought their boats across in the daytime. A Canadian customs inspector reported to his superior officers in 1929 that on a single day, January 14, he had seen six large boats, each loaded to the gunwales with booze, leave Windsor for Detroit. A Canadian revenue collector thus described conditions at the Ontario port of Bridgeburg on the Niagara River not far from Buffalo, as he observed them in April, 1929:

> There are twelve boats plying between here and Buffalo, New York, the river at this point being about half a mile wide. . . . The boats are all loaded and clearance granted about 5 P.M., and they are compelled to leave by 6 P.M. Some of these boats carry from eight hundred to one thousand cases . . . No effort, as far as we can see, is made by the United States authorities to seize any of these boats, as the United States Customs are always notified by us an hour or two before the boats leave, giving them the names of the boats and the quantity of liquor or ale on board. We have had high customs officials from Buffalo, special agents, and officers connected with the Coast Guard come over to the Canadian side and watch these boats load and pull out. It is a well-known fact that some of these boats land within a few hundred yards of the United States Customs office, and unload without being disturbed. . . . Our officers who check these boats out were informed by one of the rumrunners that they had no trouble in landing their cargo, as they were assisted by the officers of the dry squad on the American side.

3

When the Eighteenth Amendment went into effect it was the duty of the Coast Guard to keep liquor smugglers away from American shores on the Atlantic, the Pacific, the Gulf of Mexico, and the Great

Lakes. But on the advice of dry leaders who ridiculed the notion that there would ever be any organized attempts to bring liquor into the country, Congress refused to strengthen the service. Undermanned and underequipped, the Coast Guard, despite occasional well-publicized seizures, was almost helpless against Rum Row until 1924, when the United States and Great Britain agreed to a convention whereby the Coast Guard's right of search and seizure was extended to all British vessels within one hour's running distance of the American coast. To establish the new limit, the Coast Guard sent out its fastest boat; the story goes that the vessel ran out of fuel at the end of the run and was towed home by a rumrunner. During the next four years similar conventions were negotiated with Norway, Denmark, Germany, Sweden, Italy, Panama, Netherlands, Cuba, Spain, France and Belgium.

Early in 1924 Congress appropriated thirteen million dollars for the reconditioning of twenty second-class destroyers which the Navy was instructed to transfer to the Coast Guard and authorized the reorganization of the service and an increase in personnel. An extensive program of building was also begun, and by 1928 the Coast Guard could muster five hundred sixty vessels, including thirty-three cruisers, twenty-five destroyers, and 243 large offshore patrol boats, but exclusive of the small craft at the lifesaving stations. The personnel had been increased to eleven thousand officers and enlisted men. With the aid of the new international conventions, this force pushed the rum fleet some forty miles out to sea, and conducted a continuing campaign of harassment. The service captured three hundred thirty booze boats in 1926, almost as many in 1927, and one hundred ten in 1928 in a special two-months drive off the coast of Florida. In 1928 the government announced that Rum Row had been dispersed and that smuggling by sea was no longer a menace to the enforcement of the dry laws. This was decidedly optimistic. It was true that the schooners and other ships were no longer anchored in long lines off the coast, but the big syndicates carried on as usual. They operated quietly and with considerably more care, but they brought in about as much liquor as ever until the Eighteenth Amendment was repealed.

The Customs Service was likewise reorganized and strengthened during the early 1920s. Particular attention was paid to the service's Border Patrol, which guarded the rivers and the land boundaries between the official ports of entry. In 1925 the Customs Service received additional help—a convention signed by the Canadian and American governments, under the terms of which the customs officers of both countries notified their opposite numbers across the border when a boat cleared with dutiable goods. However, the rum boats kept coming, and the smugglers continued to corrupt the customs guards and other officers. In 1927 the government decided to make a big push at Detroit, and the Customs Service concentrated in that area a hundred picked men of the Border Patrol and more than half of the patrol's boats, while the Prohibition Bureau doubled the number of agents working out of its Detroit headquarters. The campaign was a flat failure. During the year ending March 31, 1928, according to the records of the Ontario Provincial Government, boats carrying 3,388,-016 gallons of liquor were legally cleared at Windsor for Detroit. Of this quantity American agents seized only 148,211 gallons, or less than 5 per cent. In 1930 the Secretary of the Treasury proposed in his annual report that the Army mount guard from the Atlantic to the Pacific, and that the Canadian border be closed to all travel except at a few points to be designated by the President.

CHAPTER THIRTEEN

What America Drank

Almost all of the liquor held in the warehouses when prohibition began was whiskey, manufactured by distillers who had been in business for many years and who took a natural pride in their product. The processes by which it was produced were essentially the same as those used today; good whiskey in pre-Volstead times would be good whiskey now, and would conform very closely to modern standards. It was all made, as it is today, from grain, finely ground, mixed with pure water, and cooked into a mash. A portion of the mash, the quantity depending upon the ultimate flavor desired, is malt, which is any grain, but usually barley, that has been moistened, allowed to sprout, and then dried. It transforms the natural starches of the grain into fermentable sugars. No actual sugar has ever been used in the manufacture of legal whiskey. When the mash has cooled, it is transferred to vats and yeast is added to induce fermentation. When this is completed, the mash is distilled, and the alcoholic vapors are condensed and run into tanks, or cisterns. Most whiskey is bottled at from 85 to 100 proof, although under the law it may be as high as 110. The legal minimum is 80, below which the product cannot be called whiskey. Proof is simply a term used to indicate the amount of alcohol, which is one half of the proof; that is, 100-proof whiskey is 50 per cent alcohol. The rest is water and a multitude of compounds called "congeners," which give the whiskey most of its body and flavor. Those compounds are destroyed if the mash is distilled at 190 proof or higher, and the resultant distillate cannot be legally labeled whiskey.

All whiskey, when it comes from the still, is almost pure white. It gets its color from the charred new oak barrels in which certain types are aged for varying periods of time. Aging is one of the most important processes in the manufacture of whiskey; it's what makes good liquor out of the raw distillate. The char on the inside of the barrel not only colors the whiskey; it also smooths and mellows it and removes many impurities. The usual aging period is from four to eight years; if left too long in the barrel, the liquor is apt to acquire a bitter taste. There is always considerable loss through evaporation and leakage, and for many years scientists have been trying to discover something that might speed up the aging process. So far nothing has been found that will age whiskey as well as time and a charred oak barrel.

Federal laws and regulations recognize more than thirty different types of whiskey, and provide a precise legal definition for each type, to which the distiller is strictly held. Only a few have ever been of interest to the average consumer. Whiskey, plain whiskey, is defined as "an alcoholic distillate from fermented mash grain (any grain or combination of grains may be used) distilled at less than 190 proof in such a manner that the distillate possesses the taste, aroma, and characteristics generally attributed to whiskey." No aging is required for plain whiskey; it can be sold, raw and colorless, direct from the still, provided the proof is brought within the legal limits. There has never been much demand for plain whiskey, and except at times when aged liquors are unavailable, as during the year or so that followed the repeal of the dry laws, it is seldom seen. Other young whiskeys that rarely appear in the market are those labeled rye, bourbon, or wheat, with no further identification. These whiskeys must be distilled at 160 proof or less—a higher proof would destroy the identity of the dominant grains—and must be stored in charred barrels. However, the law imposes no time limit on the storage. A month, or even a day, would be enough to satisfy the government, although it wouldn't produce a very palatable beverage.

Straight whiskey is distilled at 160 proof or less from any grain, and must be aged in charred new oak barrels for at least two years. If it is to be labeled straight rye, straight bourbon, or straight wheat, the mash from which it is manufactured must contain a minimum of 51 per cent rye, corn, or wheat, respectively. Straight corn whiskey, which is popular in some parts of the South, is distilled from a mash containing not less than 80 per cent corn. It may be aged in old charred barrels or in plain wooden containers. Bottled-in-bond whiskey is a straight whiskey, usually rye or bourbon, but it cannot legally be less than four years old, and must be bottled at 100 proof. The most common whiskey is blended whiskey, which is defined as "a mixture which contains at least 20 per cent by volume of 100-proof straight whiskey, and, separately or in combination, whiskey or neutral spirits." A blending agent, usually sherry or prune juice, is also added, but this cannot amount to more than 2½ per cent of the total volume. Less is generally used. If a blended whiskey is identified as rye, bourbon, or wheat, at least 51 per cent of the straight whiskey must be of these types. There is also a blend called spirit whiskey, a poor thing, in which the proportion of whiskey may legally be, and usually is, as low as 5 per cent. When manufactured at all, this whiskey is intended for the low-priced field. Neutral spirits, according to the government's definition, are "distilled spirits distilled from any material at or above 190 proof." Neutral grain spirits are distilled from grain only. These liquors are at least 95 per cent alcohol, and both body and flavor are completely lacking. Absolute alcohol, distilled at 200 proof, is supposedly 100 per cent alcohol; actually, about 1 per cent is water.

Since 1864 all legal whiskey has been manufactured under rigid controls imposed by the federal government, supplemented by state restrictions. A distillery may be owned by an individual or a corporation, but it is controlled by a federal official called the "storekeeper-gauger," whose duties and powers are almost exactly the same today as they were seventy-five years ago. The distilling rooms, the cistern rooms, the grain bins, and all operating parts of the distillery are kept locked, and the keys are in the possession of the storekeeper-gauger. No one may enter, no work begin, and no whiskey may be moved, not even from one part of the plant to another, until he has given permission and unlocked the premises. Every detail of production is carried out under his supervision, and what he says is law. He weighs, grades, and inspects every ounce of grain or other material that comes into the distillery, and every ounce of whiskey or spirits that leaves it. His eagle eye is closed only when he has finally affixed the green revenue stamp to the bottle and released it for sale. Then the whiskey comes under a great mass of federal, state, and city legislation, regulating distribution, 'display, advertising, sale, and consumption. Whiskey's only escape from the law is to slide more or less gently down the human gullet.

Similar safeguards and restrictions surrounded the manufacture of all other beverages containing alcohol, as they do today. More space is given here to whiskey because the contrast between good whiskey and bootleg was much greater than that between other liquors. Also, whiskey was by far the most sought-after drink during prohibition, and its principal component, alcohol or neutral spirits, was used in enormous quantities in the production of brandies, rums, gins, jacks, cordials, liqueurs, and other popular tipples. The beer produced in the dry era, although it was apt to be green and productive of grogginess and stomach-aches, was pretty much the same as pre-prohibition beer. The quality was uneven and the taste atrocious, but in those dizzy days who cared about taste? The same was true of wine, although internal discomfort often followed the use of the so-called wine tonics, which were loaded with phosphates and other chemicals and sold with the sanction of the government. A great deal of prohibition wine was fortified with raw alcohol, which didn't help it any. Unpalatable as they were, however, there is no record that prohibition wine or beer ever killed anybody. On the other hand, bootleg whiskey, gin, brandy, liqueurs, and cordials numbered their victims by the thousands. Other thousands died, then or later, of kidney ailments and other disorders induced by hooch, but for which the bad liquor was not directly blamed.

2

An enormous proportion of the good liquors on hand when prohibition began eventually found its way into bootleg channels—an estimate of the quantity would be little more than a wild guess. The ultimate consumer saw very little of it, or of the real whiskey and other good liquors smuggled into this country from Canada and the Bahamas. The prohibition director for Minnesota said in 1925 that his agents had seized 350,000 gallons of rye, bourbon, and scotch in two years, and that only one case, or less than three gallons, was real distillery liquor. There was never any reason to believe that the percentage was much higher in any other state. The consumer did, of course, have the pleasure of drinking whatever good liquor he had hoarded in anticipation of the drought, but judging from the immediate prosperity of the big bootleg rings, these supplies were soon exhausted.

Occasionally, in order to keep or acquire a good customer, a bootlegger sold a case of good whiskey, for which he usually received from eighty to one hundred ten dollars. But he was not often so foolish. Nearly all of the real booze went into the manufacture of bad hooch. One case of good whiskey could easily be turned into from three to five cases of bootleg, each worth in the retail market from fifty to seventy dollars. Of course there was a lot of so-called whiskey that sold for much less, but even the bootleggers admitted that it was terrible stuff. Some retail bootleggers did their own cutting, but most of this work was carried on in large, well-equipped plants in city basements or country hideaways. There were thousands of these places throughout the country. In 1928 the Detroit *News* said that in that city one hundred and fifty large cutting plants were running full blast, many on three shifts. This estimate, based on a survey of the entire liquor situation, didn't include numerous smaller places which, in the aggregate, produced enormous quantities of liquor. At least as many were operating in Cleveland, New Orleans, Los Angeles, Buffalo, San Francisco, St. Louis, and other large cities. Estimates for New York, Chicago, and Philadelphia usually ranged from five hundred to one thousand. During the first five months of 1927 federal agents raided a hundred in New York alone.

A typical cutting plant, though not a really big one, was operated in the Columbia Heights section of Brooklyn during the early years of the dry era by a bootlegger who may as well be called Tony, since that became a sort of generic term for illicit liquor dealers, especially in New York.[1] Before prohibition Tony ran a small saloon near the Brooklyn Borough Hall, but realizing that the drys were going to win, he invested every cent he could raise in whiskey. When wartime prohibition began on July 1, 1919, Tony closed his saloon and started bootlegging. Since in those early days he sold good stuff, he soon built up a big business. In the late summer of 1920 he bought a brownstone house not far from his old bar and opened a cutting plant in the basement. He used the first or street floor for storage, and occupied the upper floors with his family. Most of his business was wholesale, but he had also kept his retail trade, and sold in large and small lots. He specialized in whiskey, both cut and synthetic, but produced an occasional case of gin or applejack for a favored customer.

All of the work in the cutting plant was done after midnight, behind heavily curtained and barred windows, and was taken care of by Tony himself, his wife, their two sons, both of high-school age, and one helper. He employed two outside men, relatives, to handle sales and deliveries, and for rush orders of small lots sometimes pressed his wife's young nephew into service. His liquor and supplies were hauled by a small trucking company in which he had bought a half interest. No noisy machinery was used in the plant, and no stills or cooking vats with their penetrating odors, and there was slight danger of detection. He operated for several years before his neighbors knew what he was doing, although they used to wonder at the frequent coming and going of so many trucks. The police and the prohibition agents, of course, knew all about the place; Tony had made arrangements with them before he started in business. A third outside man, also a relative, maintained contact with the law officers and tried to keep them happy, but they were a suspicious lot and came around once in a while to check on Tony's business and make certain that they were getting their fair share. The contact man also paid off the gangsters who protected Tony's shipments from hijackers. The profits of such a business were fantastically high, but the overhead was high also, and with the passage of time got higher and higher, as the gang leaders, the cops, and the dry agents increased their demands. One morning a visitor found Tony furiously angry; a prohibition higher-up had muscled in on the graft.

"I had to buy that big crook an automobile and a fur coat," said Tony. "God knows what he'll want next."

Tony's equipment and supplies included mixing vats, a tank of sea water, a cask of cider (for applejack); tables spread with labels and revenue stamps, boxes of corks of various sizes and designs; racks of small vials containing creosote, iodine, oil of juniper, oil of bourbon, oil of rye, and other flavoring extracts and essences; a few barrels about one third filled with wood chips, some charred; bottles of all kinds, including pinch bottles for fancy scotch; several large drums of alcohol, and a dozen or so cases of real whiskey. That is, the whiskey was supposed to be real; it smelled, tasted, and looked like rye or bourbon, and was correctly stamped and labeled. But Tony always refused to have any of it analyzed. "What the hell!" he said. "It might not be so good, and then I'd feel bad." Although Tony was very stingy with his "real whiskey," he once gave a friend a bottle, and the friend took it to a chemist for analysis. It was labeled Old Crow, a fine whiskey, but it wasn't Old Crow. It was 50 per cent whiskey, and the rest was water and alcohol. The latter, for a wonder, was pure. According to the label, this whiskey was 100 proof; actually, it tested less than 90. Tony also refused to permit any of his alcohol to be analyzed; it all came from a syndicate of gangsters who had told him that if he didn't buy from them his house would be dynamited and his children kidnaped. "I don't trust those guys very much," he said. Some of Tony's alcohol was denatured industrial stuff, but most of it had been distilled by Brooklyn and Long Island moonshiners who worked for the syndicate. When he was asked if he knew what was in the mash, Tony said:

"Oh, they use sugar, garbage, anything they've got. One shiner I know goes around buying up spoiled potatoes from the farmers. He says they ferment nice and quick. Make an awful smell, though."

As in all cutting plants, Tony's manufacturing procedures were very simple. He poured whiskey into a vat, and warm water was stirred into it by one of his sons. When the mixture had cooled, enough alcohol was added to bring up the proof. Tony bottled everything at about 85 proof, although the label might say 100 proof. Burnt sugar or caramel provided the necessary color, and oil of rye or bourbon gave the hooch, almost, the flavor of these whiskeys. To give the stuff a bead, a little glycerin or fusel oil was added. Some cutters, however, used a sulphuric-acid compound. A city chemist in Chicago, while analyzing a batch of this compound, spilled a little on a kitchen sink in his laboratory. It quickly ate away the enamel. Most consumers considered the bead very important; it was the first thing they looked for, and its presence was regarded as absolute proof that the liquor was fine, mellow old whiskey, even if it almost ripped out their tonsils when they swallowed it. It was generally believed that only aged whiskey had a bead, and that only nature could put it there.

If the whiskey in the vat was to go on the market as scotch, Tony added creosote instead of the oil of rye or bourbon. Creosote is an oily antiseptic obtained by the distillation of wood tar, and is a fine preservative for timber. It has never been recommended for the human stomach. Some of the scotch, especially that which went into the pinch bottles, was dipped into the tank of sea water after bottling, and the bottles were allowed to dry slowly. This stained and discolored the label, and gave the bottle a very disreputable appearance. This liquor was usually delivered wrapped in burlap, which was the way most of the smuggled booze was shipped. Tony's salesmen assured their customers that the scotch had been dropped overboard from a transatlantic liner and picked up by one of Tony's motorboats. Naturally, all this increased the price from ten to fifteen dollars a case, and the consumer was glad to pay it, for what could be more convincing than a stained label and a piece of old burlap? For customers who demanded that their whiskey have more fire and bite than the usual stuff, Tony added iodine to the mixture. The medical dose of iodine, which is a virulent poison, is a few drops; some bootleggers loaded their hooch with as much as two ounces to the quart. The customer seemed to love it. "Boy!" he'd say. "This is good, strong stuff. Burns hell out of my throat!" In the larger cities manufacturers of hooch sometimes used embalming fluid to give their whiskey an even greater kick. Tony told a visitor that he had never used it, although one of his relatives was an undertaker who had offered him a large supply at attractive prices.

"I knew a guy down on Long Island put some of that stuff in his booze," he said. "He lost some good customers."

"They didn't like it, eh?"

"I guess not," said Tony. "They died."

The cut whiskey made by Tony and his ilk was actually a poor grade of spirit whiskey. Very little contained more than 10 per cent of real whiskey, and most of it, according to government analyses of thousands of gallons of confiscated hooch, had even less than the 5 per cent established by federal regulations as the legal minimum. Synthetic whiskey, of course, contained no real whiskey at all; it was made of water, alcohol, coloring, and flavoring, and glycerin, fusel oil, or sulphuric acid for the bead. Occasionally Tony poured some of his synthetic whiskey into one of the barrels partly filled with wood chips, and kept it there for a few days or a week. This was supposed to deepen the color and enhance the flavor. It also increased the price, for it was sold as genuine "aged in the wood."

Cut and synthetic brandy, rum, gin, liqueurs, and whatever else the bootlegger wished to add to his stock, were also made by the processes used in the whiskey-cutting plants. The only difference was in the materials. A great deal of synthetic gin was sold during the first two or three years of the dry era, but in the last decade most consumers made their own. From their bootlegger they bought the alcohol, and sometimes the oil of juniper and the glycerin, although the latter supplies, not being illegal, could also be obtained from the many retail stores which catered to the home liquor-maker. The manufacture of bathtub gin—sometimes when large quantities were desired it was really made in a bathtub—became an elaborate ritual. There were several schools of thought on the subject. Some contended that the glycerin and the oil of juniper should be added to the alcohol before the water; others insisted that it should be put in afterward, drop by drop. Some held that gin should be pungent and aromatic, so they added a bit of oil of coriander and other flavorings. Some used warm water; some cold. Some thought the gin should set for a few hours before being used, to age and mellow; others that it should be drunk as soon as possible, before something happened to it, like the plug being pulled out of the bathtub. The adherents of the latter school didn't start their operations until the party had assembled. All the guests crowded around to watch, and there was much gabbing, sampling, mixing, stirring, and adding this and adding that. By the time everybody was pie-eyed the gin was ready to drink, and it was guzzled with gusto and to hell with the distressing aftereffects. None of this stuff was really gin, which is a distilled beverage that, although there are several methods of production, usually begins with a fermented mash of juniper berries and goes through several complicated processes. For one thing, in the manufacture of good gin only distilled water is used.

To supply the needs of the cutting plants, and of the amateurs who wished their homemade liquor to resemble the real thing as much as possible, a whole new industry sprang up. In most large American cities, and in Canada, Cuba, Trinidad, and elsewhere, printing plants operated special shifts for the production of counterfeit internal-revenue stamps, and labels and wrappings of American and foreign whiskeys, cordials, brandies, et cetera, as well as prescription blanks, withdrawal permits, and other documents necessary to procure and sell legal liquor. Sometimes a printer would find himself with an oversupply of various items, whereupon he offered them at reduced prices and occasionally put on a promotion campaign. In the late 1920s a New Yorker who specialized in the production of fake labels accumulated a large stock of labels for William Penn Rye, a minor whiskey which before the Eighteenth Amendment went into effect was seldom seen in first-class saloons. In collusion with several cutters, retail dealers, and speakeasy bartenders, the printer began to circulate rumors that an enormous quantity of pre-prohibition William Penn had been stolen from a government warehouse and would soon be placed on the market without being cut or otherwise doctored. The news even got into some of the newspapers, the gossip columnists being just as gullible in those days as they are now, though not as omniscient. When the liquor appeared, correctly labeled William Penn Rye, it created a sensation; thousands of cases were sold at high prices to delighted consumers. A Brooklyn bootlegger quoted one buyer as saying, "This is fine whiskey! I can drink it without ginger ale!" And William Penn continued to be a big seller even after the New York *Telegram,* a lively newspaper which was always poking its reportorial nose into odd corners and sniffing out proof that all was not well with prohibition enforcement, had it analyzed. The chemist's report showed that it contained a little of almost everything except whiskey.

Government agents seized enormous quantities of these printed supplies. In a raid on a big printing plant on Rose Street in New York, in 1927, federal men confiscated more than eight hundred thousand liquor labels and almost one hundred thousand internal-revenue strip stamps. This was not an especially large haul, but it was regarded as important by federal officials because the owner of the plant was convicted and sentenced to three years in prison. It was usually difficult to get a verdict of guilty in such cases, largely because the manufacture of whiskey and other liquor labels was not illegal— they were sold openly in many stores. Counterfeiting internal-revenue stamps, however, was decidedly against the law. It was calculated to cheat the government out of tax money, and in the lexicon of the bureaucrat there is no more heinous crime.

The men engaged in the new business apparently thought of everything. They sold the cutting plants tanks, barrels, and other equipment. Their salesmen offered bottles of every description, including non-refillable types and the distinctive containers used for famous brands of liquor; corks bearing faithful reproductions of trademarks; labels for every known variety of booze, some already stained by sea water; and burlap and straw for packing. One outfit in Detroit even manufactured whiskey cases with the names of well-known distilleries burned into the wood; new cases for American and Canadian liquor, and battered ones for foreign goods. Another, in Chicago, made special clothing for retail liquor peddlers who sold in factories and on street corners—suits with a multitude of pockets, each large enough for a pint bottle, cunningly built into them. In some of these garments a bootlegger could carry as much as forty pints of hooch. And on the fringes of the industry were the small-time operators who hired boys to hunt for discarded bottles in trash heaps and ash cans, and to save in flasks whatever residue of liquor remained in them.

3

During a congressional committee hearing in 1926 General Lincoln C. Andrews, Assistant Secretary of the Treasury in charge of prohibition enforcement, described the manufacture of cut and synthetic whiskey, and pointed out that the former contained very little real whiskey and the latter none at all.

"But I am assured," he said, "that alcohol is just as wholesome as whiskey."

"Well," said Senator James A. Reed of Missouri, "that is a gratifying bit of information."

General Andrews failed to disclose who had given him this assurance. As a generalization it may have been correct, although it is doubtful if many physicians would have prescribed raw alcohol for their patients instead of whiskey. But there was nothing wholesome about the alcohol used by the cutting plants or sold directly to the consumer by the bootleggers. Occasionally some good alcohol got into fake whiskeys, but not often, for pure alcohol was high proof, heavily taxed, and expensive. No sensible cutter would have used it without adulteration. Almost all of the bootleg alcohol was dangerous, if not downright poisonous. Some of it came from moonshine stills, some from redistilled industrial alcohol, and some, a minor part, was smuggled in from Cuba, where it was made of sugar-cane refuse and blackstrap molasses. Drinkers who recall the Cuban gin which appeared on the American market during the second World War will have an idea what the Cuban alcohol was like. However, the alcohol used in making wartime gin was far superior to that handled by the bootleg trade.

A gallon of moonshine alcohol cost about fifty cents to manufacture, and was sold to the ultimate consumer at from twelve to sixty dollars, depending upon supply and demand. A favorite material, especially in the cities, was corn sugar, although many producers eked out their mash with other materials. Corn sugar possessed two distinct advantages—it gave off little odor while cooking, and left almost no residue. Also, the yield was generally good—one gallon of 100-proof alcohol from ten pounds of sugar. Properly handled, corn sugar will make a good grade of alcohol, but the vast majority of moonshiners knew next to nothing about the preparation of mash, proper fermentation, regulation of temperatures, and the innumerable other details of the art of distilling. Moreover, the illicit manufacture of alcohol was a very unsanitary business, carried on by dirty people in dirty surroundings. The tubs, cooking vats, and other equipment were seldom cleaned, and emitted a foul odor even when not in use. As a result of all this, moonshine alcohol was heavily loaded with poisonous aldehydes and other harmful substances. There were also other reasons why very little of it was fit to drink. It was not uncommon for prohibition agents to find in the cooking and fermenting vats, especially in the tenements, chunks of bone, decayed meat and other garbage, and carcasses of rats, cats, and mice, with dead cockroaches and other insects floating about on top of the mash. It was supposed that these creatures, attracted by the odor, had fallen into the mash and drowned. The alky cookers either didn't know they were there or didn't bother to fish them out. They certainly didn't improve the quality of the product.

Despite the enormous production of the moonshine stills, the cutting plants continued to use redistilled industrial alcohol whenever possible; it was usually of a higher proof than moonshine, and a little cheaper. The average wholesale price of a gallon of industrial alcohol, in the legitimate market, was about twenty cents, and a gallon could be transformed into drinkable liquor worth sixty-four dollars. From a carload, or forty thousand quarts, the bootlegger could make at least 120,000 quarts of hootch, easily salable at from six to twelve dollars a quart, and sometimes more. To render the specially de-natured alcohol unfit for beverage purposes, the regulations of the Prohibition Bureau provided for the addition of lavender, soft soap, oil of wintergreen, oil of peppermint, iodine, tobacco solution, sul-phuric acid, carbolic acid, menthol crystals, acetone, brucine sulphate, camphor, and numerous other ingredients, used singly or in combina-tion, according to the needs of the industry for which the alcohol was intended. For example, alcohol for use in the manufacture of liniments was denatured under two formulas, 23B and 23b. The former called for the addition of ten gallons of acetone to each hundred gallons of alcohol. Under the latter the denaturing plants added to each hundred gallons of alcohol fifteen pounds of camphor, two pounds of menthol crystals, and three pounds of carbolic acid. As a beverage, this con-coction was not very tasty. Completely denatured alcohol contained benzine, pyridine, ether, kerosene, gasoline, mercuric acid, benzoin, formaldehyde, bichloride of mercury, and methyl alcohol, commonly called wood alcohol. These ingredients, some of them virulent poisons, were used in six formulas, all of which contained varying percentages of wood alcohol. In some, notably Formula No. 6, wood alcohol alone was used. To protect the people who might be tempted to drink the stuff, the regulations of the Prohibition Bureau contained these pro-visions:

> Every package of completely denatured alcohol containing less than five wine gallons, sold or offered for sale by the denaturers or deal-ers, must have affixed thereto a label on which must be printed in plain, legible letters (red on white), the words, "Completely dena-tured alcohol," and, in addition, there shall be printed in large let-ters, in red ink, under the skull and bones symbol, the word "POISON," together with the following statement: "Completely denatured alcohol is a violent poison. It cannot be applied externally to human or animal tissues without serious injurious results. It can not be taken internally without inducing blindness and general physical decay, ultimately resulting in death."

The continued use of poisons in denaturing industrial alcohol, although it was well known that millions of gallons annually were being used for beverage purposes, aroused a great burst of rage among the wets in the middle 1920s, especially early in 1928, when the newspapers reported a large increase in the number of deaths from alcoholic poisoning. Wet members of Congress, many important newspapers, and organizations devoted to the destruction of prohibition denounced the government's policy as "fiendish," and accused the Prohibition Bureau of brutally and deliberately murdering thousands of American citizens. The New York Legislature, in one of its frequent pot shots at the Eighteenth Amendment, adopted a resolution calling upon Congress to pass a law prohibiting the use of harmful denaturants. The drys, just as vigorously, defended the use of wood alcohol and other poisons on the ground, as Wayne B. Wheeler said on behalf of the Anti-Saloon League, that "the government is under no obligation to furnish people with alcohol that is drinkable when the Constitution prohibits it. The person who drinks this industrial alcohol," he continued, "is a deliberate suicide." The W.C.T.U. in Philadelphia declared that any proposal to substitute harmless ingredients for wood alcohol was nothing more than an attempt to modify the Volstead Act.

Officials of the Prohibition Bureau pointed out that there was nothing new about poisoning industrial alcohol. Laws passed in 1906, and the Volstead Act also, required the use of the most effective denaturants available, and chemists had not yet discovered anything equal to wood alcohol. General Lincoln C. Andrews tried to soothe the indignant wets by telling a congressional committee in 1926 that Formula No. 6, most often used in denaturing alcohol, had been discontinued. He neglected to inform the committee, however, that another had been immediately substituted which increased the quantity of wood alcohol from 2 to 4 per cent. A few years later, after the hullabaloo had subsided, this was further raised to 10 per cent.

Some of the industrial alcohol which came into the hands of the bootleggers was used by the cutters without further treatment. Most of it, however, was sent to cleaning plants and put through a process of redistillation. It was comparatively easy to remove a few of the denaturants, but to get rid of others required great skill and elaborate apparatus, which not one in a thousand bootleggers possessed. Some of the ingredients added to the alcohol under government regulations could be removed only by expert chemists working in well-equipped laboratories. Wood alcohol was the most difficult of all. As Dr. James M. Doran said, "Being closely related chemically to ethyl alcohol, having a boiling point only slightly below that of ethyl alcohol, and having physical properties closely resembling ethyl alcohol, it is a substance that cannot easily be removed." None of this bothered the bootleggers very much, if at all. They ran the alcohol through a still and sent it along to cutters, usually in the same contaminated containers in which it had been received at the cleaning plant. They trusted the cutters to disguise whatever remained of the taste and odor of the denaturant with heavy infusions of flavoring. Usually this could be done, but the poisons remained in the liquor, and if the cutter himself added a little wood alcohol or embalming fluid to increase the kick, the stuff became deadly. In 1924 and 1925 government chemists analyzed more than fifty thousand samples of whiskey and gin which had been seized by the prohibition authorities. None contained more than a small percentage of real whiskey, and almost 99 per cent showed traces of denaturants. Of 480,000 gallons of confiscated booze analyzed in New York in 1927, 98 per cent contained poisons.

Late in 1928, following an epidemic of deaths from wood-alcohol poisoning—sixty were killed in New York that year, forty-two in October alone—the New York *Telegram* collected 504 samples of liquor from four hundred speakeasies and had them analyzed. Wood alcohol, from a trace to 3 per cent, was found in fifty-five of the samples. Seventy were less poisonous, though definitely harmful even in small quantities, and 362 were classified as synthetic or cut. Seventeen samples were genuine, but of poor quality. Since the *Telegram's* exposé gave the names of many of the speakeasies, among them such famous resorts as the Court House Restaurant and Tony's, it attracted considerable attention. Hundreds of telephone calls were received from people who said they intended to quit drinking at speakeasies; they

would like, please, the address of a good bootlegger. Indignant statements were issued by politicians and dry leaders, who denied everything and then demanded new laws and larger appropriations. The
Telegram gave the police a list of the speakeasies from which the
samples had been obtained, and it was promptly passed along to the
federal authorities. Prohibition agents scurried around like mad for a
few days and made fifty raids, announcing that the scoundrels who ran
the joints would be dealt with most severely. A few were fined small
amounts, but nobody went to jail and most of the speakeasies reopened
within forty-eight hours. The bartenders and operators of the joints
treated the whole thing as a big joke. Only one displayed any indignation, as far as the *Telegram* could learn, and that for a curious reason.
When a reporter dropped into this man's place the day after the publication of the analyses, he said:

"You people had a bum chemist on that deal."

"What're you kicking about?" asked the reporter. "He said your
stuff was all right."

"That's what I mean," said the bartender. "It ain't right to take
the word of a guy like that. Why, I haven't sold a drop of good liquor
since 1920!"

4

The liquors manufactured by the cutting plants from moonshine and
industrial alcohol were standard products usually available everywhere
in the country. There were occasional shortages, however, and in
some sections prices were so high that many consumers couldn't afford
to buy the comparatively high-class booze put out by the bootleg rings.
These people drank whatever they could get that contained alcohol,
and they managed to dredge up some fearful concoctions. For two or
three years there was a run on anti-freeze solution; it was frequently
stolen from the radiators of automobiles, and addicts claimed that a
little rust improved the flavor and gave their bodies needed iron. The
supply dwindled when the bootleggers learned to renature it and
diverted huge supplies to their stills. Canned heat, or solidified alcohol,

was melted and drunk; it was a very nasty but powerful tipple, and the end results were not good. In the cities and towns there was a great demand for bay rum, perfume, hair tonic, and toilet waters and similar preparations, all of which contained a large percentage of alcohol in addition to various denaturants. Sales of this stuff slackened when the government compelled manufacturers to lace their product with tartar emetic. One swallow of a compound containing tartar emetic will usually cause a violent internal upheaval, compared to which seasickness is a pleasure.

Rubbing alcohol, available at any drugstore without a prescription, was also drunk, and since it contained at least one virulent poison, caused many serious illnesses and several deaths. For years all rubbing alcohols had been clearly labeled, in large letters, "POISON! For external use only!" During prohibition the government changed the regulations and permitted manufacturers to omit the word "Poison!" Mrs. Mabel Walker Willebrandt, Assistant Attorney General, called attention to this ruling, in 1929, and expressed wonderment at it. But it was never explained. And today, almost seventeen years after the repeal of prohibition, the word "Poison!" is still omitted, although the user is warned that "if taken internally serious gastric disturbances will result." The bottle also bears a cautionary notice that if a druggist sells rubbing alcohol for other than external uses he will be required to pay a beverage tax on it.

In addition to all these drinks there were many regional liquors which were popular in some parts of the country and virtually unknown in others. Their only merits were cheapness and a plentiful supply. Farm hands in the Middle West drank a fluid drawn from the bottom of a silo, where silage had rotted and fermented for perhaps several years. No viler beverage can be imagined. In Washington and the surrounding sections of Virginia and Maryland a drink called Panther Whiskey was well-liked. It was moonshine, new, raw, heavy with esters and fusel oil, and three small drinks would knock a man out. Another concoction used in that area, which appears to have been a little better, was known as Old Stingo. Some Washington bootleggers bottled Old Stingo and sold it as Old Lewis Hunter Rye, an excellent whiskey before prohibition. In this guise it brought ten to twelve dollars a bottle. In Richmond, Virginia, those who wanted a cheap liquor drank White Lightning; a chemist who analyzed several samples reported that the best he could say for it was that it was "dangerous." In some of the small towns and country districts of Virginia a lot of Jackass Brandy was used; it was supposedly made from peaches and sold for four dollars a quart. A few drinks usually caused severe intestinal pains, and sometimes internal bleeding.

In Maryland drinkers who didn't care much what happened guzzled a drink called Old Horsey, which is exactly the way it is said to have smelled. Bootleggers in Baltimore sold, especially to oystermen, a liquor known as Scat Whiskey. It cost five or six dollars a bottle. Most of this stuff was made on a farm near Baltimore, where bootleggers had set up a big still which turned out one thousand gallons of hooch a day for several years. Instead of the copper which is the only safe metal through which to run alcohol vapors, the still was equipped with lead coils, as were thousands of other moonshine plants throughout the country. The acids in the distillate picked up the lead, and it was deposited in the liquor as acetate of lead. This is a dangerous cumulative poison; a little may do no harm, but it remains in the body until enough has accumulated to cause lead poisoning, which is a very serious ailment. Scat Whiskey was loaded with it. A popular drink on the Philadelphia water front was a terible thing variously known as Happy Sally and Jump Steady. It sold for fifty cents a half pint. Most of it was made in a section of South Philadelphia called Moonshine Valley, which also produced Soda Pop Moon. This was sold in soda-pop bottles for three dollars a quart, and analyses showed that it contained isopropyl alcohol, a violent poison. Many men who had drunk Soda Pop Moon were treated in Philadelphia hospitals; their tongues were paralyzed, and they had been thrown into a stupor which lasted for several hours.

Throughout the South, Squirrel Whiskey was popular; a few drinks, it was said, would make a man climb a tree. As a matter of fact, mountain moonshine had been known as Squirrel Whiskey for many years, but in the old days the mountaineers made it from grain, and though new and raw, it was really whiskey. It had little in common with the prohibition product. In parts of Indiana a drink popularly known as Goat Whiskey sold for one dollar a pint; it was so called because there was a widespread suspicion, never verified, that one of the ingredients was an old billy goat. A lot of Goat Whiskey was also sold in South Dakota; so much, in fact, that by 1926 the price there had dropped to one dollar a quart. Incidentally, one of the largest stills ever seized in Indiana was operated by a man appropriately named Floyd Death, an Adams County deputy sheriff. Another well-known drink in that part of the country was Red Eye, which came only in pint bottles, at two dollars each, and was usually sold by peddlers on street corners. A similar concoction, called Straitsville Stuff, was plentiful in Ohio at three dollars a quart; it was manufactured in underground stills in the coal-mining regions.

In the Middle West country people and small-towners drank a lot of Pumpkin Wine, although it was fairly weak. It was made by scooping out the inside of a pumpkin and filling the cavity with wine, hard cider, or alcohol, together with raisins or whatever else happened to be handy. The opening was then sealed with paraffin, and the pumpkin was set aside for a month. By that time the liquor was ripe. In upper New York State summer residents were partial to Cherry Dynamite, which was made by pouring alcohol over ripe black cherries and putting the mixture aside over the winter. This was usually served as a liqueur; it was very powerful and lived up to its name. Somewhat similar drinks were made by amateurs all over the country. All kinds of fruit were used, but berries, peaches, and apricots were thought to be best. Assuming that the alcohol was pure, drinks of this type consumed in small quantities were not harmful.

In the Negro districts of New York, Washington, Chicago, and other large cities a very poor grade of moonshine sold for as low as two dollars a quart, and Nigger Gin cost about the same. The latter could be had in cheap speakeasies for ten or fifteen cents a slug, and was used as a windup drink to keep a jag going after money had begun to get scarce. In *Collier's Weekly* for May 2, 1925, a writer described what happened when he put his nose to a bottle of Nigger

Gin. "There was a brief wave of heat as from a match," he said, "then a flash of sweetish, pungent, bitter vapor which seemed to leave all the membranes of the throat covered with a lingering, nauseating mustiness." A drink almost as terrible was sold in Kansas City speakeasies for twenty-five cents; it was sometimes known as Sweet Whiskey, and was made by boiling sweet spirit of niter, also called spirit of nitrous ether, a distillation of alcohol combined with nitric and sulphuric acids. A considerable quantity of niter was found in samples analyzed in the early 1920s, and the report of the chemist said that it would soon destroy the kidneys. In Chicago many speakeasies sold a very dark concoction called Yack Yack Bourbon, which was loaded with iodine, burnt sugar, and other flavoring matter. In 1923 enterprising bootleggers bottled this stuff and sold it in Chicago hotels, especially to southerners, who are very fond of bourbon. One Birmingham businessman told a reporter for the Chicago *Daily News* that he paid sixteen dollars for a quart of Yack Yack, and drank about a pint. "I'm not feeling rational yet," he said. "I'm still uncertain and subject to fits."

Out in Colorado and some parts of the Southwest, bootleggers did a big business in Sugar Moon, made from beet sugar. This seems to have been a little better than most moonshine, but it was raw and very strong, and a few drinks caused intoxication and produced a bad hangover. A lot of this liquor was delivered in one-gallon wooden kegs which had been charred on the inside, and the buyer was advised to let it age awhile before drinking. This was a good idea, but the trouble was that most of the barrels were not well made, and unless the hooch was used within a few weeks, almost all of it was lost through leakage or evaporation. On the Pacific coast and in the Southwest, cut and synthetic whiskey, as well as all grades of moonshine, were usually in good supply; and there was a lot of so-called American Whiskey, hurriedly manufactured in Mexico and sent into this country through San Diego, El Paso, and other border points. This stuff was generally distilled from potatoes, rotten cactus, or whatever else was available, and artificially flavored and colored. Almost none was real whiskey. In the Los Angeles movie colony a popular party beverage during prohibition was a sort of punch called the Hollywood Special. Each guest brought a bottle of whatever he happened to have—gin, whiskey, moonshine, beer, wine, anything—and the preparation of the punch began with the host pouring a quart of alcohol over a big cake of ice. The other bottles were then poured, one at a time, and as each was emptied, everybody sampled the mixture. It is local tradition that the punch was never completed.

Probably the worst drink that appeared during prohibition was fluid extract of Jamaica ginger, popularly known as Jake, which was almost 90 per cent alcohol. During the final years of the dry era large quantities were consumed in the Middle West, the South, and some parts of the East. Jake was occasionally used medicinally for stomach disorders, and could legally be sold at retail only on prescription. Drugstores and wholesale houses could obtain it only on federal permits issued by the Prohibition Bureau in Washington, but nobody seemed to have any trouble getting it; in 1928, for example, the government released two hundred barrels to a druggist in a small Texas town. This was enough to last him, if disposed of legitimately, for at least a hundred years. In many states drugstores sold Jake to all comers for thirty to fifty cents for a two-ounce bottle, and boot-leggers peddled it at about the same prices. The principal buyers were poor people, and boys and girls, who couldn't afford more than one drink at a time and wanted something that would start them off with a bang. Since it was much too strong to be guzzled straight, Jake was usually mixed with ginger ale, soda pop, or a fountain drink. As far as is known, nobody died from drinking it, but even small quantities nearly always caused a terrible form of paralysis. It was described by William G. Shepherd in *Collier's Weekly* for July 26, 1930:

> The victim of "jake paralysis" practically loses control of his fingers. . . . The feet of the paralyzed ones drop forward from the ankle so that the toes point downward. The victim has no control over the muscles that normally point the toes upward. When he tries to walk his dangling feet touch the pavement first at the toes, then his heels settle down jarringly. Toe first, heel next. That's how he moves. "Tap-click, tap-click, tap-click, tap-click," is how his footsteps sound.

. . . The calves of his legs, after two or three weeks, begin to soften and hang down; the muscles between thumbs and index fingers shrivel away. . . .

Although a few cases were reported in 1928 and 1929, the use of Jake on a large scale apparently began in Kansas early in 1930. The first victims were looked upon as comical figures. They were called "jake trotters," and were said to be "jake jazzed," or to have "jake feet." Their peculiar locomotion was laughed at as the "jake dance" or the "jake step." The merriment subsided, however, when health authorities discovered that in the city of Wichita alone there were more than five hundred cases of Jake paralysis, and many more in other parts of Kansas. In the summer of 1930 the Prohibition Bureau estimated that the number of victims throughout the county exceeded fifteen thousand, including eight thousand in Mississippi, one thousand in Louisiana, eight hundred in southern Tennessee, about four hundred in Georgia, and several hundred in Rhode Island, Connecticut, and Massachusetts. Many of them ultimately regained partial use of their hands and feet, but as far as the record shows, none completely recovered.

5

When it came to estimating the consumption of alcoholic liquors in the United States during prohibition, the wets, drys, and government officials seem to have enjoyed themselves enormously; with no facts to hamper them, they let their fancy roam wide and free. The most important estimators, or at least the ones whose findings appeared most frequently in newspapers and propaganda material, were John C. Gebhart, secretary of the Association Against the Prohibition Amendment; Hugh F. Fox, secretary of the United States Brewers' Association; Robert E. Corradini, research secretary of the World League Against Alcoholism; and the division of research and education of the Prohibition Bureau, which remained anonymous to the end. These wizards used a great variety of secret formulas involving assumptions of which few, if any, were based on known facts. They assumed that so much corn sugar was used by illicit distillers, that so many tons of hops were turned into illegal beer, that so many tons of grapes were used by the bootleg wineries, that so many moonshine stills were in operation, that so many homes possessed brewing and distilling apparatus, that so much liquor was smuggled into the country, that so much industrial alcohol was diverted to bootleggers, et cetera. Retiring into the silences with these assumptions and, perhaps, a few crystal balls, they emerged in due time with estimates of consumption which were released with great fanfare by the organizations which employed them. Their charts and tables were very impressive, partly because they reduced nearly everything to terms of absolute alcohol, which made them harder to understand, and partly because they scorned the easy method of round figures; they calculated down to the last gallon. For example, Rober E. Corradini estimated that the absolute alcohol contained in the distilled spirits consumed in 1928 amounted to 13,547,593 gallons. How this was arrived at, in the absence of accurate reports from the bootleggers, who were notoriously unco-operative, was never fully explained.

Naturally enough, John C. Gebhart and Hugh F. Fox found that the United States was getting plenty of booze. The former estimated that the production of distilled liquors in 1927 was at least 180,-000,000 gallons; this was twelve million gallons more than the record pre-prohibition year of 1917. His minimum estimate of the per capita consumption of distilled spirits was 0.93 gallons, but his maximum was 2.66 gallons, more than any year since 1860. Fox estimated that in 1930 the total consumption of all kinds of liquor was 1,317,931,386, or 1.611 gallons per capita of absolute alcohol. As might have been expected, the estimates of Corradini and the Prohibition Bureau had little in common with those of Gebhart and Fox; it is a bit difficult to believe that they dealt with the same subject. Corradini found that in 1927 the consumption of wine, beer, ale, and distilled liquors, reduced to absolute alcohol, was only 34,265,859 gallons, or 0.85 gallons per capita. The Prohibition Bureau was easily the winner of the estimators' sweepstakes; it was only with considerable difficulty that its experts found any liquor at all. Charmed by its own conclusions, the bureau announced in 1930 that "it appears that the consumption of alcohol liquors in the United States is growing less from year to year." The bureau's estimate of the per capita consumption of absolute alcohol in 1930 was 0.062 gallons, or a few spoonfuls.

None of these estimates was worth much more than the paper on which it was printed. All that is certain about the consumption of liquor in the United States during the dry era is that anybody who wanted it, and was able to pay for it, could get it.

CHAPTER FOURTEEN

Prohibition's Fairest Flower

The appalling moral collapse which followed in the wake of the Eighteenth Amendment and the first World War caused the almost complete breakdown of law enforcement throughout the United States, and made it possible for the underworld to take over the importation, manufacture, distribution, and sale of illegal liquor. Already well organized for other purposes, the criminal gangs required only a comparatively short time to perfect the setup of their new booze departments, to establish sources of supply, and to secure their operations against undue interference. In many cities the gang leaders held formal conferences, usually attended by the police, at which definite divisions of territory were agreed upon, each gang to be supreme in its own area. In considerably less than two years the whole vast machinery of underworld domination was running smoothly and peacefully, and the money was pouring in at the rate of millions of dollars a month. The shooting began when greedy captains encroached upon the districts held by others.

With prosperity came expansion and consolidation, and by the middle 1920s, by force of arms and through the payment of huge sums to politicians and officials, the gang chieftains had become virtually all-powerful. Honest men everywhere were appalled by the spectacle of politicians, judges, mayors, district attorneys, high police officers, prohibition agents of all ranks, and even governors and high federal officials, cringing and kowtowing before big-shot gangsters; running their errands, obeying their commands, protecting them from the consequences of all manner of crime, gratefully accepting their handouts, attending their social functions, and acting as honorary pallbearers at their gaudy funerals. It is little wonder that the United States acquired an international reputation, which it richly deserved and from which it still suffers, as the most lawless nation on earth.

2

No large city escaped the ravages of the gangs, but nowhere else did they attain such power as in Chicago. All the evils of prohibition came to a head in the Illinois metropolis, and were symbolized by the pudgy figure of Al Capone, affectionately known as "the big fellow" and "the big shot." Although he was a pander, a dope peddler, a racketeer, a briber, an extortionist, and a savage and merciless murderer, Capone became one of the great popular heroes of his time. Millions of Americans ignored his crimes and admired him for disdaining a law which was becoming increasingly unpopular; they sympathized with him when he objected to being called a bootlegger and a racketeer. "I call myself a businessman," he complained. "I make my money by supplying a popular demand. If I break the law, my customers are as guilty as I am. When I sell liquor, it's bootlegging. When my patrons serve it on silver trays on Lake Shore Drive, it's hospitality."

Capone received fan letters from all over the world, and foreign authors traveled thousands of miles to interview him and to write learnedly about his place in American life. Visitors to Chicago considered their trip a failure unless they caught a glimpse of the "big fellow," the bulge of holstered pistols under his armpits clearly visible as he lolled in his twenty-thousand-dollar seven-ton armored automobile upholstered in heavy silk, a fifty-thousand-dollar diamond sparkling on his finger and a big cigar between his fat lips. Spectators were thrilled by the sight of the thug who sat beside Capone's chauffeur, a submachine gun across his lap, and by the touring cars crowded with armed hoodlums which preceded and followed the great man. He carried fifty thousand dollars in cash in his pockets, and when he went out for pleasure he scattered money like dandruff—one thousand dollars to a café singer who pleased him, one hundred dollars as tip to a waiter, fifty dollars to a panhandler, twenty dollars to a hat-check girl, five dollars to a newsboy. He gave diamond-studded belts and solid gold cigarette cases to his favorites, bet twenty thousand dollars to fifty thousand dollars on a single roll of the dice and on a horse race. He once said that in less than eight years he had "fooled away" more than seven million dollars.

He was openhanded in other ways too. He disbursed a corruption fund of several million dollars a year, and gave lavishly to the campaign funds of his friends the politicians. According to the president of the Chicago Crime Commission, he spent $260,000 to help elect Mayor William Hale Thompson, the political blatherskite who became notorious by threatening to "punch King George in the snoot." Capone was greatly pleased when Mayor Thompson dismissed the killing and corruption in Chicago with an airy wave of his hand and, "It's all newspaper talk." Capone could well afford these enormous outlays. His net profit from his various enterprises—liquor, prostitution, dope, racketeering, and what not—was conservatively estimated by the Chicago Crime Commission at sixty million dollars a year. At least two thirds came from booze. The income tax? That was for lesser mortals. Or so he thought. It was a thought that eventually put him behind bars.

3

Capone became the richest, best-known, and most powerful of American gang leaders, but he wasn't the smartest. That distinction must go to Johnny Torrio, who was probably the most efficient organizer of criminal enterprises on a large scale that this country has ever produced; he came very close to being the mythical mastermind. Torrio created Chicago's bootleg empire and ruled it for five years with a minimum of shooting. He abdicated when the going got a bit tough, and turned it over to Al Capone as a going concern doing a gross business of more than seventy million dollars a year. Capone added new territory and greatly increased the revenues, but during the six years of his reign he was constantly engaged in suppressing insurrections and repelling invasions.

Torrio was born in Italy in 1877, but was brought to this country as an infant, and lived in New York and Brooklyn until he was about thirty-three years old. He ran a saloon in Manhattan, bossed several brothels, and led a bunch of hoodlums in James Street, an affiliate of Paul Kelly's famous gang. When he moved to Brooklyn he opened another bar near the Navy Yard and joined forces with Frankie Yale. He went to Chicago about 1910 to captain the bodyguard and act as general assistant to Big Jim Colosimo, a top figure in prostitution and white-slave circles. Colosimo had been a street cleaner and precinct captain for the Democratic machine in Chicago's First Ward until 1902, when he married Victoria Moresco, a brothelkeeper. He took charge of her house, and under his astute management the bordello became one of the most popular places in the Levee, the old segregated district which was larger than San Francisco's Barbary Coast and New Orleans's Storyville combined and twice as vicious. Colosimo and his wife acquired other houses of prostitution, and in 1909 or 1910 opened a café on South Wabash Avenue which was a celebrated resort for many years. By that time Colosimo was the biggest vice operator in Chicago and possessed great political influence.

Colosimo brought Torrio to Chicago for two reasons. In the first place, he needed expert assistance in the management of his growing prostitution business, and he knew that women as an article of commerce had been Torrio's chief interest for half a dozen years. In the second place, Colosimo was in serious trouble with the Mafia and the Black Hand, which had been preying upon him ever since he got "up in the bucks," as the gangland phrase had it. Torrio was widely known as an arranger of murders, although as far as the authorities ever knew, he committed none with his own hand. He seldom carried a gun, in fact, and often boasted that he had never fired a pistol. Scarcely anyone believed him. Colosimo himself had killed three extortionists, and Torrio's hired gunmen disposed of several others. It soon became extremely dangerous to blackmail Colosimo, and after a couple of years the Mafia let him alone.

For a few years Torrio worked contentedly as a subordinate, gradually building up his personal political and police connections and becoming acquainted with the workings of the Chicago underworld. When Colosimo fell in love with a young café singer, and thereafter had time for little else, Torrio began moving in on the bemused big shot, and by about 1918 Colosimo had become little more than a front, although he was still supposed to be the boss and continued to absorb most of the profits. In 1919 Torrio began to urge Colosimo to send more prostitutes into Cook County outside of Chicago; he had already established brothels in the suburban town of Burnham, through the wholesale corruption of county and village officials, and they were doing a big business. Colosimo, however, was satisfied with things as they were. When prohibition went into effect, Torrio wanted to get in on the ground floor of the illicit-liquor trade, but Colosimo poohpoohed the idea. "Stick to women," he advised. "That's where the money is. There's no future in bootlegging. Prohibition won't amount to anything."

As matters turned out, it was Colosimo who had no future. Early in May 1920 Frankie Yale came to Chicago and, according to the police, collected ten thousand dollars in cash from Johnny Torrio. On the afternoon of May 11, Yale hid in the cloakroom of Colosimo's café on South Wabash Avenue, and when Big Jim walked into the resort, alone, and started down the hallway to his office, the gunman shot him in the back of the head. Colosimo's funeral was the first of the ornate burials which became common in gangland during the 1920s and which helped focus attention upon the unholy alliances between politicians and criminals. The honorary pallbearers included three judges, an assistant state's attorney, a member of Congress, a state representative, and nine aldermen, all assembled to do honor to the great pander and marching in close companionship with the most notorious thugs and hoodlums in Chicago. Torrio wrote a check for the funeral expenses, and for the magnificent floral tribute which he had sent, and then turned to business. He had a lot to do. And one of the first things he did had terrific consequences—he answered a letter from his young friend Alphonse Capone, then working as a dishwasher and part-time bartender in Frankie Yale's cabaret at Coney Island, in Brooklyn. Capone wrote that he wanted to leave Brooklyn, and asked Torrio for a job.

Torrio knew all about Capone. Although he was only twenty-three, the youthful hoodlum was an adept in the use of both pistol and blackjack, and had already made an enviable name as a gunman and slugger on the Brooklyn water front. Torrio wired Capone to come to Chicago, and put him to work as bouncer in a Burnham brothel. Capone displayed so much zeal and aptitude that within a few months he was appointed manager of the Four Deuces, a resort which Torrio had opened at 2222 South Wabash Avenue. The Four Deuces was an unusual place even for Chicago—a saloon and cabaret on the ground floor, Torrio's office on the second, gambling on the third, and prostitution on the fourth. Late in 1921 Capone became Torrio's principal assistant and chief gunman. As a blind he ran a secondhand furniture store next door to the Four Deuces, under the name of Alfred Caponi. In underworld circles he was generally known as Scarface Al Brown. The general public knew little about him for several years.

4

When Johnny Torrio set about organizing the Chicago liquor business in the late summer of 1920, he found the prohibition situation made to order. Hundreds of saloons and roadhouses had remained open and were selling whatever they could get, a few small cutting plants and alley breweries had begun operations, the members of the Unione Siciliana were cooking alcohol in the tenements, independent bootleggers were active, and several gang leaders, notably Frankie Lake and Terry Druggan, of the Valley Gang, were making big talk about taking over breweries and distilleries. But everything was helter-skelter; there was no direction, and dangerous rivalries were building up. The Chicago police were doing nothing; marking time, it was called. Torrio had little fear of the police; he often said, "I own the police," and events proved that this was no idle boast. Mayor William E. Dever told a congressional committee in 1926 that at least 60 per cent of the Chicago cops were in the liquor business; citizens who frequently saw policemen riding liquor trucks as guards felt that he was being a little conservative.

The Prohibition Bureau had 134 agents working out of its Chicago headquarters, but they were also required to cover all of Illinois, Iowa, and eastern Wisconsin; the result was they covered little or nothing. A state enforcement law was pending in the Illinois legislature; it was a strong measure when introduced, very similar to the Volstead Act, but was weakened by amendments, most of which were pushed through by members from Chicago. Incidentally, when Charles H. Weber, a state legislator from the sixth Chicago district, was sued for divorce, his assets as listed by his wife included one brewery, one gambling house, one speakeasy, one roadhouse, one Rolls-Royce automobile, one Minerva automobile, one yacht, and two speedboats.

As finally enacted, the state law, which went into effect on July 1, 1921, was virtually worthless. It provided for no central administration and no state-wide police unit, and appropriated no money. Responsibility for enforcement was vested in the state's attorneys of the 102 counties, and most of them ignored it. As late as 1930 the Wickersham Commission investigated fifty-three of Illinois's most populous counties, and found only twelve state's attorneys who were actively trying to enforce the law and co-operating with the federal authorities. The law also provided for permits to manufacture, transport, and sell medicinal whiskey and industrial alcohol, but not beer. Supposedly these were issued only to those who already possessed federal permits, but no application was ever investigated, and anybody could get one with a little political pull. As a matter of precaution, the gang leaders each had several. Throughout the prohibition era the state issued an average of nine thousand basic permits a year and fifteen thousand special ninety-day purchase permits.

Torrio decided to make his big play in beer. Chicago had always been a great beer-drinking city, and beer was what the people wanted when they visited speakeasies. Torrio, and later Capone, provided it in overwhelming measure. They controlled the hard-liquor trade also, absorbing most of the alcohol manufactured by the Unione Siciliana as well as that produced by independent moonshiners, but their big money was made in beer. As his first move, Torrio formed an alliance with Joseph Stenson, member of a well-known Chicago family, and took over the five breweries which Stenson had operated before prohibition. These plants were supposedly dismantled, but were running on a small scale and supplying a few speakeasies. With Stenson's assistance, Torrio acquired other breweries, leasing some and buying others outright. He also got control of several distilleries. With supplies assured, he called the leaders of the principal gangs into conference, and with little difficulty persuaded them to go into the booze business under his general supervision. He promised them political protection, which most of them already had, as much beer as they could sell at fifty dollars a barrel, and whatever hard liquor they required at the going price. A few of the gang captains subsequently acquired breweries and distilleries and operated as manufacturers and wholesalers, but most of them continued to depend upon Torrio and Capone for supplies and devoted themselves to building up markets and developing outlets. Torrio predicted that everybody would make a fortune, and almost everybody did.

At Torrio's suggestion, Chicago and Cook County were divided into small kingdoms, and each gang leader agreed not to invade another's territory. The North Side, one of the richest sections of the city, went to Dion O'Banion, a former choirboy whose gang specialized in bank holdups and burglary. Since he had two large Chicago wards "in his pistol pocket," and faithfully delivered the vote each year to the Democratic ticket, his protection was of the best. He was caught red-handed in several big holdups, but nothing ever happened to him. As a side line, to satisy his love of the beautiful, O'Banion ran a flower shop on North State Street in partnership with William E. Schofield, who was never accused of participation in any of O'Banion's criminal enterprises. The Chicago police said that O'Banion killed, or ordered killed, at least twenty-five men. His first lieutenant was Hymie Weiss, who invented the "one-way ride" and coined the phrase.

Torrio retained for himself a portion of the West Side, including the suburban towns in which he had established brothels and roadhouses, and divided the rest of that area among Myles and Klondike O'Donnell, Frankie Lake and Terry Druggan, and the six Genna brothers— Sam, Jim, Pete, Angelo, Tony, and Mike—better known as the Terrible Gennas, who were high in the councils of the Unione Siciliana. The Gennas became the biggest alcohol manufacturers and distributors in Chicago; in 1925 their holdings were valued at more than five million dollars, and their gross sales of raw booze amounted to $350,000 a month, of which $150,000 was profit. They bought policemen in wholesale lots; every month four hundred uniformed cops called at their warehouse in Taylor Street to be paid off. They also made regular payments to five police captains, and to a score of detectives from police headquarters and the state's attorney's office.

A portion of the South Side also remained a part of Torrio's personal empire, and Al Capone was appointed subchief to rule it. The remainder was allotted to Danny Stanton, Ralph Sheldon, Polack Joe Saltis, and Frank McErlane, who was noted for his fat red face and small, piglike eyes; and a few others of lesser importance. The Illinois Association for Criminal Justice called McErlane "the most brutal gunman who ever pulled a trigger in Chicago"; he committed at least a dozen murders with a sawed-off shotgun loaded with slugs. He was equaled in ferocity, however, by John Scalisi and Albert Anselmi, who killed for the Gennas and later for Capone. Scalisi and Anselmi used to rub their bullets with garlic, the theory being that if their victim didn't die of his wounds, gangrene would kill him. Each of these gang captains commanded from a dozen to fifty experienced murderers, and when necessary, Torrio and Capone could call upon several hundred first-rate gunmen. About 40 per cent were paroled convicts. There were plenty of these gentry around; the Illinois State Board of Pardons and Paroles, under heavy political pressure, had released nine hundred and fifty criminals in less than three years.

In the allocation of territory Torrio made one mistake—he ignored the four O'Donnell brothers, Edward (Spike), Steve, Walter, and Tommy, who were known as the South Side O'Donnells to distinguish them from Myles and Klondike O'Donnell of the West Side. The reason for this omission was never divulged, but it was probably the absence of Spike O'Donnell, who was serving a prison sentence for a daylight bank robbery. Spike O'Donnell was an accomplished criminal with a long record as sneak thief, pickpocket, burglar, footpad, and gunman; he had twice been tried for murder, and had been suspected by the police of complicity in several other killings. His three brothers were capable thieves and gunmen, but they had never worked except under his direction, and would undertake nothing without his leadership. So they made no protest when Torrio froze them out. While waiting for Spike to return, they supported themselves by petty thievery and holdups in the parks, and by working for Capone at the Four Deuces and as guards on liquor trucks. Early in 1923 Spike O'Donnell was pardoned by Governor Len Small, who had received a petition signed by a judge of the criminal court of Cook County, six state senators, and five state representatives. Spike was understandably indignant over the shabby treatment his brothers had received, and as soon as he could get things organized he hijacked several Torrio beer trucks. Then he imported gunmen from New York, made arrangements with Butch Crowley in Joliet, and began running beer into the South Side areas ruled by Polack Joe Saltis and Frank McErlane.

Torrio imediately ordered his gunmen out to teach the South Side O'Donnells a lesson. A band of killers led by McErlane cornered five O'Donnell gangsters in a saloon on Lincoln Street, but succeeded in killing only one. They got two more about ten days later; these unfortunates were forced into an automobile by Hymie Weiss, who jovially invited them to "take a one-way ride." This was the first of the famous ride murders, and it was repeated on December 1, 1923, with two more victims. Ten different attempts were made to kill Spike O'Donnell; he was shot several times, but recovered. The O'Donnells fought back as best they could, but were hopelessly outnumbered and outgunned. Early in 1924, when the score stood at seven to two in favor of the Torrio-Capone gunmen, Spike O'Donnell disbanded his gang and left Chicago. He returned a year or so later, made peace with Al Capone, and thereafter operated in a small way as a Capone henchman. To help out, he was given a contract to supply the city with coal.

5

The Chicago police twice interfered with the orderly development of Torrio's booze machine. In November 1921 the Chicago *Tribune* made a survey of prohibition enforcement and reported that at least four thousand saloons were running full blast and selling all kinds of liquor. This was real news to the city authorities, and the chief of police was astounded and outraged. He announced immediately that he would invoke the new state law and "make Chicago so dry that a sponge can be wiped across it without picking up a drop of liquor." The cops went into action with a great blast of publicity. In one day five hundred arrests were made and several hundred speakeasies closed. A few breweries were raided, with reporters on hand to watch. A special "dress-suit squad" prowled the hotels and restaurants trying to catch "exclusive society violators of the law" taking a drink. City chemists complained that the police were seizing liquor faster than they could analyze it. Everybody had fun.

Torrio and his allies viewed these antics with amused tolerance. They sympathized with the police and understood perfectly that such gestures had to be made in order to satisfy the newspapers and the citizens who had the naïve idea that laws should be enforced. They co-operated by withdrawing their delivery trucks and virtually suspending operations until the commotion subsided, which it did within two weeks. In a month the whole thing had been forgotten. A similar but even shorter outburst occurred in 1923, when Mayor William E. Dever, who had been elected on a reform ticket, tried to dry up Chicago and close the speakeasies, which by that time numbered about twenty thousand. The police made more than seven hundred arrests in three days, and many saloons went out of business. The gangsters followed the same procedure as before, and after a few weeks the uproar died down and they resumed their normal pursuits. Mayor Dever tried energetically throughout his term of office to enforce the law and destroy the gangs, but the odds against him were too great. Honest policemen closed breweries, distilleries, and speakeasies and brought in the bootleggers and gunmen, but the booze joints reopened and the courts and politicians freed the criminals.

6

While the guns were blazing in the war with Spike O'Donnell, which was really little more than a skirmish as only nine men were killed, Torrio proceeded with his plans to bring all of Cook County under his domination. Since the death of Jim Colosimo he had established brothels in Stickney, Berwyn, Chicago Heights, Forest View, and a dozen other suburban towns, and he now cast a covetous eye upon Cicero, the biggest city in the county outside of Chicago and the fifth largest in the state. It had a population of about fifty thousand. Most of Cicero's saloons had remained open when prohibition began, and were being supplied with beer and other liquors by Myles and Klondike O'Donnell. Several hundred slot machines, owned by a Democratic politician named Eddie Vogel, were in operation, but other forms of gambling were not permitted, and there was no commercialized vice.

In the fall of 1923 Torrio sent prostitutes into Cicero and opened a brothel on Roosevelt Road. They were promptly thrown out by the Cicero police. Torrio sent in another batch of harlots, and the police wrecked the bordello and locked up the women. Two days later the sheriff of Cook County raided the town and confiscated Vogel's slot machines. Torrio then suggested a compromise, and a treaty was arranged which was carefully observed for more than three years. Vogel got his slot machines back, and the two O'Donnells received exclusive beer and liquor privileges on Roosevelt Road and several other parts of Cicero. Torrio took over the remainder of the city for gambling and liquor selling, and as a base for his Cook County operations. He agreed not to import prostitutes.

When the occupation terms had been arranged, Torrio turned Cicero over to Al Capone, who now emerged as an authentic big shot and a full partner in all of Torrio's enterprises. Capone established his headquarters at the Hawthorne Inn, occupying an entire floor, with armed gangsters at every entrance and bulletproof shutters at the windows. He proceeded cautiously until the municipal election of April 1, 1924, when he set out to assure the re-election of his pal Mayor Joseph Z. Klenha and the rest of the Democratic ticket. It had been expected that Mayor Klenha would be defeated by a strong Republican slate pledged to law enforcement. But Capone imported two hundred gunmen and sluggers from Chicago, and his hoodlums took charge of the election. "Automobiles filled with gunmen paraded the streets," said a report of the Illinois Association for Criminal Justice, "slugging and kidnaping election workers. Polling places were raided by armed thugs and ballots taken at the point of the gun from the hands of voters waiting to drop them into the box. Voters and workers were kidnaped, taken to Chicago, and held prisoners until the polls closed." Before the day was over, five men had been killed and a score of others knifed or blackjacked. Capone himself fought a pistol battle with a detachment of Chicago policemen who had been sent into Cicero to help preserve order.

The Democratic ticket headed by Mayor Klenha was elected by record-breaking majorities, to nobody's surprise, and Capone became the undisputed ruler of Cicero. He immediately transformed the city into the wildest place in the country. Trigger-happy gangsters came to Cicero for recreation, the number of saloons multiplied by five or six, and almost two hundred big gambling houses ran wide open day and night, with screaming barkers urging passers-by to step in and play. There were no open brothels, but several such dives ran under cover, and hundreds of free-lance harlots prowled the streets. Both women and gambling houses were either owned by Torrio and Capone or paid them tribute, usually 50 per cent of their gross business. Capone's word was the law of Cicero; his orders were obeyed promptly by the police and all city officials. Once when Mayor Klenha failed to show proper respect, Capone knocked him down on the steps of

City Hall and kicked him when he tried to get up. He lay there until Capone gave him permission to rise. When the city council threatened to pass an ordinance which Capone didn't like, hoodlums invaded the meeting, blackjacked one of the councilmen, and ordered the others to go home. The editor of the Cicero *Tribune* was beaten because he published an anti-Capone editorial.

With the capture of Cicero, Johnny Torrio reached the peak of his career. In partnership with Al Capone he operated twenty-five large and prosperous brothels, twice that many gambling houses and immoral cabarets, sixty-five breweries, and a large number of distilleries. In addition he owned many moonshine stills and little alley breweries, and was running large quantities of whiskey and other hard liquors into Chicago from Detroit and New York. The Torrio-Capone net income was estimated at thirty million dollars a year from liquor and about fifteen million from gambling, prostitution, and other interests. They were sitting on top of their evil world, there was peace in gangland, and the future looked rosy.

But great trouble was brewing. Dion O'Banion was moodily nursing grudges. The mercurial ruler of the North Side had sent a score of his best hoodlums to aid Capone in the conquest of Cicero, and he had received nothing but a curt word of thanks. His pride was hurt, and he began threatening reprisals. Torrio gave him a large cut of the Cicero take, but he still sulked. He complained that the Gennas were selling bad liquor in his territory at low prices. He demanded that they be kept out of the North Side. Torrio replied that nobody could tell the Gennas what to do. O'Banion retorted that if Torrio was afraid, he would attend to the matter himself, and to show his disdain for the dangerous Sicilians, he hijacked several Genna trucks and stole thirty thousand dollars' worth of their whiskey and alcohol. The Gennas immediately set out to kill O'Banion and everyone associated with him, but were held back by Torrio and Mike Merlo, head of the Chicago branch of the Unione Siciliana and the most influential Sicilian in Chicago. They realized that a war between O'Banion and the Gennas would eventually involve every gangster in Chicago, and, besides, would be bad for business. The Gennas subsided out of deference to

Merlo, and O'Banion proceeded to make matters worse by double-crossing Torrio in a brewery deal; he sold the plant to Torrio and then tipped the federal agents that he and Torrio would be there on a certain night, May 19, 1924, getting out a shipment of beer. The agents raided the brewery and arrested Torrio, O'Banion, and several gangsters. O'Banion had expected to be picked up; he knew that since he had no record as a prohibition violator, he would only be fined, whereas Torrio, as a second offender, might be in considerable trouble. When Torrio was brought into court he pleaded guilty and was fined five thousand dollars and sentenced to nine months in jail. He appealed, and it was almost a year before he was locked up.

Because he didn't want to precipitate a war, Torrio did nothing about O'Banion's treachery, and the North Sider began to get grandiose ideas of his importance. When Hymie Weiss, the brains of the O'Banion gang, urged him to make peace with Torrio and the Gennas, he said contemptuously, "Oh, to hell with them Sicilians!" He might as well have committed suicide, for every Italian and Sicilian in Chicago accepted the slur as a deadly insult; O'Banion's death became simply a matter of time. During the summer of 1924 Torrio, Capone, and the Gennas made several plans for the extinction of O'Banion, and each time Merlo intervened, counseling patience. But Merlo died on November 8, 1924, and O'Banion's enemies moved quickly. A few minutes before noon on November 10, the day of Merlo's funeral, three men walked into O'Banion's flower shop, where the gang leader was working on a wreath. A Negro porter, the only other person in the store, saw O'Banion walk toward them, smiling, and extend a hand in greeting. One of the men jerked O'Banion off balance, and the two others shot him six times. The identity of the three men was never known to the police. Hymie Weiss always insisted that the murderers were Mike Genna, John Scalisi, and Albert Anselmi, but it seems doubtful, in view of the bad blood between them, that O'Banion would have welcomed the Sicilians or offered to shake hands with them. He would have been more apt to reach for his gun. Many Chicago newspapermen believed that the principal killer was Frankie

Yale, who was himself slain in Brooklyn in 1928 by order of Al Capone.

Hymie Weiss succeeded O'Banion as leader of the North Side gang, with Schemer Drucci and Bugs Moran as his chief lieutenants, and immediately announced that he intended to kill Torrio, Capone, and the six Genna brothers. Capone and the Gennas retorted in kind, but Torrio, badly frightened, hurriedly left for an extended tour of Cuba and the West Indies. He returned to Chicago about the middle of January 1925, and on the twenty-fourth, as he crossed the sidewalk in front of his home on the South Side, two men rushed from behind a parked automobile and opened fire with automatic pistols and a shotgun. They shot Torrio five times in the jaw, chest, right arm, and abdomen. Torrio recovered after three weeks in the Jackson Park Hospital, where he was guarded by the police and a squad of gunmen detached from Capone's personal bodyguard, and on February 9, 1925, appeared in United States District Court. There he paid the fine of five thousand dollars imposed upon him in the brewery case, and was sent to the Lake County Jail at Waukegan to serve his nine months' sentence. About a month later, in a transaction involving several million dollars, he transferred his brothels, breweries, distilleries, and other properties to Capone, who thus became the biggest of the big shots. Torrio was released from prison in the fall of 1925, and a strong escort of gunmen rushed him to Gary, Indiana, where he boarded a train for New York. He sailed for Italy a few days after his arrival in the metropolis. He was back in the United States within a few years, but as far as the police knew never returned to Chicago. The federal government made no attempt to prosecute Torrio for his less serious crimes, such as murder, bootlegging, and pandering, but hounded him for years about his income tax. He was finally convicted of evasion in 1939.

The killing of O'Banion made war inevitable, and the attack upon · Torrio touched it off; even if he hadn't wanted to, Capone was compelled to fight or lose control of his vast booze organization. All the alliances so carefully fostered by Torrio were broken, and new lines were drawn. There were no neutrals; as Mike Merlo had predicted, every gangster in Chicago was involved. Gang captains who had been firm friends for several years robbed one another's trucks, breweries, and distilleries and started shooting on sight. Several of Capone's crack gunmen, among them Frank McErlane and Myles and Klondike O'Donnell, deserted the big fellow and enlisted under the banner of Hymie Weiss. But the Gennas and others remained loyal, and in the end it became more or less the Italians and Sicilians against the field. The war went on for more than five years, and five hundred men were killed, three hundred in 1926 and 1927. The dead included such celebrated gunmen as Hymie Weiss, Schemer Drucci, John Scalisi, Albert Anselmi, and three of the Genna brothers. Of the big shots, only Capone survived.

7

In April 1926, while gangsters' guns were roaring all over Chicago, Mayor William E. Dever and United States Attorney Edwin A. Olson of the Chicago district went to Washington to testify before a congressional committee. Neither Mayor Dever nor Olson mentioned Al Capone or the gang war then raging in Chicago and Cook County, although the mayor said that organized bootleggers were "a bad lot" and had given him considerable trouble up to 1924. Each, however, had many good words to say about his own administration. Olson said that since he took office in January 1923 he had closed twenty-six breweries, and that not one gallon of illegal beer was now (1926) being manufactured in his district. He said he had reduced withdrawals of sacramental wine from 885,000 gallons a year to sixty thousand gallons, and had cut whiskey and alcohol withdrawals almost in half. "There have been no outstanding liquor-law violations in six months," he said. "Criminals find it less hazardous to commit daylight robbery with a gun." He declared also that there was no political fixing in Chicago, because he always put the fixers in jail. Olson had no very high opinion of the Chicago police; he declared that there were five thousand moonshine stills in the city, and that the cops, if they wanted to, could root them out in twenty-four hours.

Mayor Dever said that he resented Olson's slur upon the police; he was prepared to defend the good name of Chicago against all comers. He told the committee that when he became mayor in 1923 he found fifteen breweries and between fifteen thousand and twenty thousand speakeasies, all running wide open. He shut down the breweries and closed four thousand saloons; the others, he said, quit through fear of the police. He implied that in 1926 there were no speakeasies in Chicago. He declared that he had driven the liquor business out of existence as "a going, profitable, commercialized traffic," and said the federal government made little or no effort to enforce the law in Cook County outside of Chicago. As far as moonshine stills were concerned, Mayor Dever said that no man knew how many Chicago harbored. "But that the stills are there," he said, "and in threatening numbers, I have not the least doubt."

8

Hymie Weiss and his North Side gunmen made a dozen attempts to slaughter Al Capone, and the big fellow had many narrow escapes; several times he was saved by the heavy steel and bulletproof glass of his armored car. One of these efforts to wind up Capone's career was as spectacular an operation as the country has ever seen. On the afternoon of September 20, 1926, while Capone and one of his bodyguards, Louis Barko, were lunching in a restaurant adjoining the Hawthorne Inn at Cicero, eleven touring cars loaded with Weiss gunmen rolled through the street crowded with shoppers and pedestrians and bombarded the building with pistols, sawed-off shotguns, and machine guns, firing more than a thousand shots. At the first blast both Capone and Barko flung themselves to the floor, and Capone was not injured, although bullets struck all around him and Barko was hit in the shoulder. A woman and her infant son, sitting in a car in front of the inn, were slightly wounded, and bullet holes were found in thirty-five other parked cars. Woodwork and doors inside the hotel were splintered and windows shot out, and most of the furniture in the lobby was damaged.

A few days after the attack on the Hawthorne Inn, the Chicago police undertook to make peace in gangland and brought representatives of Capone, Weiss, and other important leaders together at the Hotel Sherman. Capone expressed his willingness to quit fighting, but Weiss refused to entertain any proposition unless Capone agreed to turn over Scalisi and Anselmi to him for punishment, which meant torture and death. Capone indignantly declared that he "wouldn't do that to a yellow dog," a statement of principles which gave the police a big laugh. Capone himself took care of Scalisi and Anselmi three years later, when they began to put on airs, swaggered about boasting that they were the most powerful men in Chicago, and tried to take over the Unione Siciliana. A banquet was given to celebrate their exploits, and they were bludgeoned to death as they sat drinking wine.

When Hymie Weiss spurned Capone's peace overtures at the Hotel Sherman meeting, he signed his own death warrant. Less than two weeks later, on October 11, 1926, he was machine-gunned by two Capone hoodlums as he drove up to his headquarters above O'Banion's flower shop. Weiss was succeeded by Schemer Drucci, who met a disgraceful end; he was killed in April 1927 by a policeman. Bugs Moran then assumed the leadership of the North Side gang, and established his headquarters in a garage at 2122 North Clark Street. There the war reached a bloody climax on St. Valentine's Day, February 14, 1929. Six members of Moran's gang, and a young optometrist who was an old friend of Moran's and enjoyed hanging out with gangsters, were in the garage waiting for a big shipment of liquor from the Purple Gang at Detroit. A touring car stopped outside about the middle of the afternoon, and passers-by saw five men, three wearing police uniforms, get out and walk leisurely into the garage. Once inside, they produced guns, disarmed the Moran gangsters and the more or less innocent optometrist, and lined them up facing a wall with their hands above their heads. Then one of the two men in plain clothes sprayed them with machine-gun bullets, while the other cut loose with a shotgun and one of the pseudo policemen shot every man with a pistol as he lay on the floor. The police learned that the murderer who handled the machine gun was Fred (Killer) Burke of St.

Louis, a member of the Egans Rats gang and an expert gunman. The men with the shotgun and the pistol were believed to have been Scalisi and Anselmi. Bugs Moran escaped death by only a few minutes. He was on his way to the garage, using a short cut through an alley, when he saw the five men enter the garage. Assuming that the police were making a raid, he returned to his home a few blocks away.

The St. Valentine's Day massacre alarmed underworld chieftains all over the country. Gang leaders in other cities had already begun to take sides, and it was obvious that unless something was done quickly the underworld everywhere would blaze into furious fighting that would completely disrupt liquor operations and other enterprises. Early in May 1929 some thirty Chicago gangsters, representing all of the important outfits, met at Atlantic City in a conference supposed to have been arranged by Frank Costello of New York, who, in addition to his bootlegging and rumrunning business, had become the slot-machine king of the East. Big shots from New York, Boston, Philadelphia, Newark, and other cities were also present, and the conference settled all of gangland's difficulties. It not only made new territorial allotments in Chicago, with a formal treaty signed by all gang captains; it also divided the whole eastern seaboard into spheres of influence. There were minor outbreaks in Chicago during the next few years, and the usual run of gang killings and private murders, but the war between Capone and the North Siders was ended.

On his way home from the peace conference Capone and his chief bodyguard, Frank Rio, stopped over in Philadelphia, and on the night of May 16 they were arrested by the Philadelphia police and charged with carrying concealed weapons. The two men were rushed into court, where they pleaded guilty and were each sentenced to one year's imprisonment. In some sixteen hours after he arrived in Philadelphia, Capone was in jail for the first time in his life. This extraordinary incident has never been explained. It has always been believed, however, that the arrest had been arranged by Capone, who didn't trust Bugs Moran and wanted a safe refuge until he could see how the peace treaty was going to work out. In any event, he served his term, with time off for good behavior, and was released on March 17, 1930.

Capone returned to Chicago to find that the city, as far as he was concerned, had experienced an extraordinary revulsion of feeling; he was no longer a hero, but a bum against whom every man's hand was raised. Police Captain John Stege put a guard of twenty-five uniformed cops around Capone's house on Prairie Avenue, with orders to arrest the gang leader on sight. But Capone didn't go home; he went instead to the Hawthorne Inn at Cicero, where he spent four days transacting business and answering mail. Then, with his lawyers, Capone called upon the police, the state's attorney, and the federal authorities. Nobody had a warrant for his arrest, and there were no charges against him. Captain Stege withdrew his police guard, but assigned two uniformed cops to watch the gang chieftains. They stuck close to his heels for several weeks. Capone could easily have had them killed, but he was too smart; he knew that if he did so he would almost certainly go to the gallows.

The change of sentiment in Chicago and elsewhere was due partly to a great wave of resentment at the excesses of the bootleggers and the underworld which was sweeping all over the country. Principally, however, it was due to the Chicago Crime Commission and the Chicago Association of Commerce Sub-Committee for the Prevention and Punishment of Crime, popularly known as the "Secret Six." These organizations had been fighting Capone and his fellow gangsters for years without much visible success until the Crime Commission hit upon a publicity idea which captivated the entire nation. This was the famous list of public enemies, headed by Al Capone as Public Enemy No. 1, which was sent to the authorities with a recommendation that the gangsters be hounded relentlessly in every possible way. The commission suggested that if they couldn't be convicted as murderers, thieves, or panders, they should be proceeded against as undesirable aliens, tax evaders, vagrants, and inmates of gambling joints and disorderly houses. The Crime Commission and the Secret Six hammered away with a pitiless barrage of publicity, with "public enemies" as their chief weapon. The phrase quickly caught the public fancy and became popular everywhere; newspapers took it up and the radio broadcast it, and it began to appear as the title of books, plays, motion pictures, and magazine articles. It stirred up the country and brought good results. Within four years fifteen men who had been branded as public enemies had been convicted of various crimes, nine had died, and the cases of nine more were pending in the courts. The rest, the Crime Commission announced, were "on the run."

Worried by the avalanche of publicity, visibly annoyed by the dogged watchfulness of the two uniformed cops, and incensed because he was now pointed out as "Public Enemy No. 1" and not as the "big fellow," Capone left Chicago early in 1931 and started moving about the country. He was searching, he said, for a quiet place in which to settle down in peace. But he was unwelcome everywhere he went. He tried Los Angeles and was ordered by the police to leave within twenty-four hours. When he appeared in the Black Hills of South Dakota, the governor threatened to call out the National Guard. He was warned to keep away from Cuba and the West Indies. He finally got to Florida, where he owned property, after his lawyers had obtained an injunction restraining the Florida authorities from bothering him. He lived fretfully and unhappily on his estate at Miami for a few months, but was again in Chicago in the late summer of 1931. On October 6 of that year he was arrested by federal agents for income-tax evasion, and his trial began soon afterward. When Capone appeared in court accompanied by an armed bodyguard, the judge promptly sent the hoodlum to jail for contempt. On October 18, 1931, the jury found him guilty on five counts, and the court imposed a fine of fifty thousand dollars, with twenty thousand dollars additional for costs, and sentenced him to prison for eleven years. His bail was continued, pending appeal, until May 5, 1932, when he was sent to the federal prison at Atlanta. Two years later he was transferred to Alcatraz Island in San Francisco Bay. He was released in 1939 and, after treatment in a Baltimore hospital for paresis, went to his home at Miami. He died there on January 28, 1947.

CHAPTER FIFTEEN

The End of the Noble Experiment

During the struggle over the ratification of the Eighteenth Amendment and the passage of the Volstead Act, the liquor interests of the country fought alone except for sporadic and ineffectual assistance from a few hotelkeepers' associations and real-estate boards, and the American Federation of Labor, which demanded modification of the act to permit the manufacture and sale of beer. Millions of Americans were opposed to prohibition but were unorganized and lacked spokesmen to present their side of the question. The champions who in later years led and largely financed the fight for repeal were silent; many, in fact, were outspoken in favor of the Eighteenth Amendment. Alfred E. Smith, a saintly figure in the annals of the wet movement, had nothing to say for several years. Smith ran for his first term as governor of New York in 1918, after the Eighteenth Amendment had been ratified by fourteen states and while it was pending before the New York Legislature. Yet, as far as the record shows, neither he nor his Republican opponent, Charles S. Whitman, so much as mentioned prohibition. Charles Merz summed up the situation in *The Dry Decade:*

. . . the opposition [the wets] had no funds, no organization, and no real leadership except in so far as these elements were supplied by the liquor interests. . . . There were no independent organizations in the field whose motives were disinterested and whose constituents were drawn from the rank and file of ordinary citizens. . . . In 1917 it was the brewers and distillers who invoked the argument of home rule and championed the doctrine of state's rights. . . . It was the Distillers' Association of America which carried the fight to the state legislatures in an effort to prevent ratification, organized emergency committees, and attempted unsuccessfully to force a referendum vote in fourteen states. It was the United States Brewers' Association, and not an association interested in the theory of the Constitution or the bill of rights, which briefed the case against the Volstead Act and submitted its brief to the President with a petition for his veto. It was the firm of Feigenspan, New Jersey brewers, which employed Elihu Root and William D. Guthrie to carry a last desperate appeal to the Supreme Court of the United States.[1]

It was not until the summer of 1919, after forty-five states had ratified the Eighteenth Amendment and so made it a part of the Constitution, that any sort of public protest was heard. Then a few mass meetings were held in New York and elsewhere; twenty thousand people marched through the streets of Baltimore clamoring for beer; ten thousand union men demonstrated for three hours before the Capitol at Washington; resolutions demanding beer were adopted by the American Federation of Labor and the Confederated Labor Union of New York; and a small group of anti-prohibitionists tried to promote a national "Daisy Day," when everyone opposed to prohibition should wear a daisy in his buttonhole. Nothing came of any of these outbursts. They quickly subsided, and were soon forgotten.

Organized opposition to prohibition was slow getting under way. The Association Against the Prohibition Amendment was founded in 1918 by Captain William H. Stayton, who had been active in the affairs of the Navy League, and was incorporated in the District of Columbia in December 1920. Captain Stayton headed the association until 1928, when he became chairman of the Board of Directors and was succeeded as president by Henry H. Curran, who had held many public offices, among them that of Commissioner of Immigration at the Port of New York. The Crusaders, composed of young men, appeared early in 1922, and in 1923 the Moderation League and the Constitutional Liberty League of Massachusetts took the field. Most of the initial financing of these and other groups of lesser importance was provided by the brewers and distillers. None accomplished much until 1926, when they combined with the American Federation of Labor to present evidence to a congressional committee which held hearings on the problems of enforcement.

Between 1927 and 1930 the American Legion came out for repeal and the labor unions abandoned their long-standing demand for beer and urged that the Eighteenth Amendment be wiped out. The Voluntary Committee of Lawyers, incorporated in New York in 1927, opposed the amendment on the ground that it violated the Bill of Rights and was "inconsistent with the spirit and purpose of the Constitution." The Bar Association of New York adopted resolutions in 1928 calling for the repeal of the amendment and the return of the whole liquor question to the states. Similar action was taken by the bar associations of New Jersey, Detroit, St. Louis, San Francisco, and Portland. The American Bar Association in 1930 adopted a repeal resolution by a vote of 13,779 to 6,340. The last of the important organizations which fought for repeal was the Women's Organization for National Prohibition Reform, which was founded in May 1929 by Mrs. Charles H. Sabin, wife of a New York banker. Mrs. Sabin, who was the first woman member of the Republican National Committee, resigned to become president of the W.O.N.P.R., the membership of which increased from seventeen in 1929 to 1,326,862 in 1932.

The appearance of Mrs. Sabin and her crusading ladies in the prohibition arena was particularly shocking to the drys, because it violated the ancient tradition that women were always on the side of the Lord, and the prohibitionists were as firmly convinced as ever that their cause was the cause of God. Prominent dry leaders assailed the Sabin cohorts in characteristic terms. Dr. Mary Armour, president of the Georgia W.C.T.U., and widely known as "The Georgia

Cyclone," was quoted in the New York *American* of May 30, 1929, as saying, "As to Mrs. Sabin and her cocktail-drinking women, we will out-live them, out-fight them, out-love them, out-talk them, out-pray them, and out-vote them." Dr. D. Leigh Colvin, prominent in the councils of the Prohibition party and later its candidate for President, described the members of the W.O.N.P.R. in the New York *Times* of May 23, 1932, as "Bacchantian maidens, parching for wine—wet women who, like the drunkards whom their program will produce, would take pennies off the eyes of the dead for the sake of legalizing booze."

All of the anti-prohibition organizations which entered the fight during the first half dozen years of the dry era advocated modification of the Volstead Act, and not repeal of the Eighteenth Amendment. A vast majority of both wets and drys were inclined to agree with Senator Morris Sheppard of Texas, author of the dry amendment, that "there is as much chance of repealing the Eighteenth Amendment as there is for a hummingbird to fly to the planet Mars with the Washington Monument tied to its tail." And with Clarence Darrow, a famous Chicago lawyer and prominent wet, who said, "The repeal of the Eighteenth Amendment is pure nonsense. One might as well talk about taking his summer vacation on Mars." Very few, if any, wet leaders had anything good to say about that old devil whiskey, but they talked a lot of pious nonsense about the glories of beer and light wines, predicting that if unlimited quantities of these could be made available, the American people would forget their appetite for hard liquors. And all the wets who could make themselves heard above the tumult of propaganda reacted with horror at every suggestion that the saloon might eventually return; they pledged their very souls to prevent such a calamity. However, many thought it should be possible for the people, especially the workingman who was perishing without his legal beer, to buy liquor by the drink. Nobody ever figured out how this could be accomplished except through the medium of something very similar to the saloon.

The first organization to abandon the double talk about modification and revision of the Volstead Act and demand outright destruction of the Eighteenth Amendment seems to have been the Women's Committee for Repeal of the Eighteenth Amendment, which in 1927, "tired of taking a halfway position," changed its name from the Women's Committee for Modification of the Volstead Act. The idea of repeal, however, had been advanced before. In 1924 Edward A. Alexander, a New York lawyer, began urging Democratic leaders to ask Congress to submit a repeal amendment to state conventions elected by popular vote, a method of amending the Constitution which had not been used for more than a hundred years. The New York Democratic organization, shuddering at the political perils involved, refused to have anything to do with Alexander's suggestion, but a resolution embodying his proposal was introduced in Congress in 1926 by Senator Edward I. Edwards of New Jersey. A somewhat similar measure, providing for a nation-wide referendum on the liquor question, was introduced by Senator Walter E. Edge, also of New Jersey. Neither got out of committee and, except for a few newspaper stories, attracted little attention, although Senator Edge's resolution was approved, with amendments, by Senator William E. Borah of Idaho, a powerful dry leader.

2

By the middle 1920s prohibition had become almost a national obsession; it overshadowed all other questions. The people talked of little else. Books and pamphlets about it rolled off the presses by the thousands. It was a rare magazine which didn't publish at least one article about it in every issue. The newspapers were filled with it; one New York paper alone printed almost seventeen thousand prohibition items in eight years, and a large proportion were on the front pages. As we have seen, the federal courts and prosecution agencies devoted a disproportionate amount of time to it. As William Howard Taft had predicted, it was the principal issue in every election campaign. To state and municipal officials it was a continuing headache. Mayor William E. Dever of Chicago spoke for many when he told a congressional committee in 1926, "It is an everyday—yes, an hourly—difficulty with us in Chicago . . . our attention is engrossed from morning until night with this particular subject. It is almost impossible to give anything like good government along general lines, this one subject presses so strongly upon our attention. . . . I find myself immersed in it, to the very great damage of the city, from morning until night."

It was clear, as the prohibition experiment groggily approached its last half dozen years, that the Eighteenth Amendment and the Volstead Act could be enforced only if all of the forty-eight states cooperated without stint and regardless of expense; or, lacking that cooperation, if Congress appropriated enough money to set up a new judicial system, to hire thousands of additional prosecutors, to build hundreds of new prisons, and to establish a huge national police force with virtually unlimited powers of search and seizure. Dr. James M. Doran, Prohibition Commissioner, told Congress in 1927 that if the federal government assumed the entire responsibility, enforcement would cost at least three hundred million dollars a year. It was obvious that no such sum would ever be provided, and it was equally obvious that the states would do little or nothing. The state legislatures, or most of them, cheerfully passed almost any laws the drys wanted, but consistently refused to implement them with money or administrative machinery.

Congress, and the executive branch of the federal government as well, dillydallied throughout the first decade of the prohibition era. No really constructive step was taken by the White House until Herbert Hoover was elected President in 1928. Neither President Harding nor President Coolidge brought pressure to bear upon Congress or made any important suggestions relating to enforcement; in general they confined themselves, in their messages and speeches, to complaints of the states' failure to help and to platitudes about the sanctity of the law and the duty of every American to obey it. Early in May 1926 President Coolidge signed an executive order which might have had far-reaching results; it authorized the appointment of "any state, county, or municipal officer . . . as a prohibition officer of the Treasury Department." This order aroused such a storm of protest, on the ground that it was destructive of state's rights and possessed calamitous possibilities, that it was never put into effect, although it was not withdrawn. During the first four years, when there was great need of clarifying and other legislation, Congress passed but one prohibition law—the Willis-Campbell Act which prohibited the prescribing of beer. The lawmakers did, however, devote considerable time to defeating bills legalizing beer, fifty-nine of which were introduced in one session, and to measures which would have extended prohibition to the Hawaiian and Philippine islands and to Americans residing in consular districts in China.

The largest congressional appropriation for enforcement in any one year was less than fourteen million dollars, and the annual average was not more than ten millions. Dry members of Congress, as well as the leaders of the Anti-Saloon League and other dry organizations, continued to insist that everything needful had been done when the Eighteenth Amendment was adopted and the Volstead Act passed; that the newspaper reports of gangster killings, liquor wars, bootlegging, clogged courts, corruption, and crowded jails were greatly exaggerated, if, indeed, such things existed at all; and that to give the Prohibition Bureau more money would be to waste the taxpayers' substance. They were vastly encouraged by a statement made by Commissioner Doran in 1929, in which he pointed out that actually prohibition had been a very profitable operation. He said that during the first nine years the government had spent $141,179,485 on enforcement, and had received, in fines, penalties, and taxes on liquor, $460,502,792.76. This was a clear profit of $319,323,307.76, and was in addition to the economic benefits which prohibition had bestowed upon the nation, estimated by Dr. Irving Fisher of Yale University, a noted economist and dry propagandist, at six billion dollars a year. It was obvious that all was for the best in this best of all possible dry worlds.

Secure in their Panglossian dreamworld, the drys ignored the plain fact that a nation-wide shift of public sentiment was in progress. It was clearly shown in official referendums, of which nineteen were held in eleven states between 1920 and 1929; and in numerous unofficial polls conducted by magazines, newspapers, labor unions, and other organizations. The largest of the latter were those of the *Literary Digest* in 1922 and the Newspaper Enterprise Association in 1926. In the *Digest* poll 922,382 ballots were counted, and 61.4 per cent were for modification of the Volstead Act. The N.E.A. was assisted by 326 newspapers in forty-seven states, and 1,747,630 votes were received. Of these, 81.1 per cent favored repeal or modification. In both polls a large majority were for modification. Ten of the official referendums were on the repeal or enactment of state laws, and six were won by the drys. Nine dealt with the Eighteenth Amendment and the Volstead Act—eight with modification and one with outright repeal—and the wets won seven, some by large majorities. In New York the vote was 1,763,070 to 598,484 in favor of an appeal to Congress for modification of the Volstead Act, and in Illinois a similar proposition carried by a majority of 284,039. Eight states, with one fourth of the country's population, voted on various aspects of the liquor problem in 1926, and 59.4 per cent of the ballots cast were wet.

The Association Against the Prohibition Amendment and other wet organizations made a great to-do about these polls and referendums in their propaganda, but the dry leaders insisted that they were worthless, since they were not binding upon Congress, where the final decisions were made. The Anti-Saloon League accused the newspapers and magazines of rigging their polls, of permitting thousands to vote two or three times, and of manipulating the final figures. The drys declared that they had boycotted all of the referendums except the ones in which they were victorious, and called attention to the fact that despite the growth of wet sentiment, the people continued to elect dry congressmen. Wayne B. Wheeler, general counsel of the Anti-Saloon League, said that each of the four Congresses chosen after the ratification of the Eighteenth Amendment had been drier than its predecessor. Even in the "wet year" of 1926, while the wets gained about twenty-five seats in the House of Representatives, the drys elected twenty-nine out of thirty-five senators. The drys maintained large majorities in both houses until 1932; the wet strength never exceeded 30 per cent, and most of the time was less than 20 per cent. The wets attributed their failure to gain more of a foothold in Washington to the refusal of Congress to reapportion the country after the 1920 census, as required by law. A more probable reason, however, was that the people were not yet ready to vote nationally as they talked and voted locally, a political phenomenon not uncommon in this country. There can be no doubt, however, that millions of Americans were getting very tired of the dry paradise.

3

The most important development of the mid-twenties was the radical change in the character of the wet leadership. The brewers and the distillers had faded into the background, and were replaced by railroad presidents, bankers, industrialists, businessmen, lawyers, educators, and authors. To read the names of the directors of the Moderation League, the Association Against the Prohibition Amendment, and similar organizations was almost to call the roll of American financial, industrial, and business power. The annual report of the Association Against the Prohibition Amendment for 1929 listed 227 members of its national board of directors, almost every one of whom was a rich man and a prominent figure in American life. Among them were fifteen of the twenty-eight directors of General Motors Corporation, and such nationally known tycoons as General W. W. Atterbury, president of the Pennsylvania Railroad; Pierre, Lammot, and Irénée du Pont; John J. Raskob, a Du Pont vice-president and chairman of the Democratic National Committee; Edward S. Harkness, a director of the New York Central Railroad and of the Southern Pacific; Arthur Curtiss James, capitalist and a director of a dozen corporations; Nicholas F. Brady, capitalist; Henry B. Joy, former president of the Packard Motor Car Company; Charles H. Sabin, of the Guaranty Trust Company; Newcomb Carlton, president of Western Union; Haley Fiske, president of the Metropolitan Life Insurance Company; Elihu Root, noted lawyer and former Secretary of State; and Percy S. Straus, president of R. H. Macy & Company.

On the other hand, the dry leadership had deteriorated. The Rev. Earl L. Douglass, in his *Prohibition and Common Sense,* published in 1931, described it as "limping, to say the least. There are many able leaders among the drys," he continued, "but there is also a great lack of unity. . . . There has not existed among them that spirit of unity and co-operation which victory requires. There has been too much talk and too little action. Conferences of dry workers have too often resulted in nothing but the passage of resolutions." The drys suffered an irreparable loss when Wayne B. Wheeler died in 1927; they were never able to replace him, and his sagacious counsel and unusual qualities of leadership were sorely missed. Bishop James Cannon, Jr., who as chairman of the legislative committee of the national Anti-Saloon League was already an important figure, became the recognized leader of the drys, but he was no Wheeler. The bishop was a shrewd politician, well equipped to crack the whip over Congress and to stir up the rabble, but he was violent, abusive, greedy for power, and given to wholesale denunciation which frequently verged on absurdity. Whoever disagreed with him or strayed from his holy path was a sinner of the blackest hue. His influence began to decline in the late 1920s when he was exposed as a bucketshop gambler and a hoarder of flour and other foodstuffs during the first World War. He was also accused of numerous other shenanigans definitely not becoming to a man of the cloth.

Moreover, once the Eighteenth Amendment had been safely tucked away in the Constitution, the drys had considerable difficulty collecting money. For this there were three main reasons—the decline of their organizations in hustle and efficiency, the apathy of prominent drys who still thought that the battle for a boozeless America had been won in 1920, and the defection of wealthy contributors who had gone over to the wet side. Pierre du Pont, for example, had been an ardent prohibitionist until about 1925, when he became active in the work of the Association Against the Prohibition Amendment.

Thanks to Du Pont and many other rich men who gave freely, the wets had plenty of money, and their astute leaders eventually built up a propaganda machine which was at least as powerful as the steam roller which the Anti-Saloon League had used to force the Eighteenth Amendment through Congress and the state legislatures. The drys professed to be terribly shocked at the huge sums spent by the wets, and were horror-stricken when an annual report of the association showed expenditures of $818,723.41 in a single year. As a matter of fact, this was less than half as much as the Anti-Saloon League annually poured into propaganda and political activity in the days when the drys were sweeping everything before them.

In other respects, also, the drys were at a disadvantage. Since it was impossible for them to admit that anything could be wrong with either the Eighteenth Amendment or the Volstead Act, they were compelled to defend the status quo; and, by inference, the bootlegger, the speakeasy, the rumrunner, and all the other evils with which the country had been afflicted since the ratification of the amendment. When the wet propagandists published official government reports and figures showing the extent of the illicit liquor traffic and the crime and corruption which made it possible, the drys could only scream that the booze hounds were lying, or take refuge in the feeble argument that prohibition was a great social experiment and deserved a fair trial. When the drys produced famous economists who proved that the prosperity of the 1920s was due entirely to prohibition, the wets trotted out even more renowned calculators who proved that the drys didn't know what they were talking about and were possibly a little insane. None of these flights of economic fancy were much more reliable than the estimates on liquor consumption.

The drys sent out a great deal of propaganda intimating that Pierre du Pont and the other millionaire wets were actuated solely by a selfish desire to get rid of some of their taxes. They made a considerable hullabaloo about a circular, supposedly sent out by Pierre du Pont to large taxpayers, which said that the application of the British liquor system in the United States "would permit of the total abolition of the income tax both personal and corporate." At a congressional committee hearing a dry senator dug out of the files of the Association Against the Prohibition Amendment a memorandum which referred to "Irénée du Pont's statement that one of his companies would save ten million dollars in corporate taxes if we could have, say, the British tax on beer." The wets retorted that the Du Ponts, and all of the other rich men working for the destruction of the Eighteenth Amendment, were inspired by the purest and loftiest of motives; that their main interest was the preservation of American freedoms imperiled by prohibition. Of course, the wets admitted, a reduction in taxes was not to be despised; it was one of the fundamental hopes of mankind, and even a Du Pont should not be censured for wistfully contemplating such a possibility. Such exchanges made more hay for the wets than for the drys.

4

Armed with the prestige of his high ecclesiastical office, Bishop Cannon attended the Democratic National Convention in June 1928 as the representative of thirty-one dry organizations and as the most powerful prohibitionist in the country. He was unable to prevent the nomination of Alfred E. Smith for President, which had been his principal objective, but succeeded in getting a strong enforcement plank into the party platform—it pledged "the party and its nominees to an honest effort to enforce the Eighteenth Amendment and all other provisions of the Federal Constitution, and all laws enacted pursuant thereto." Bishop Cannon, a lifelong Democrat, endorsed the platform, and, by implication, the nominee. He bolted, however, when Smith sent a telegram of acceptance in which he declared that while he would run on the platform adopted, he wanted the Volstead Act modified to give more power to the states. Bishop Cannon denounced Smith's message as "an action of brazen, political effrontery" and "a shameless proposition of political double-dealing," and announced that he and other dry leaders would support the Republican candidate, Herbert Hoover. The Republican convention adopted an enforcement plank very similar to that of the Democrats, but in his speech of acceptance Hoover said that he did not favor repeal of the Eighteenth Amendment. "I stand for the efficient enforcement of the laws enacted thereunder," he said. "Modification of the enforcement laws which permit that which the Constitution forbids is nullification. This the American people will not countenance." It was before he was nominated, in a letter to Senator William E. Borah in February 1928, that Hoover referred to prohibition as "a great social and economic experiment, noble in motive and far-reaching in purpose."

Bishop Cannon established headquarters in Richmond, and directed a violent anti-Smith campaign in fourteen southern and border states, eight of which voted Republican, some for the first time in history. The bishop leaped into the fight with characteristic frenzy —he devoted most of his time to beating Smith, gave liberally of his own money, and made speeches in every southern state. Hoover overwhelmed the Democratic candidate, receiving 444 electoral college votes to 87 for Smith, and rolling up a popular plurality of 6,300,000. The drys immediately hailed the election as a great triumph for prohibition; they pointed out that not only had they decisively defeated the country's leading nullificationist, but had also elected forty-eight of fifty-three governors, obtained dry majorities in nearly every state legislature, and had increased the number of senators and representatives. In the new Congress the drys had a majority of 80 to 16 in the Senate and 328 to 106 in the House.

The election, however, was more than a victory for the drys; it was also a victory for intolerance. It is quite likely that Hoover would have beaten Smith on the dry issue alone, for the wet sentiment in the country, though growing rapidly, was not yet strong enough even for modification. But if no other factors had been involved, the race probably would have been close. After all, Smith never threatened the Eighteenth Amendment; he had gone no further than to advocate comparatively minor changes in the Volstead Act. It seems unreasonable to believe that this would have caused the South to break a tradition of a hundred years' standing and vote Republican. Smith undoubtedly lost many votes because of his close connection with

Tammany Hall, but his poor showing was due in large measure to the fact that he was a Roman Catholic. Bishop Cannon was almost wholly responsible for bringing Smith's religion into the campaign. As Virginius Dabney said in his biography of the bishop, "He hauled in the religious issue, and he emphasized it, played upon it, and reiterated it until this political campaign throughout the southern states was transformed into what was tantamount to a religious war."[2] It was Bishop Cannon who industriously spread the rumor that if Smith became President the east wing of the White House would be reserved as the American residence of the Pope. And the bishop at least encouraged a widespread whispering campaign against Smith's character and personal habits. The Democratic candidate was accused, among other things, of drinking from four to eight cocktails a day.

One of President Hoover's first acts after he entered the White House was to appoint a National Commission on Law Observance and Enforcement, which had been authorized by Congress in the first deficiency appropriation of March 4, 1929. George W. Wickersham, former Attorney General, was named chairman, and the other members were: Newton D. Baker, former Secretary of War; William S. Kenyon, Paul J. McCormick, and William I. Grubb, federal judges; Kenneth Mackintosh, former Chief Justice of the Supreme Court of Washington; Roscoe Pound, dean of Harvard Law School; Ada L. Comstock, president of Radcliffe College; Henry A. Anderson of Virginia; Monte M. Lemann of New Orleans, and Frank J. Loesch of Chicago. Anderson, Lemann, and Loesch were prominent lawyers. Loesch was also head of the Chicago Crime Commission and took an active part in the war against Al Capone.

This body, which was popularly known as the Wickersham Commission, studied the problems of prohibition enforcement for almost two years, and made a final report to the President in January 1931. Its extensive records, consisting of special reports by committees and investigators, newspaper and magazine articles, and numerous documents and exhibits provided by the Prohibition Bureau and by wet and dry organizations, were later published in five large volumes. The commission's main conclusions were presented in a few brief paragraphs:

> The Commission is opposed to repeal of the Eighteenth Amendment.
>
> The Commission is opposed to the restoration in any manner of the legalized saloon.
>
> The Commission is opposed to the Federal or state governments, as such, going into the liquor business.
>
> The Commission is opposed to the proposal to modify the National Prohibition Act so as to permit manufacture and sale of light wines or beer.
>
> The Commission is of opinion that the co-operation of the states is an essential element in the enforcement of the Eighteenth Amendment . . . and that the support of public opinion in the several states is necessary to insure such co-operation.
>
> The Commission is of opinion that there is as yet no adequate observation or enforcement.
>
> The Commission is of opinion that the Federal appropriations for enforcement of the Eighteenth Amendment should be substantially increased. . . .

The commission suggested a few changes in judicial procedures and in methods of handling the medicinal liquor problem, but made no radical recommendations. In addition to the general report which all signed, each member of the commission made a separate statement. Newton D. Baker favored the immediate repeal of the Eighteenth Amendment and the return of the whole question of liquor control to the states. Monte M. Lemann said that since there was little reason to believe that the government could obtain the active support of the people, he saw no alternative but repeal. The other members favored further trial, with perhaps slight revision of the amendment. Judge William S. Kenyon suggested that the people be permitted to vote on a repeal amendment.

Although the report of the commission was a thorough, well-documented exposition of what was going on in the country, it was a great disappointment. The wets insisted that it didn't go far enough, and the drys said it went entirely too far; the few neutral observers complained that it was so loaded with "ifs, ands, and buts" that it made very little sense. The St. Louis *Post-Dispatch* summed it up by recalling the story of the company of soldiers who were being harangued by their captain before going into battle. "Boys!" he shouted. "Will ye run or will ye fight?" And the men yelled, "We will!" However, there was something in the report for everybody, and both wets and drys used it according to their lights. Within a few months it had been so twisted and revised and interpreted that scarcely anyone knew what it really contained. And so it sank quietly into limbo, while the bottleggers continued to thrive, enforcement conditions grew worse and worse, and the people became increasingly restive.

5

It was the depression which finally broke the back of the dry camel. The wets exploited this national disaster to the utmost. Their trained economists shouted that it was altogether due to prohibition, and who was to prove that it wasn't? In every conceivable medium of propaganda the wets belabored the obvious facts that legalizing liquor would create thousands of much-needed jobs and greatly increase dwindling federal revenues. These arguments helped to convert many politicians who had hitherto been true to their dry principles; they held the belief, later shown to be somewhat naïve, that what the government didn't have the government couldn't spend. It was clear within six months after the Wickersham Commission had made its report that the Eighteenth Amendment was surely headed for oblivion; the only question was, when? The end came considerably quicker than almost anyone had anticipated. The Democrats were so confident that early in March 1931 Alfred E. Smith and John J. Raskob tried to compel the party's national committee to make a public announcement de-

manding the immediate repeal of the amendment. They were stopped
by Franklin D. Roosevelt, who contended that it was too early for
the party to commit itself. Nobody doubted, however, that when
the Democratic convention met in 1932 it would adopt a repeal plank.
And so it did, unanimously and amid great disorder, with boos and
hisses for the few dry delegates who tried to protest. The plank said,
"We favor repeal of the Eighteenth Amendment," and demanded that
Congress immediately submit a repeal amendment to state conventions
elected by popular vote. Safeguards were urged to prevent the return
of the saloon, and to enable the dry states to protect their territories
from the inroads of the liquor traffic. The Republican convention
wasn't quite so bold; it didn't specifically commit the party or its candidate to repeal. Otherwise the Republican plank was the same as that
of the Democrats. What most of the voters seemed to remember,
however, was what Roosevelt said when he made his dramatic appearance at the Democratic convention to accept the nomination. "I say
to you," he shouted, "that from this date on, the Eighteenth Amendment is doomed!"

President Roosevelt took the ax to prohibition as soon as he entered
the White House, issuing an executive order which reduced the appropriation of the Prohibition Bureau from $8,440,000 to $3,600,000
and that of the Bureau of Industrial Alcohol from $4,000,000 to
$2,500,000. Nine days after his inauguration the President asked
Congress to modify the Volstead Act to permit the manufacture and
sale of beer with an alcoholic content of not more than 3.2 per cent.
Congress immediately did so, and the new law became effective on
April 7, 1933. Once more beer trucks rumbled through the streets
without gangster escorts, and thousands of speakeasies flung their
doors wide and became legal beer saloons. Meanwhile Congress had
passed a resolution submitting a repeal amendment to state conventions, the Senate on February 17 and the House on February 20,
1933. The fight for delegates to these conventions began at once,
although the dry forces were so demoralized that they didn't put up
much of a fight. A great deal of the credit for hurrying things along,
and for getting out the vote, was given to the "Bacchantian maidens"

of the Women's Organization for National Prohibition Reform, who scurried about the country by the hundreds of thousands. On April 10 the first state convention was held in Michigan, and the repeal amendment was ratified unanimously. Utah, the thirty-sixth state, voted for ratification by three to two on November 7, and on December 5 the convention made it official. The Twenty-first Amendment thus became a part of the Constitution, and the noble experiment was at an end.

6

When President Roosevelt signed the proclamation notifying the country that repeal had been ratified, he said, "I ask the wholehearted co-operation of all our citizens to the end that this return of individual freedom shall not be accompanied by the repugnant conditions that obtained prior to the adoption of the Eighteenth Amendment, and those that have existed since its adoption. . . . I ask especially that no state shall by law or otherwise authorize the return of the saloon either in its old form or in some modern guise."

Well, of course, there are now no "saloons" in the United States. Instead there are bars, taverns, grills, and cocktail lounges. But by and large it is the same old rose with the same old smell. Anyone who will walk along Bourbon Street in New Orleans, North Clark and South State streets in Chicago, and any of several streets in New York, and observe what the seller of liquor-by-the-drink is doing with his second chance, is almost bound to recall one of Will Rogers's famous sayings:

"The poor dumb clucks. They ain't learned a thing!"

Bibliographical Note

When I started work on this book more than two years ago, it was my intention to publish a complete bibliography of temperance and prohibition literature. The notion was abandoned when it became clear that such a record would fill at least another book as large as this one. It seemed pointless, when such a vast quantity of material was available, to print the titles of a hundred or two hundred references. A few books, however, deserve special mention: *Permanent Temperance Documents of the American Temperance Society,* Boston, 1835; *The Liquor Problem in All Ages,* by Daniel Dorchester, D.D.; New York, 1884; *The Cyclopedia of Temperance and Prohibition,* New York, 1891; *Prohibition, Modification of the Volstead Law,* compiled by Lamar T. Beman, A.M., LL.B.; New York, 1924; *The Origins of Prohibition,* by John Allen Krout, New York, 1925; *The Inside of Prohibition,* by Mabel Walker Willebrandt, Indianapolis, 1929; *The Noble Experiment,* by Irving Fisher, assisted by H. Bruce Brougham, New York, 1930; *The Dry Decade,* by Charles Merz, New York, 1931; *Dry Messiah, The Life of Bishop Cannon,* by Virginius Dabney, New York, 1949.

The principal sources for the period of actual prohibition were the daily newspapers, the magazines, the reports of the Wickersham Commission, the records of the various congressional committees, and the publications of the Brookings Institution. Also, some of the propaganda put out by dry and wet organizations, some of the reports and statements issued by government agencies and officials, and a few of the fulminations of important political figures on both sides. It must be remembered, however, that the fourteen years from 1920 to 1934 were not only the era of unparalleled crime and corruption; they were also the era of the Big Lie. The drys lied to make prohibition look good; the wets lied to make it look bad; the government officials lied to make themselves look good and to frighten Congress into giving them more money to spend; and the politicians lied through force of habit.

Footnotes

Chapter One

1. *The Liquor Problem in All Ages,* by Daniel Dorchester, D.D. New York and Cincinnati, 1884. Pages 133–34.
2. *The Backwoods Preacher, An Autobiography,* edited by W. P. Strickland. London, n.d. Page 119.
3. Quoted in *Temperance Reform and Its Great Reformers,* by Rev. W. H. Daniels, A.M. Cincinnati, 1879. Pages 63–64.

Chapter Three

1. Quoted in *Temperance Reform and Its Great Reformers,* by Rev. W. H. Daniels, A.M. Cincinnati, 1879. Page 587.
2. *Prohibition in the United States,* by D. Leigh Colvin. George H. Doran & Company, New York, 1926. Pages 53–54.

Chapter Five

1. *Prohibition in the United States,* by D. Leigh Colvin. George H. Doran & Company, New York, 1926. Page 147.

Chapter Six

1. *Temperance and the Changing Liquor Situation,* by Deets Pickett. The Methodist Book Concern, New York, 1934. Pages 45–46.

Chapter Seven

1. *Dry Messiah, The Life of Bishop Cannon,* by Virginius Dabney, Alfred A. Knopf, Inc., New York, 1949. Page 130.

Chapter Nine

1. Quoted in the report of the Wickersham Commission, Vol. V, page 201.
2. From *The Inside of Prohibition,* by Mabel Walker Willebrandt, copyright 1929. Used by special permission of the publishers, The Bobbs-Merrill Company, Inc. Page 113.
3. Ibid., page 145.

Chapter Eleven

1. Ibid., page 48.

Chapter Twelve

1. *The Real McCoy,* by Frederic F. Van de Water, Doubleday, Doran & Company, New York, 1931.

Chapter Thirteen

1. Tony was no myth. I knew him well. When I was working on the New York *Herald* during the early 1920s, and living in Brooklyn, I used to stop on my way home occasionally and have breakfast with him. I do not recall that he ever gave me more than one bottle of liquor.

Chapter Fifteen

1. *The Dry Decade,* by Charles Merz. Doubleday, Doran & Company, New York. Pages 208–9.
2. *Dry Messiah, The Life of Bishop Cannon,* by Virginius Dabney, Alfred A. Knopf, Inc., New York, 1949. Page 181.

Index